The
EVERYTHING®
Guitar Chords Book

Dear Reader,

Chords are one of the most fundamental elements of playing guitar. Chances are, one of the first things you learned to play was a chord. Many players find themselves repeating the same basic chord shapes over and over in their music, yearning to break free. The guitar has a hidden magic—one that contains more chords and chord possibilities than you could ever imagine learning in a single lifetime. The fingerboard's landscape of harmony is deep and powerful. This book is designed to be your guide through the maze that is fingerboard harmony.

There are a lot of chord books out there. What makes this one different? Instead of going overboard with every possible shape for every possible chord, I chose to be realistic. As a professional musician, I typically draw upon four or five comfortable shapes for a C Major chord, even though theoretically there are eighty-eight shapes for it.

In this book you will find five shapes for each chord, listed from low to high, to give you variety in your voicing. Feel free to explore; the chords range from simple to exotic, comfortable to difficult.

I hope you enjoy this book and never run out of uses for it.

Warm Regards,

Marc Schonbrun

The EVERYTHING Series

Editorial

Publishing Director	Gary M. Krebs
Associate Managing Editor	Laura M. Daly
Associate Copy Chief	Brett Palana-Shanahan
Acquisitions Editor	Gina Chaimanis
Development Editor	Jessica LaPointe
Associate Production Editor	Casey Ebert
Music Engraver	Marc Schonbrun
Technical Editor	John Baboian

Production

Director of Manufacturing	Susan Beale
Associate Director of Production	Michelle Roy Kelly
Cover Design	Paul Beatrice
	Erick DaCosta
	Matt LeBlanc
Layout and Graphics	Colleen Cunningham
	Holly Curtis
	Sorae Lee
	Daria Perreault
Series Cover Artist	Barry Littmann

Visit the entire Everything® Series at *www.everything.com*

THE
EVERYTHING®
GUITAR CHORDS BOOK

Rock · Blues · Jazz · Country · Classical · Folk

Over 2,000 chords for every style of music!

Marc Schonbrun

Adams Media
Avon, Massachusetts

Bill, thanks for teaching me my first chord: A Minor.
Look at what you started . . .

——————————————————

An Everything® Series Book.
Everything® and everything.com® are registered trademarks of F+W Publications, Inc.

Published by Adams Media, an F+W Publications Company
57 Littlefield Street, Avon, MA 02322 U.S.A.
www.adamsmedia.com

ISBN: 1-59337-529-8

Printed in The United States of America.

J I H G F E D C B A

This book is available at quantity discounts for bulk purchases.
For information, please call 1-800-872-5627.

Contents

Acknowledgments

Thank you to my family: Mom, Dad, David, Bill, Trish, and the Kennedys; Pablo and Yoshi, too! Thanks to Joe Mooney for teaching me how music works. Very special thanks to Doug Rubio for taking a gamble and never losing faith in me. Also, the Crane School of Music for educating me so well. Special thanks to Greg Utzig for opening my eyes to the possibilities of the guitar; you have had more impact on me than you realize—oh, and thanks for making sure I didn't mess the chords up! Thanks to Pat Cummings for his faith and vision. To anyone who ever showed me a chord in my life: Thanks, I stole them all.

Without Sibelius Music Notation software, this book would have been impossible to produce—thanks, Robin. Thank you yet again for such well-crafted software.

TRACKS

About the CD

The accompanying audio CD comprises one set of each chord in the key of E. No CD would have enough room for all the chords (all 2,400 of them), so the CD will serve as a reference to the sound of each type and family of chords. You can use it as an ear-training guide, or even as a guide to show you which parts of the book you may wish to explore based on your reactions to the sounds you hear. The CD concludes with the chord progressions from Chapter 9 in their entirety.

A complete list of tracks and titles can be found in the Appendix.

The CD was recorded at Herkimer Sound on a PowerMac G5.

Marc exclusively uses Brian Moore Custom Guitars, La Bella Strings, Walter Woods Amps, Flite Sound Cabinets, MOTU Digital Performer, and Native Instruments Guitar Rig.

Foreword

▶ If you are a guitar player, one of the guarantees in life is that you will have to play chords on your instrument. This multi-note instrument separates itself from single-note instruments such as the trumpet, trombone, saxophone, and flute by the fact that you can harmonize several notes at a time to create wonderful things called chords!

Chords are a large part of what brings people to the guitar. Whether you are accompanying yourself, accompanying a singer, playing rhythm guitar in a rock band, playing in a jazz quartet, jamming with some friends, or just looking for an escape from the rigors of life for a few minutes, chords provide mood and atmosphere, and add color and emotion to your music. Chords can sound cheerful (major chords), melancholy (minor chords), and aggressively powerful (power chords). They can resolve neatly, or they can leave you hanging (suspended chords). Chordal variation is one of the things that make studying the guitar such a rewarding—but also challenging—pursuit.

There are literally thousands of chords you could potentially play on the guitar. In this book, Marc Schonbrun wisely does not present the reader with every chord in existence. Such a book would be heavier than a bowling ball! Instead, he chooses to present five useful forms of the most frequently seen and heard chords in the musical world. The fact that he has presented them in all twelve keys makes it easy for the reader to find the necessary chord or chords to enhance the performance of a song.

The opening chapters of the book provide excellent explanations of how chords are built and used in different musical settings. Marc presents useful tips on how best to utilize this collection of sounds, and makes it easy for even a novice to learn from and use this book. The musical examples in the back of the book offer practical usage of the chords, and the included CD of the author playing the chords will help students to hear the correct voicings.

This reference book of chords will help guitar players of all levels enhance their overall chord knowledge, and will help to make any guitarist a more knowledgeable musician. Whether you are a veteran guitar player looking for some new sounds, or a beginning musician who wants to start out on the right foot, you will find this book to be an invaluable resource. Enjoy the ride as you embark on your journey to discover the beauty and complexity of guitar chords!

John Baboian
Associate Professor
Guitar Department
Berklee College of Music
Boston, Massachusetts

Chapter 1

What You Will Find in This Book

So many chords, so little time. How can you use a book like this? What do the little boxes tell you? How is this thing organized? Answers to these and more important questions reside in Chapter 1. Get the most out of your chords and enhance your playing by using this book as effectively as possible.

Chord Frame Diagrams

No doubt, before you bought this book, you took a quick gander through it. Based on the law of percentages, if you randomly flipped open to any page, you came to the main content of this book: the chord frame diagrams. You probably noticed that there are a lot of them. You're right, there are a ton of chords—about 2,400 in all.

This book is not as cut and dried as you may think; there is a system at play here. First, you need to learn about the actual chord frames, which dominate the layout of the book. If you don't know how to read a chord frame, you won't get much out of this book. The good news is that chord frames are simple to read, and most of you have come across them before.

How the Chords Are Displayed

Chords can be displayed as standard musical notation that every instrument can read, such as in Figure 1.1.

Figure 1.1

However, the language of music is complex, and so is the guitar. The popularity of the guitar and its highly visual fingerboard have given birth to some specialized forms of notation that only guitarists use. If you play guitar, you're no stranger to tablature, which is a shorthand way to represent guitar notation.

The six lines represent the six strings on the guitar. The lowest string is the lowest line, and it reads sequentially up from there. Numbers placed on any individual line indicate that you should play that particular fret. While the system completely lacks any mention of rhythm, which is a key element of music, its simplicity enables guitar players with little or no training to learn guitar parts easily. Chords can be displayed in tablature by simply placing multiple notes vertically together, as in Figure 1.2.

Figure 1.2

While this is another viable way to represent chords (it's the same chord as in Figure 1.1), it's still not the preferred way to list chord shapes, because it's missing some essential information: It doesn't tell you which fingers to use on which frets. The best way to show chord shapes is the chord frame box, which gives you all the information you need to play the chords properly. This is why I chose the chord frame box as the standard of language in this book. Let's talk about how to read a chord frame box.

The Basic Chord Frame Box

Because a picture is worth a thousand words, Figure 1.3 shows a sample chord frame box.

Figure 1.3

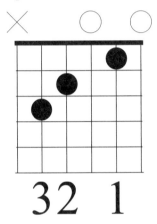

Let's break the box into its main elements.

The first thing you need to see is the six strings of the guitar, represented vertically (as in Figure 1.4).

Figure 1.4

Six Guitar Strings

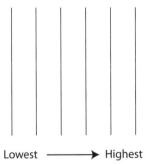

Lowest ——→ Highest

The lowest string on the guitar is always on the left side, and the highest string is on the right side. This is standard. If you are a left-handed player, these will be backward to you. As unfair as this may sound, the guitar world has made little concession for southpaws, and you'll just have to learn to flip the diagram around in your head.

On top of the vertical lines are horizontal lines that represent the frets of the guitar (as shown in Figure 1.5).

Figure 1.5

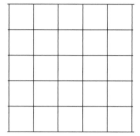

You now have a visual template for making chords. If you were to lay your guitar in your lap (strings up), you would be looking at a blank chord frame box. From here, you will learn the various elements that define the chords for you.

Other Chord Frame Information

Once you have the blank template, you need to add information about which fingers to use to make these lifeless grids into music. We do so by adding black dots into the diagrams. The black dots sit right on the vertical strings they are played on, and in between the horizontal frets they are placed on. Figure 1.6 provides clarity.

Figure 1.6

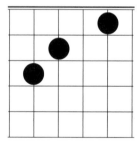

By assembling the chords this way, you can get a quick overview of where to put your fingers. If this is your first experience with chord frames, it may take a day or so to get used to them. Trust me, these boxes are very efficient and you'll be able to breeze through them in no time.

Using the Chord Frame Box

The chord frames now are infused with dots that show each chord's basic outline, but you still need a few more pieces of information in order to play the chords correctly. Once you learn how to read and interpret the chord frames, you will know where to place your fingers.

Fingering

First, you need to know which finger is responsible for which dot. Thankfully, this part is fairly obvious: Below each chord you will find a set of numbers. These numbers line up with the strings, and the dot markings tell you which finger to use to play each of the notes. This part is fairly simple (see Figure 1.7).

Figure 1.7

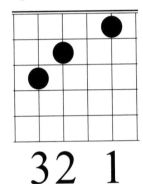

Open Strings and Dead Strings

In some chords, you play "open" strings—strings that contain no fretted fingers, but are part of the chords. To designate that a string is to be played open, a small open "O" is placed above the chord frame, directly in line with the string. In the opposite sense, there are times when you don't want a string to play at all. This is designated in much the same way, using an "X" above the string that is not to be played. Just like an open string indication, this will appear at the top of the chord frame diagram. See Figure 1.8 for the complete diagram with all the markings.

Figure 1.8

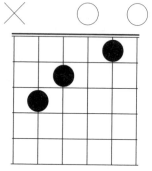

Location on the Fingerboard

You now have almost all the elements you need to play any chord in this book, but you still have to determine the exact location on the fingerboard. Each chord frame only displays five frets at a time. Most guitars have at least twenty or more frets, so how can this basic frame work for the whole guitar? That's simple—it's moveable. All you have to do is indicate where the chord frame sits. Let's look at Figure 1.9, a basic chord frame that sits in the open position (the first through fifth frets).

Figure 1.9

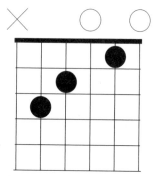

The big giveaway here is that the top horizontal line in the chord frame is a thick black line. This is to mimic the nut that your strings rest on, which is a thick piece of bone or plastic, depending on your guitar. If you see that thick black line, you know that you're in the open position.

For the chord frame to be moved, you have to be told where it's being moved. This is done with the marking "5 fr," meaning "fifth fret." What this tells you is that the first horizontal fret you see in the diagram is the fifth fret, and the five frets follow up from there (fifth through tenth frets). You'll also notice that the solid black line that indicated the open position is gone. This is another way to find out where you are if you happen to miss the fret marking. Take a look at Figure 1.10, which is a chord frame starting at the fifth fret.

Figure 1.10

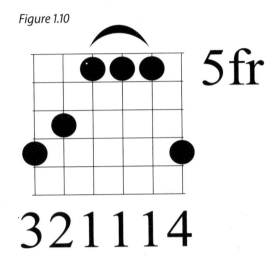

The marking is fairly prominent and easy to spot.

Now that you understand the basics of chord frames, there is a technical detail to explain: barre chords.

Barres

A barre is a technique that allows you to use the same finger for more than one string. Since you have only four fingers to fret chords with, and the guitar has six strings, you need to make efficient use of your fingers in order to play full chords. Barre chords allow you to make the most of your hands and play chords that contain five or six notes.

In the chord frame diagram you will see a barre indicated in two ways. The first is a curved line on top of the chord frame—this is the standard way to indicate a barre chord. The other way is to look at the fingering: If you see your first finger used three times in the same chord, you have a barre chord.

Just remember, your fingers are straight, and so are your frets. Though you will be playing multiple notes with the same finger, it will always be across the same frets. So if your hand is cramping up just thinking about this, have no fear; you simply flatten out your finger and lay it across the fret indicated. Figure 1.11 is an example of a barre chord.

Figure 1.11

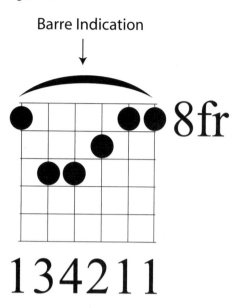

Barre chords are common. As your chord vocabulary grows, you will encounter them often. Barres can happen on any left-hand finger, but the majority of barres occur on your first finger (your strongest finger).

Optional Notes

The last visual element to talk about is optional notes. Just because a chord can span five or six strings does not mean that it necessarily has to. Throughout this book you will notice that certain notes are gray. These gray notes can occur on fingers placed on the fingerboard, or on open strings themselves. Simply, if a note appears gray, you don't have to play it. Figure 1.12 is an example of two chords, one with an optional note occurring on a finger, and the other with an optional open string.

Figure 1.12

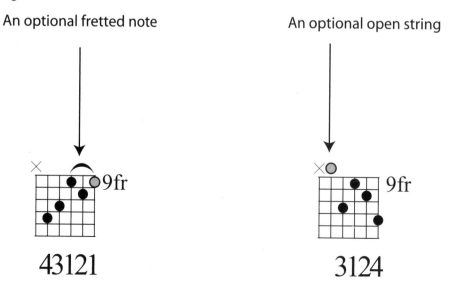

Now, let's talk about what constitutes an optional note. There are a few reasons that a note would be considered optional. Many times these "rules" go hand in hand and all are present at the same time. There isn't a way for you to know which rule is in place by simply looking at a chord grid. The gray note is optional for any of the reasons listed below; you'll see that certain optional note choices are more obvious than others.

Repeated Notes

Guitar chords typically have repeated notes within them. If the chord has a repeated note in it that isn't necessary to get the full sound of the chord, I made it optional. You can play the chord either way and you'll still be playing the exact same chord. The two chords will sound a bit different, but theoretically they are the same. This just leads to more variation in your chord playing!

Difficult Fingerings

If the optional note in question makes the chord really hard to play, either by introducing barre chords or unusual stretches, it is considered optional. Many times, difficult fingerings lead to exotic and interesting-sounding chords, so don't write them off totally. If you can slowly work up to playing all of the voicings in the book, you will get a greater picture of what's possible.

Dissonance

Dissonance is defined as a sound that is in conflict. At times in this book, certain chords are voiced in such a way that certain notes, when played as part of the chord, cause a possible conflict. I say "possible" because one man's meat is another man's poison, as the saying goes. You may not find the notes dissonant; I don't, I think that tension is beautiful. The notes that may cause dissonance also are considered optional. Don't write them off if they don't sound beautiful to you yet. Give them time to grow on you. It's common for your ears to grow as you experience different sounds. In the end, you are given the choice; leave the note out if it doesn't suit your situation.

A Note on Fingering

This book is designed for all styles of guitar, including finger style, pick style, and any other style you can think of. You will be presented with chord shapes that seem impossible in your style (for example, muted notes in the middle of a chord). With a pick, muting notes inside of chords is very difficult, but for players who use their fingers, this is no big deal. The same goes for chords with wide spreads. Not every chord will be playable with a pick, though you can break the chord into two parts with a pick by playing the lowest note, skipping the muted string, and striking the rest of the chord a split second later. If you see a chord that you can't play, try switching to a different style.

How the Sections of This Book Are Divided

Now that you can read any chord frame in this book with confidence, let's talk about the structure of the book. The chords in this book are divided into six main sections, which encompass the major categories of chords that you will encounter as a guitarist. The sections are:

- Major Chords
- Minor Chords
- Dominant Chords
- Diminished Chords
- Augmented Chords
- Special Chords

Within each category, there are subsets of individual chords. For example, if you glance at Chapter 3, you will see that "major chords" encompasses nine different types of major chords. Each individual chapter has a different number of subsections of chords. This depends on how many possible chords there are for each family. There are more minor variations than major ones. This is simply because of music theory and how the chords were laid out over time. It was also an editorial decision to give you the most common choices in each family. Certain families just had more necessary chords to complete your knowledge. Each chapter is broken down by the type of chord (which you can think of as the "family" of chords), and the chords are listed chromatically, one note at a time.

Within Each Chapter

The first chord you will see in any chapter is C, with all of its variations. Then you will see C♯/D♭ and all its variations.

You will notice that C♯ and D♭ are listed on the same page. This is because these notes are considered "enharmonic": they are spelled differently but sound the same. I list all the enharmonic notes together as "one" set of chord shapes, even though the music above each row of chords shows you two different note spellings. Here are the enharmonic notes in the book:

- C♯/D♭
- D♯/E♭
- F♯/G♭
- G♯/A♭
- A♯/B♭

All twelve possible chord roots are listed chromatically. Once you get through all twelve of the chord roots, the chapter is complete.

Each individual chord is illustrated by five example shapes. Each of the five example shapes gives you real-world examples of how to play that particular chord at five different locations on the neck.

Why Five Shapes?

The five chords are set up in order from lowest-sounding chord to highest-sounding chord. This is done so you can have some sonic variety in your chord voicing. One of the neat things about chord voicing is that while any of the five chords in any set are all considered "the same chord," they will all sound just a bit different. This is due to the nature of chord building, which you will learn about in the next chapter. The goal here is to give you the five "best" shapes for any particular chord.

You may have seen books that advertise 35,000 chords for the guitar. No one knows that many chords. This book is all about showing you the common, useful, and expected chord voicings. In some categories there are possibly hundreds of chords. For example, there are about eighty-eight possible C Major chords. How many do you think professional guitar players use? Certainly not eighty-eight. See the idea? This book is about giving you what you need to succeed as a chord player—and besides that, five chords fit nicely on a page!

The Complexity of the Guitar

The guitar is terribly complicated. Too many players never get out of the basic first position major and minor chords they are taught at early lessons or from friends. Why do so many players never reach beyond the "freshman fifteen"? (You will see this set of chords at the end of Chapter 2.) The reason for this is complicated and hard to explain. The truth is that the guitar is very logical in its layout. The strings and frets follow a predetermined order and if you study it well, you too may end up writing a book on chords.

The guitar's true complexity, and for many its unique beauty, lies in what it can't do. It's not like a piano, which is an instrument with almost unlimited chordal possibilities. The guitar is hampered by the design of the instrument, the fact that you have only four fingers, and the fact that the instrument itself has only six strings (it could have more, but then you'd be playing the lute, and not reading a guitar chords book). Those factors limit the way you can play chords on the guitar. It also yields some unique and unusual ways to play chords that other instruments, such as piano, cannot approach. As you work through this book, you will get a better picture of how the guitar is unique in this regard.

A very smart man once said, "The greatest fuel for imagination is limitation." This relates to guitar very well. There are things that you just *can't* do on the instrument. That never stopped anyone from making beautiful guitar music.

Endless Possibilities of Chords

The briefest possible definition of a chord is that it is three notes played at one time. Chords can extend to much greater numbers than three notes; some chords have six or eight notes. When you couple this with the fact that the guitar has a range close to that of a grand piano, the possibilities of what you can consider a chord and name as a chord get absurd.

The complexity of music theory and the rules for how you name chords also make life a bit difficult. You can look at a certain guitar chord one way and call it "x" one day and then call it "y" the next. All these factors combine to make chord playing on guitar a bottomless well. You could spend your whole life studying harmony and chord construction, but you don't have to; I have done that for you.

How to Use This Book

You're probably not going to learn every chord in this book. That's okay. You're not supposed to. This is a reference book. It is set up to show you how to play any chord you may encounter in your playing, no matter what your level of experience, style of music, or other factor. I set out to make this book manageable for the widest group of players. For the most part, fingerings are easy. Stretches and other uncomfortable techniques are kept to a bare minimum. The only reason to "work" for a particular chord voicing is that the end result is a beautiful chord.

In each section of five chords, you will no doubt find a few really easy-to-finger chords. If you are new to this game, go for the easy ones. As you progress and your curiosity is piqued, go back and take a look at the chords that you opted not to try.

In each section of five chords, I present five playable, usable voicings. For example, if you are working on a piece of music that calls for an A Minor 6 chord and you don't know how to play that chord, simply flip to the proper page in the book and look at the five examples of A Minor 6. Now, which one do you choose? They all sound good. It all depends on context: Which chord do you play before? Which chord do you play after? Try to pick a chord that fits into the flow of what you're doing in the rest of the piece. In the five shapes, you should find one that suits you.

Using This Book as a Tool

The other way to use this book is as a creative tool. If you find that you favor the same chords over and over again and yearn for a new sound, simply flip open the book and pick a chord at random. Try to base your progression around that chord. You may find some chords you love, and some you hate. These chords have existed for a long time; it's up to you to discover them.

Don't feel that you need to learn anything from this book in any specific way. Take what you want and what you need. The rest of the chords will be there for you when you need them.

Chapter 2

Chord Theory

Beyond just looking at chords as visual grids with dots and fingerings, there is theory and logic to what makes chords what they are. Here you will learn about basic chord construction, chord types, how to identify chords, and their relationships to scales—the lifeblood of music.

Chords Explained

Since this is a book about chords, it might not be the worst thing in the world to explain what a chord actually is. To the vast majority of guitar players, chords are "finger shapes" or "boxes" or "grips." Whatever you call them, few players think of them as groupings of notes that have order and structure. This very fact makes most guitar players look at a book that contains more than 2,000 chords and wonder how any player could possibly know that many shapes. The answer is that few players know that many individual shapes. The shapes are nothing more than combinations of notes. A simple three-note combination can yield many shapes—as many as eighty-eight shapes from the same three notes. The trick is to ignore the grandeur of "eighty-eight shapes" and remember that they all come from one thing: a pattern of notes. The best place to start is the triad.

The Triad

A chord is any grouping of three or more notes played simultaneously. Disregard the "three or more" statement, and focus on the basic chord: the triad. You Latin scholars know that "tri" means "three"; therefore, a triad is a three-note chord. The "tri" also has another meaning: Each of the notes are three notes apart from each other. So, a triad is a three-note chord based on notes that are three notes apart from each other. The musician's term for distance is an "interval," so a triad has intervals of thirds between the notes.

Let's look at a very basic triad, the C Major triad, which is composed of the notes C, E, and G (see Figure 2.1).

Figure 2.1

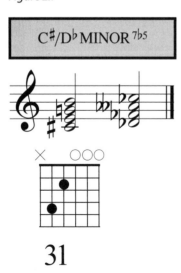

The triad is displayed three ways: in a chord grid, on a music staff, and in tablature. It's amazing how these visual systems look so different from each other, though each displays the exact same set of information.

Chord Voicings

In truth, the basic C E G triad is more of a model than anything else. Have you ever played that particular C Major chord shown in Figure 2.1? No, most likely you don't encounter that exact triad. However, some of you may have noted an alarming similarity to the regular C Major chord that all guitar players play. The C Major triad appears to be part of the "full" C chord. Let's look at both side-by-side in chord frames (Figure 2.2).

Figure 2.2

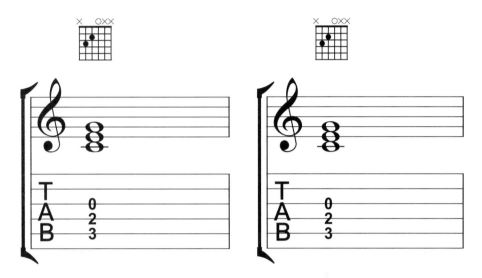

The chord on the left is the triad; on the right is the "typical" C Major chord. You can see that the first three notes are exactly the same. So what is the difference between the two? Let's look at Figure 2.2 again. However, this time, let's provide the names of the notes below the chord frames, instead of the usual fingerings (see Figure 2.2a).

Figure 2.2a

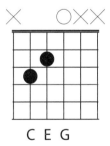

C E G

As you can see, the only difference between the two chords is that the traditional C Major chord simply "doubles" or "repeats" notes that are already in the chord. An extra C and an extra E fill out the chord more, and give you five contiguous strings to play, which is convenient for strumming chords. What you've just witnessed is the birth of a chord "voicing."

Triads will always be the perfect model of what a chord should be. Chord voicings are adaptations of those perfect models to fit within the framework of what the guitar can do. Now do you see how three notes can spawn eighty-eight or more chords?

The bottom line, in the case of a C Major chord, is that as long as it has C, E, and G in it, no matter where on the neck, and no matter what the order is, it's still a C Major chord. The only difference is that the chords are different voicings of each other, and will sound subtly different.

Basic Triads

The most basic chords in the world are triads, just like the ones discussed earlier in the chapter. A triad is simply a group of three notes, with third intervals between the notes. The two most used triads are major and minor. They are used far more commonly than are the other two triads. Simply speaking, major chords have a "happy" feeling to them, while minor triads feel "sad" or "dark." It may seem like a silly explanation, but chords can conjure up emotions, and major and minor are often used to paint sonic pictures.

There are four different types of triads that make up the whole musical universe:

- Major triads (root, third, fifth)
- Minor triads (root, ♭ third, fifth)
- Diminished triads (root, ♭ third, ♭ fifth)
- Augmented triads (root, third, ♯ fifth)

The four triads above are the four basic building blocks of western music. The words in parentheses show the theoretical blueprint for how each chord is formed. The numbers correspond to the intervals away from the root. A third is three notes away from the root, and so on. There isn't enough space here to get into the minute details of chord construction, but never fear! *The Everything® Reading Music Book* is a complete guide to music theory and goes into chord construction on a deep level. It would be a great companion to this book if you wanted to get beyond just looking at chord shapes. For now, though, it's enough to glance at the rest of the chord categories and then start playing!

Seventh Chords

Once you start from the basic categories of triads, the next step is to make them more advanced. Simply take any of the triads and add another third interval. That takes you to what are called "seventh" chords. The theoretical blueprint for a C Major 7 chord would be root, third, fifth, and seventh, or C E G B in pitch.

Chords like C Major 7, F7, and G Diminished 7 are all examples of seventh chords. A seventh chord is a four-note chord, built in thirds. Because there are so many different combinations of triads and sevenths, there are a lot of seventh chords! One more hint: They are also called seventh chords because the root of the chord is seven notes away from the highest note of the chord. Chord naming is very literal; more on this in a minute.

Dominants

There are a ton of seventh chords. Every triad can have a seventh of some sort. There are major sevenths, minor sevenths, augmented sevenths, diminished sevenths, and so on. There are subvarieties of those chords as well. However, there is an area of confusion to clear up right away: There is one extremely common type of seventh chord that musicians refer to as "dominant seventh" chords. These are the most typical and common seventh chords. If you've only been playing guitar a little bit, these are the first seventh chords that you will come into contact with. Here is what a dominant seventh chord looks like when you write it out: D7. The formula for this construction is: chord root (in this case, D), directly followed by the number 7.

All of these chords are dominant seventh chords: C7, D7, E7, F7, G7, A7, B7.

So many people think that these are the *only* seventh chords in the universe! They are very common, so they come up often. Remember that while there are many different types of seventh chords, most guitar players commonly refer to the dominant seventh chord simply as *the* seventh chord, so be aware of this to avoid confusion.

To signify one of the "other" seventh chords, you'd need to add more information, such as the "major" and "minor" in C Major 7 and C Minor 7. As long as you can spot the distinction and not get confused, you will be in good shape.

Sixth Chords

This may seem out of order, considering that I just talked about seventh chords and now I am onto sixth chords, but there is a reason! Seventh chords follow the nice triad pattern of thirds and are the next logical step from the triads. Sixth chords are in their own little family. Sixth chords appear only in Chapters 3 and 4.

Jumping back to dominant seventh chords for a second, you just learned that when you see a letter and number combination, it indicates a dominant chord; for example, C7. Unfortunately, music is full of inconsistencies, and here is one of them: A chord such as C6 belongs in the family of major chords, not in the family of dominant chords. This is an exception you need to learn. Sixth chords are major or minor and do not belong with dominant chords even though they follow the same "rule" for written expression that dominants do: a letter directly followed by a number. As to what a sixth chord is, chord names are literal, so take a guess. What makes sense? How about a triad, with a sixth note attached? C6 = C E G A, with A being six notes higher than the root of C. See, chord naming isn't that hard at all! C6 is a major chord; sixth chords also exist in the minor section, but thankfully, they are easy to spot: "C Minor 6." Just don't get them confused with dominant chords! Tip: Sixth chords are some of the prettiest sounding chords out there. Go find some to play!

Tall Chords

The next step after seventh chords is to make your chords taller. I say "taller" because as you stack the chords on the music staff, they reach vertically higher on the page. Making taller chords is as simple as adding additional third intervals. Remember, chords are made up almost completely of third intervals. This is called "tertian" (based on three) harmony, and is the foundation of the western system of harmony.

Here is how the next group of chords stacks up. After seventh chords, there are:

- Ninth chords (root, third, fifth, seventh, ninth)
- Eleventh chords (root, third, fifth, seventh, ninth, eleventh)
- Thirteenth chords (root, third, fifth, seventh, ninth, eleventh, thirteenth)

You can't go any higher than thirteenth chords because adding one more third will loop you back around to where you started by adding another root. Also realize that a thirteenth chord has seven notes in it, and you have six strings and four fingers. Part of the art of guitar chord voicing is compromising on these tall chords in order to make them playable.

You will see these chords in Chapters 3, 4, and 5 of this book. Tall chords aren't exclusively a "jazz" thing, but they are used most commonly in jazz. They have a truly unique sound that's worth checking out, even if you don't play jazz. You never know when you'll want to use them to spice up your music.

Finger Limits

Tall chords can sometimes lead to problems. The guitar is a limited harmonic instrument. This may seem hard to believe, considering that you just purchased a book that shows you more than 2,000 chords, but compared to the piano, the guitar is extremely limited. If you look at the chord pages themselves, you will see that each page has five chords, with the music staff on top spelling out the chord as it appears in written music. The guitar is rarely, if ever, capable of playing the exact written chord specified in each section. This is an important point to touch on. The music staff at the top of each set of chords is there for theoretical display only. It is never represented *exactly* that same way in the chords below. What the chords below show are voicings of the music at the top of the page. Basically, they are different versions of the chord, working within the confines of the tuning of the guitar and the number of fingers you have to play with. Remember, a thirteenth chord has seven notes in it, so you'd never be able to play that chord with four fingers and six strings; the five voicings shown are five of the ways that the guitar can play a thirteenth chord. Don't feel that this is a limitation! What the guitar can do, and what a great guitarist can do, is play the essence of the chord, the notes that best define the harmony. As I said in Chapter 1, the beauty of the guitar is overcoming this limitation and finding some unique chord voicings. The written music is the model, and the five resulting voicings are the best-case scenarios for reproducing that chord. If only there were more strings and you had more fingers—well, just more fingers; they make guitars with thirteen strings.

Odd-Looking Dominant Chords

Tall chords in Chapters 3 and 4 (Major Chords and Minor Chords) look fairly normal; nothing stands out as too odd. In Chapter 5 (Dominant Chords), you will notice some very unusual chords.

Dominant chords are broken into two categories, unaltered and altered. The unaltered chords are easy to spot: In the key of C they are C 7, C 9, and C 13. Looking at the rest of the chapter, you will see some very unusual-looking chords. For example, take a look at C 7♯9 or C 7♯5. These chords are called "altered" dominant chords. Altered dominant chords are a staple of jazz. Basically, you alter one or more of the pitches in the chord, up or down one fret, to create a new and unusual sound. If you are reading a jazz chart, you will see these chords. They are not just here for fun; they are commonly used in jazz music.

There are many varieties of altered dominant chords. This book gives you the garden-variety chords, which will get you through most any situation. When in doubt, please look at the chord simplification section found later in this chapter. It will get you through anything that might come your way.

Other Chords

You now have progressed through most of the chords that you will encounter in music. There are a few "rogue" categories of chords that you also need to handle as a guitar player. You will find them in chord form in Chapter 8. Here is the lowdown on what those chords are.

Power Chords

Ah, the power chord. What a name for a chord. No one is sure who named it, but one thing is for sure—the title is fitting. A power chord, when played through a loud amplifier, especially in a rock setting, is one of the most powerful sounds you've ever heard. It is the standard chord of metal, rock, and punk music. There's no way to play guitar and never encounter a power chord. The real name for a power chord is a "fifth chord," as in C5.

Power chords are structurally different in that they contain only two notes: the root and the fifth of the chord. This breaks the traditional notion that chords contain three notes, but leave it to a guitar player to break the rules of music. Even though a power chord contains only the root and fifth, the root is usually doubled, so typically you play three notes anyway, just not three *different* notes. Power chords can be played anywhere on the neck of the guitar, but they sound best played as low as possible. Distortion is also a plus when dealing with power chords. Another neat thing about power chords is that they have a consistent finger shape that easily slides around the fingerboard. Look at the power chord section in Chapter 8 to see what I mean.

Suspended Chords

A suspended chord is a fairly common chord in all styles of music. The basic chord is still the triad. The triad, as you learned earlier, is composed of the root, third, and fifth (C E G for C Major triad). In any chord, the third (in this case, E) is the defining member of the chord. The third of *any* chord is very important. When you take the third away completely you get a power chord, which yields a unique sound. In the case of a suspended chord, you take the third of the chord away and replace it with another tone: either the second or the fourth note above the root. This yields two possible suspended, or "sus" chords: sus 2 and sus 4. The name "suspended" is literal; these chords seem to be frozen and suspended in motion and sound. Taking away the most important tone of the chord and replacing it with something else produces a sound that isn't dissonant, just *unresolved*. Typically, suspended chords are momentary chords. You often see C Major, Csus2, and then C Major, as the suspension serves as a temporary "pass-through." Suspended chords are neither major nor minor chords. They are harmonically ambiguous because the third is missing. The third of the chord is the defining element. Without it, it's not really much of a "chord" in the traditional sense. Sus chords do have intriguing sounds and are used as chords that don't ever resolve. They are simply another color in your palette.

In your music, you will usually see exactly which suspension is called for, either the sus 2 or the sus 4. If the chord just says "C sus," it's up to you to choose one or the other. There is no right or wrong choice in that case. Most likely, the composer wanted an ambiguous sound, and both the sus 2 and sus 4 will suffice in that regard.

Triads over Bass Notes (Slash Chords)

There is one last chord type to explain before you can get the most out of this book. Slash chords, which also are called triads over bass notes, are another subset of chords. A slash chord is presented like this: C/E or C min/A♭. A slash chord is composed of two elements: On the left side is the basic chord, and on the right side is the note that should be the lowest sounding note. Usually, slash chords are used to show specific chord motions and specific voicings.

The beauty of slash chords is that typically, the right side of the slash chord (the bass note), is not played by the guitar player. Typically, the job of playing the lowest note is left up to the bass player. When encountering a slash chord, you simply play the left side of the slash and the bass player plays the right side. Together, you get the correct sound. Since theoretically any chord can be played over any bass note, I have opted to leave these out altogether, because they would muddy up this book with chords that truly may never come into play. It's enough to know that all of the chords on the left side of the slash chords are covered in this book. Slash chords are part of the greater topic of chord inversions, which you will find covered in great detail in *The Everything® Reading Music Book*.

If you are playing guitar alone, without a bass player, it isn't too hard to create a slash chord. Simply take a chord voicing you know, and try to place the appropriate bass note on your lowest string. Sometimes this is easy. Sometimes this is hard. It's really great when the bass note is an open string! A great example is A/E, which is telling you to play an A Major chord with an E in the bass. Because E is an open string, you can play this chord (shown in Figure 2.3).

Figure 2.3

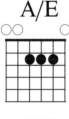

This is nothing more than a simple open A chord with an open E added to the chord.

When in doubt, just play the triads on the left side of the slash. You won't be wrong.

Chord Simplification

Jazz and pop music makes use of "extensions" on chords. Extensions are notes added to the top of the chords. Typically these extensions are intervals of a ninth, eleventh, and thirteenth. You learned earlier that these are called tall chords. Extensions can also be any combination, and in the case of altered dominants, they can be very messy chords. The good news about extensions is that you don't have to play them. Extensions provide a more colorful harmony, one that is more jazz-like. However, the basic chord still stays the same. For example, if you see C Major 13, you will know that it's in the family of C Major 7, and you can play that instead. The same holds true for any extended chord:

- C m 13, C m 11, C m 9 = C m 7 (C Minor 7)
- C 9, C 11, C 13 = C 7 (C Dominant 7)

This is the case no matter how elaborate the chord is. Here is a scary example: E 7$\sharp$9$\flat$9$\flat$5$\natural$13.

That's an actual chord! Disregard everything after the E7 and simply play an E7 chord. Even though the chord asks for more, by playing less you're not playing anything wrong— you're just playing a simpler harmony.

The one alteration that you need to watch out for is an alteration to the fifth note: $\sharp$5 or $\flat$5. The fifth is considered a core note of the chord and not an extension as a ninth or an eleventh is. When the fifth is altered, if at all possible you should try to play it, even if it means excluding the extensions (just playing E 7$\flat$5) in the example above.

Alterations and extensions are there for a reason, so whenever possible try to play the chord as best as you can. Often, the altered notes are part of melodies that other instruments are playing, so you end up supporting them by playing the notes. When you can't do that, simplify.

Chords Written as Symbols

Guitar chords don't usually appear in written music as stacks of notes. Very often, and especially in jazz and show music, you'll find chords written out as symbols of text. The player is responsible for knowing how to play that chord in a comfortable way on the guitar. Over the years, several conventions for writing out chords have been used. Unfortunately, no one standard exists.

- A major chord can appear as one of the following symbols: C, C Maj, C M, C $\triangle$.
- A minor chord can appear as one of the following symbols: C min, C m, C -.
- Diminished chords are written the following way: C °, C dim.
- Augmented chords are written this way: C +, C aug.
- Dominant seventh chords are written this way: C 7.
- Major seventh chords are written this way: C Maj 7, C M 7, C $\triangle$ 7.
- Minor seventh chords are written this way: C min 7, C m 7, C - 7.
- Diminished seventh chords are written this way: C di m 7, C ° 7.
- Half diminished seventh chords are written this way: C min 7$\flat$5, C ø 7, C - 7$\flat$5.

The Freshman Fifteen

Here are the first chords you should know by heart before going any further in this book. These are your "freshman fifteen."

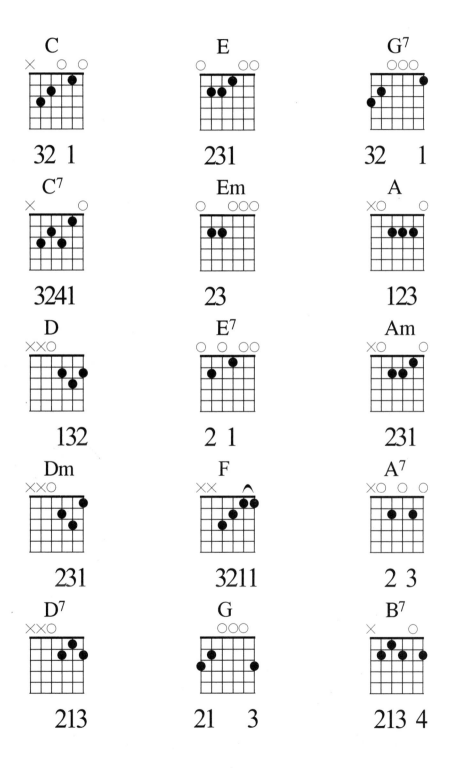

3

Chapter 3

Major Chords

So much of today's music is made up of major chords. In our society, these chords make up the "happy" sounds in music. In popular music, they are a staple with many possibilities.

27

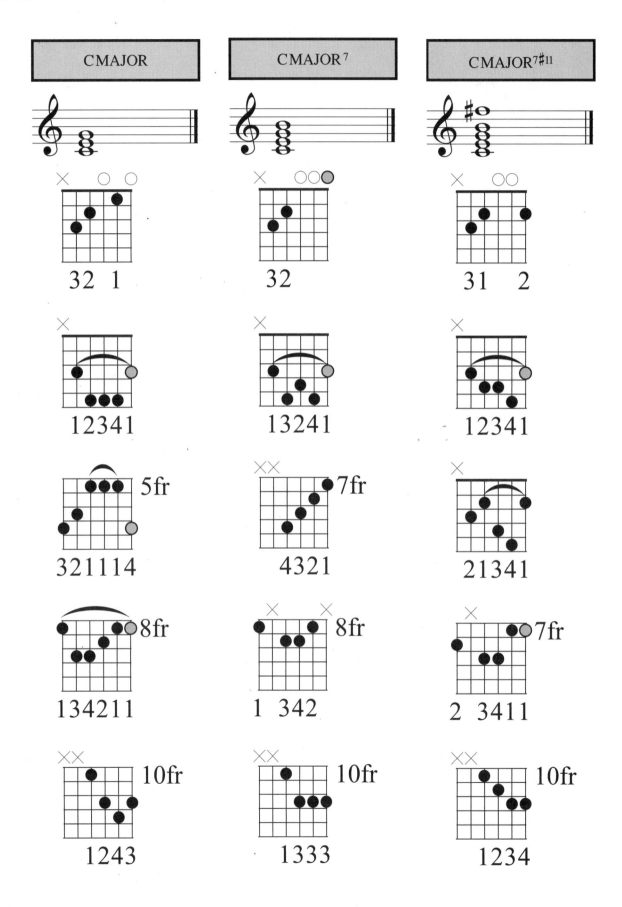

CMAJOR⁷#⁵	CMAJOR⁹	CMAJOR¹³

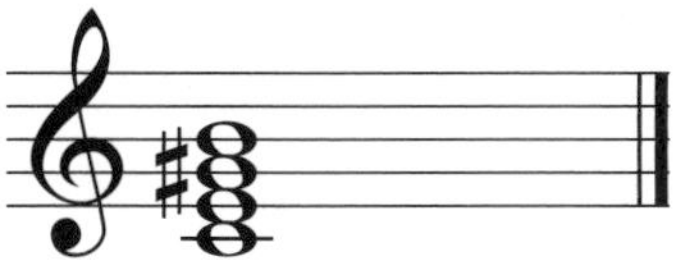

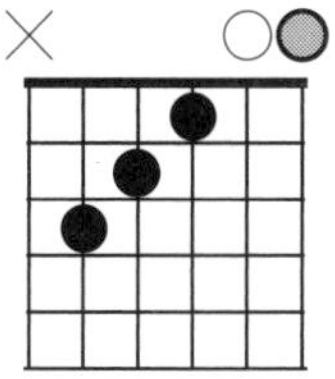

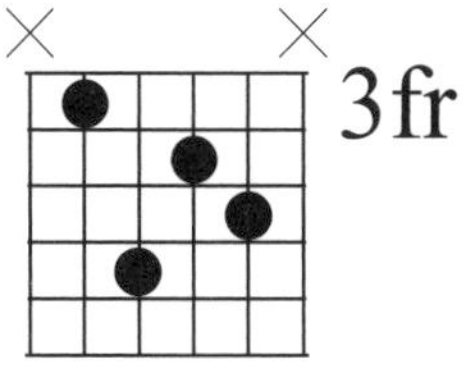

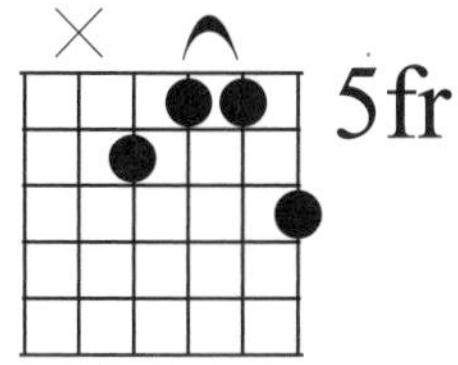

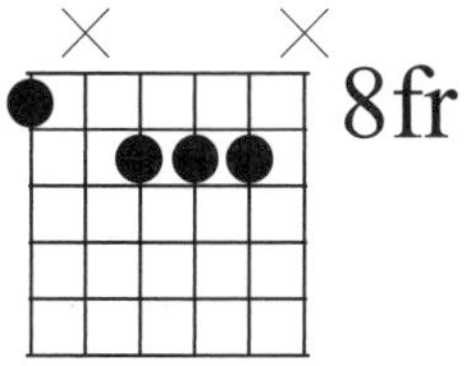

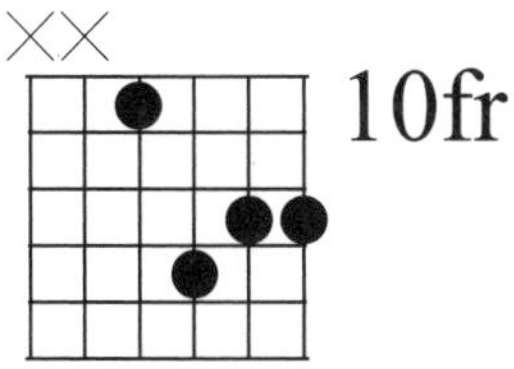

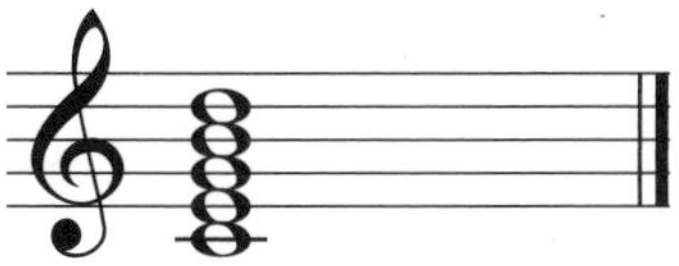

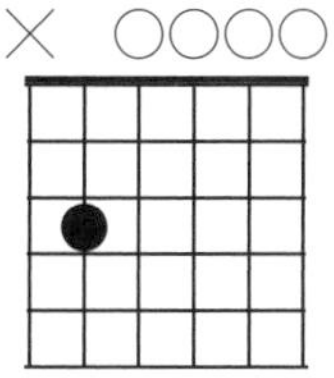

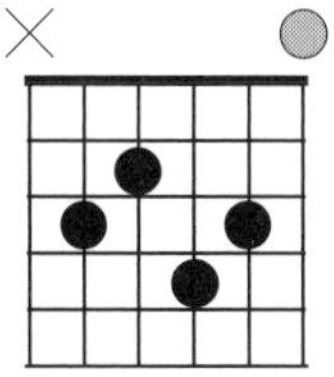

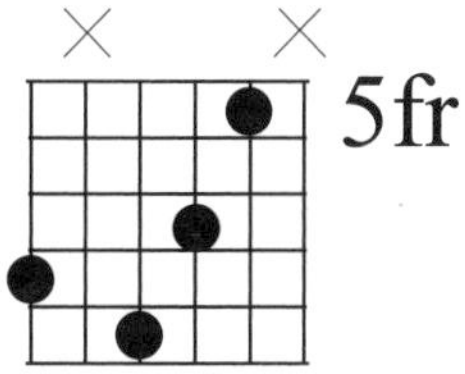

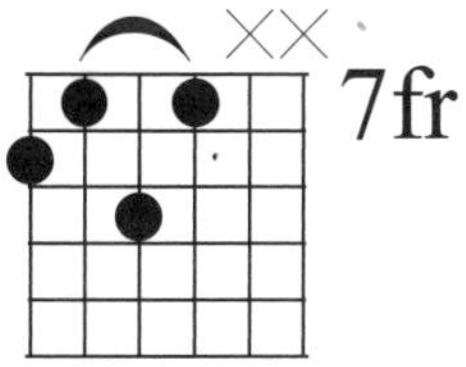

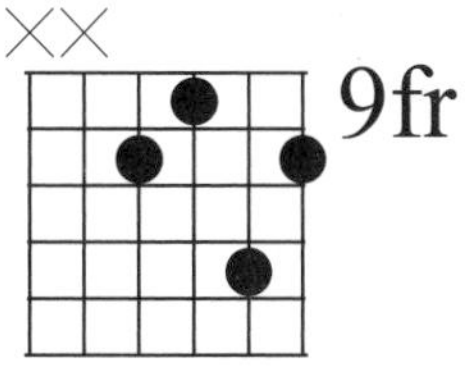

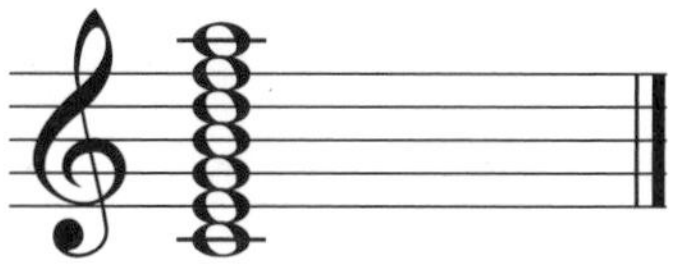

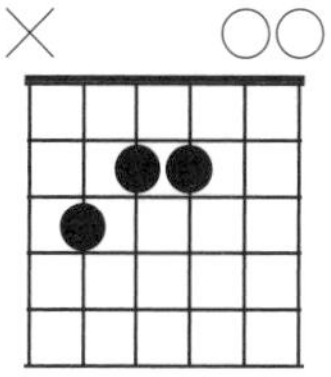

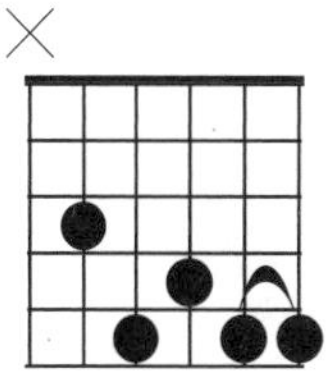

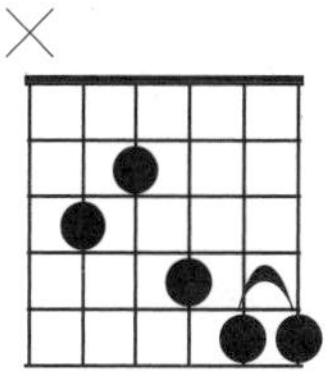

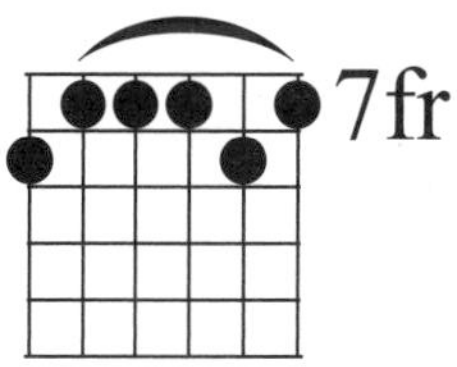

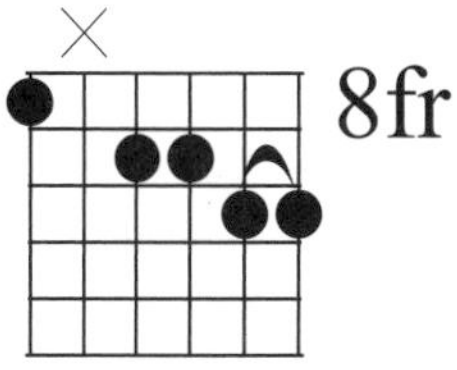

321

3

423

1423 (3fr)

2143

13244

2114 (5fr)

3 421 (5fr)

21344

1 234 (8fr)

2131 (7fr)

211131 (7fr)

1423 (10fr)

2143 (9fr)

1 2344 (8fr)

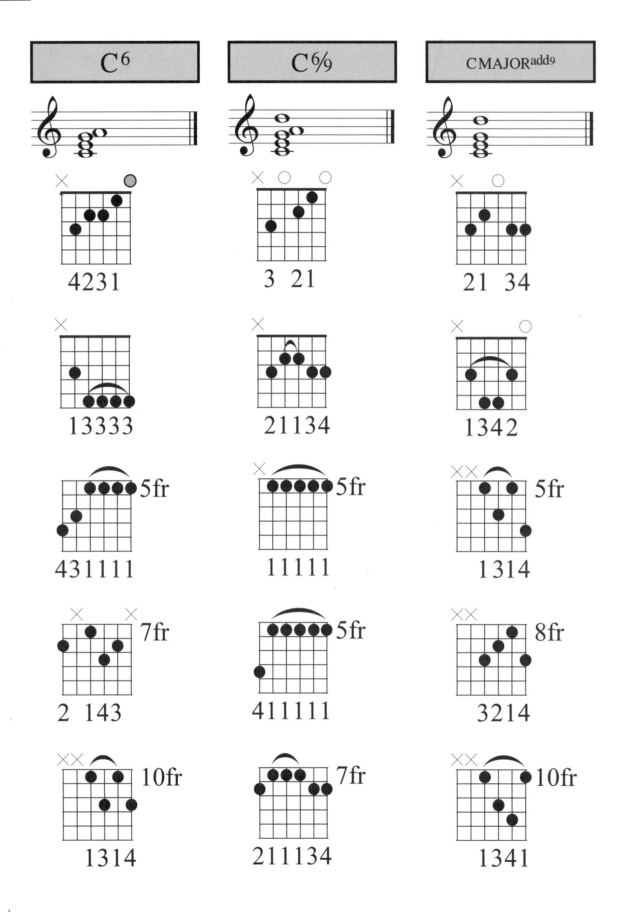

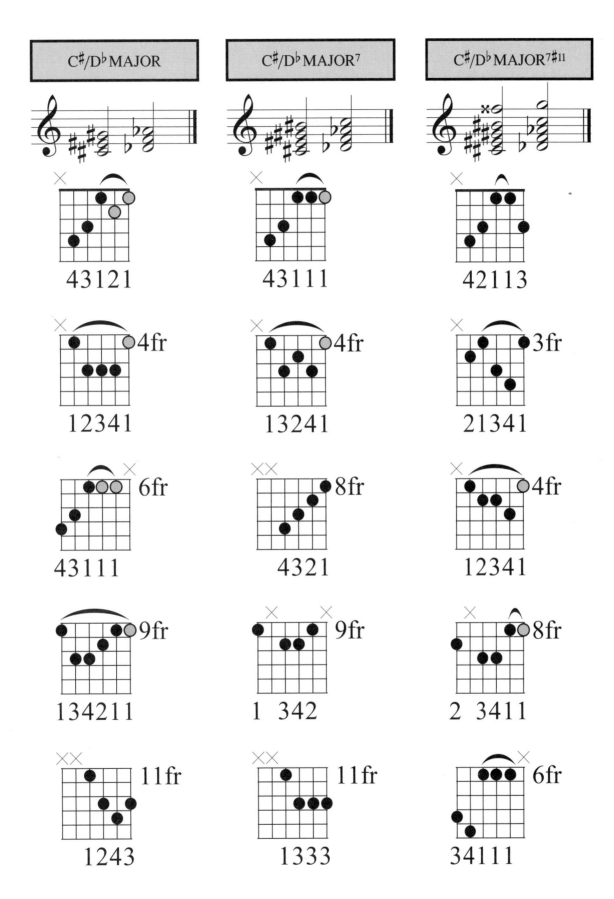

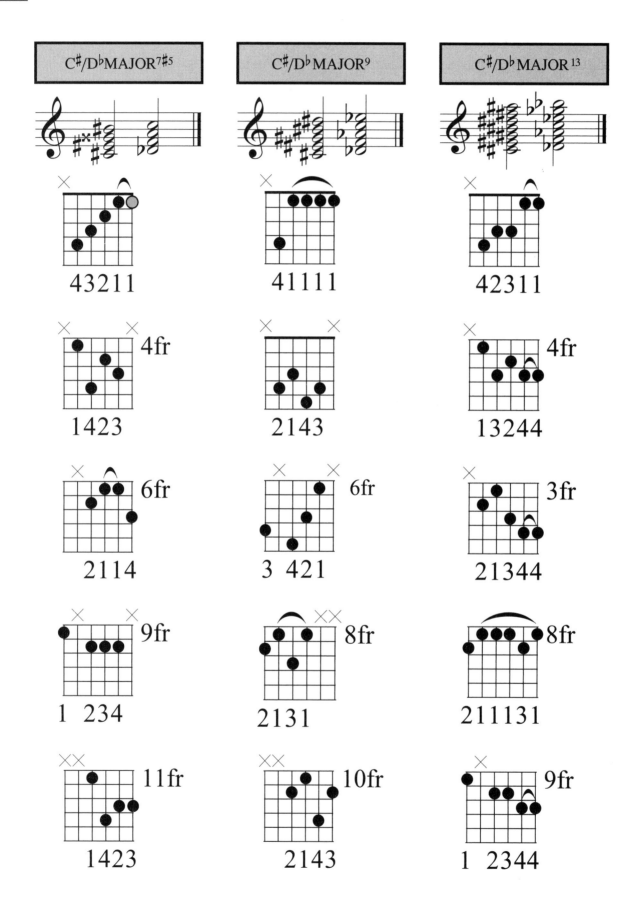

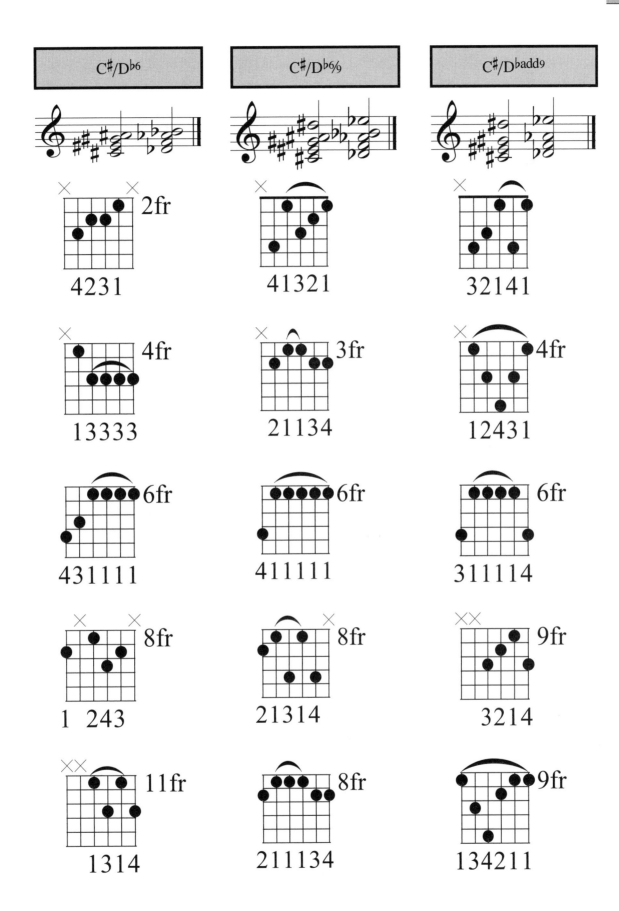

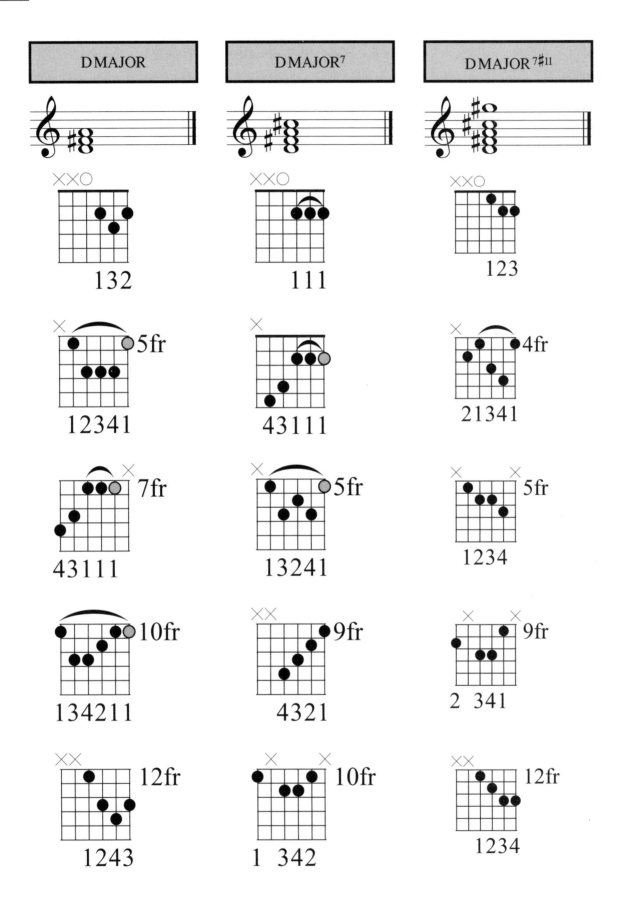

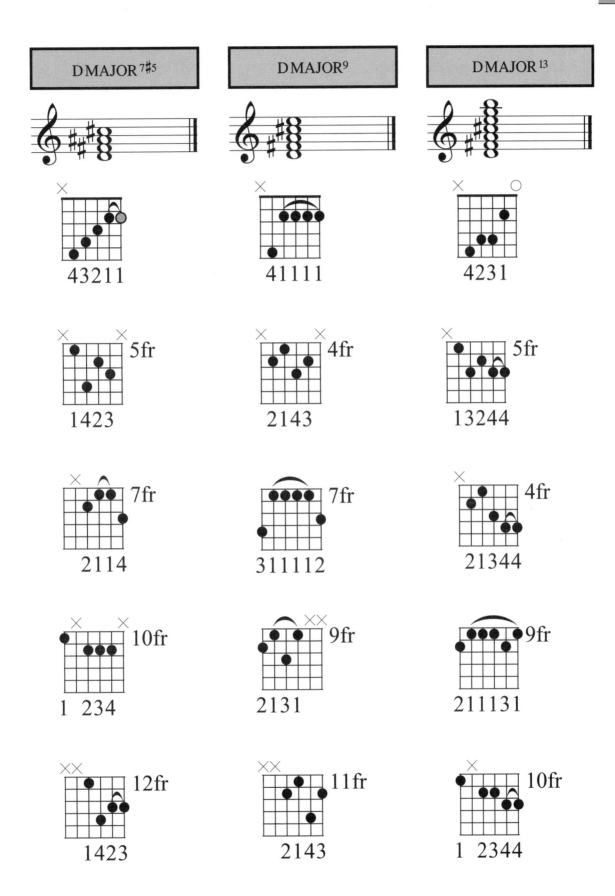

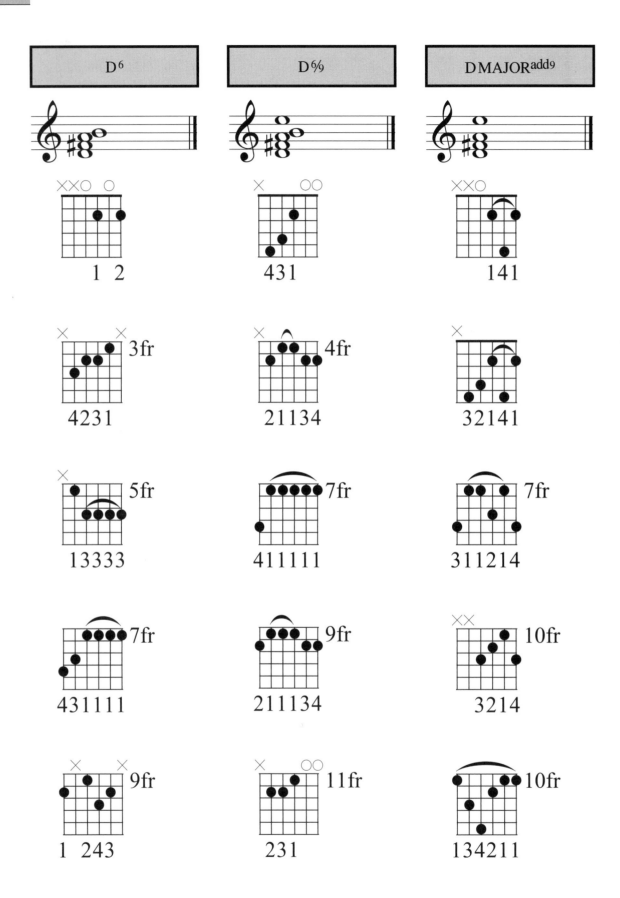

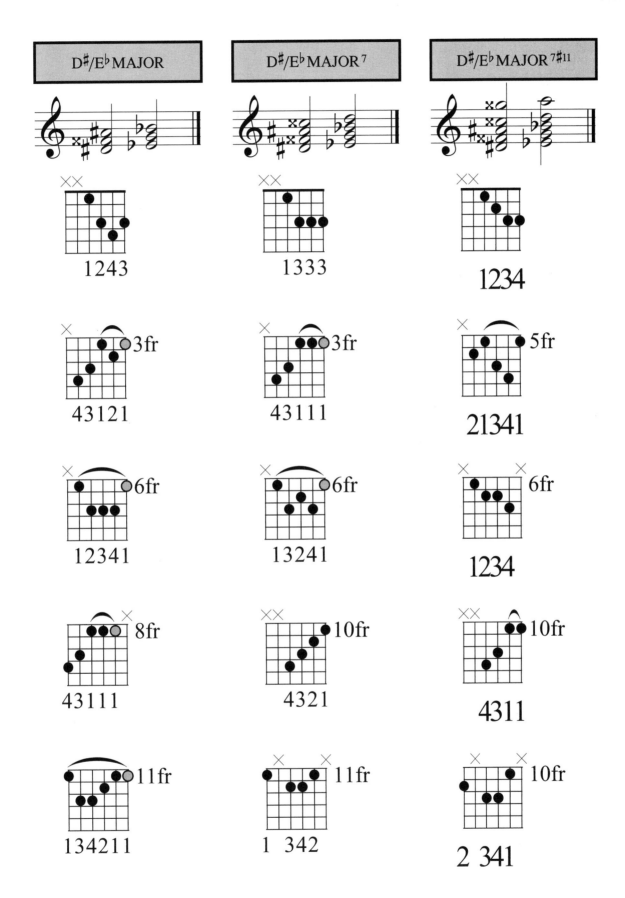

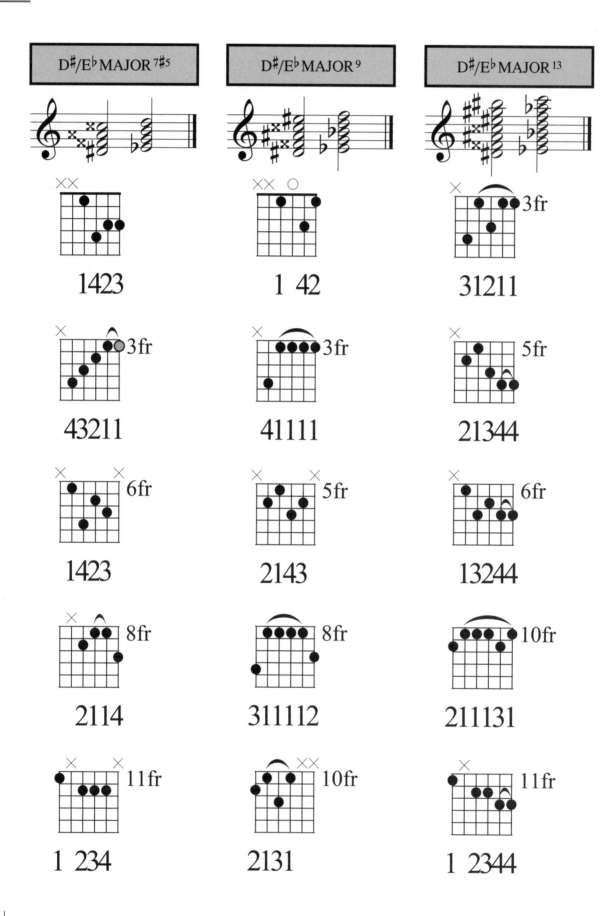

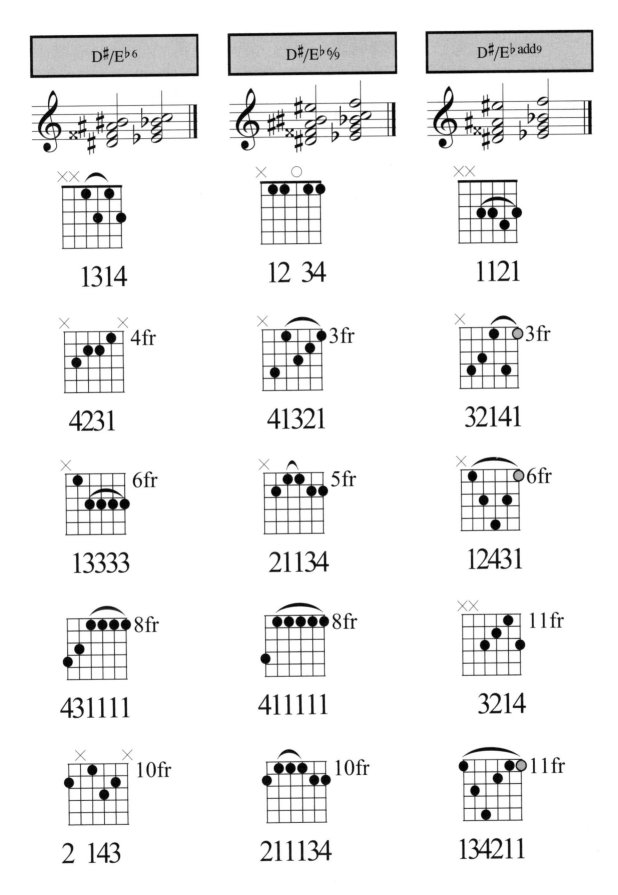

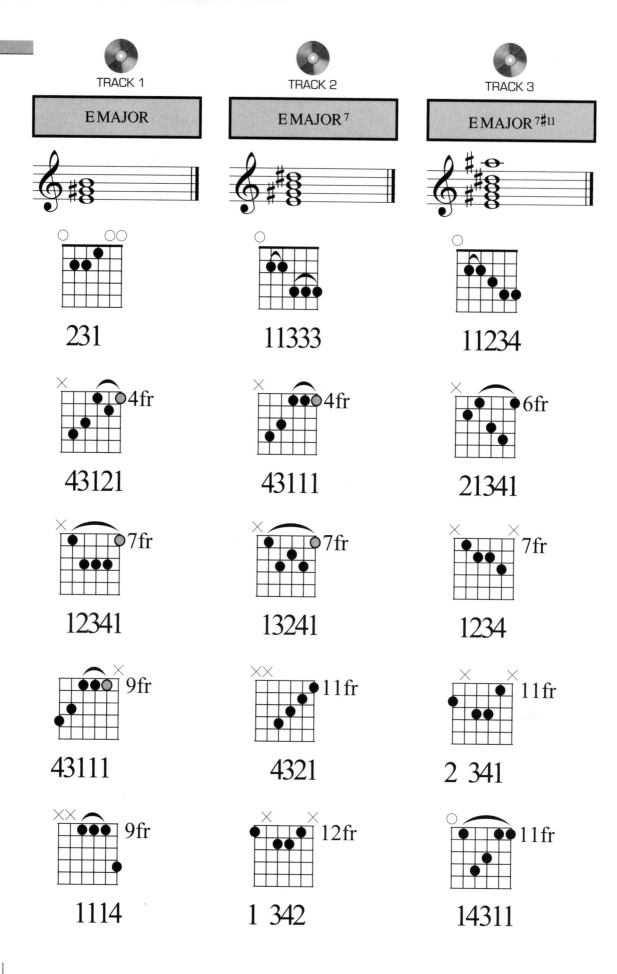

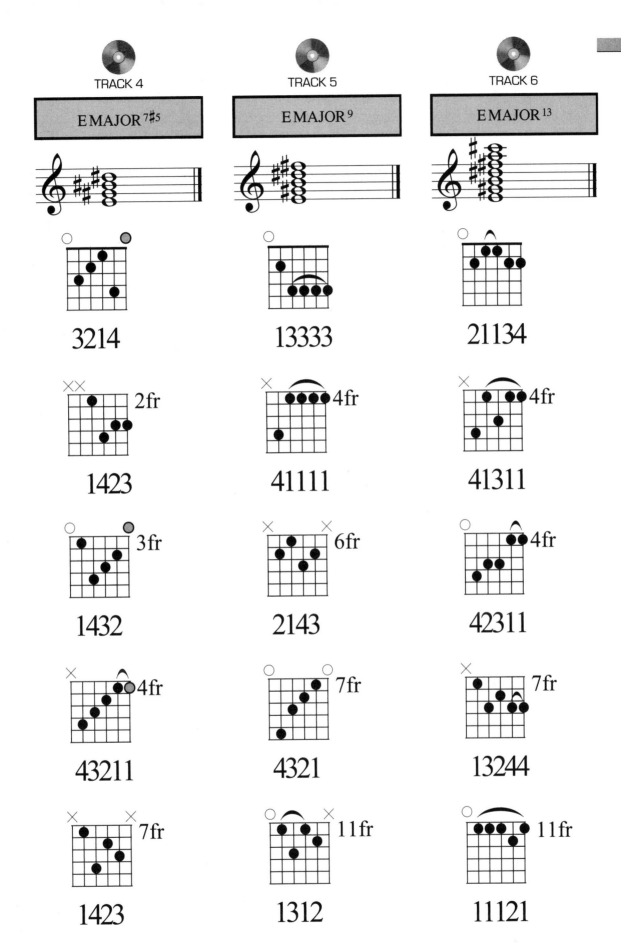

TRACK 4

E MAJOR 7#5

3214

1423

1432

43211

1423

TRACK 5

E MAJOR 9

13333

41111

2143

4321

1312

TRACK 6

E MAJOR 13

21134

41311

42311

13244

11121

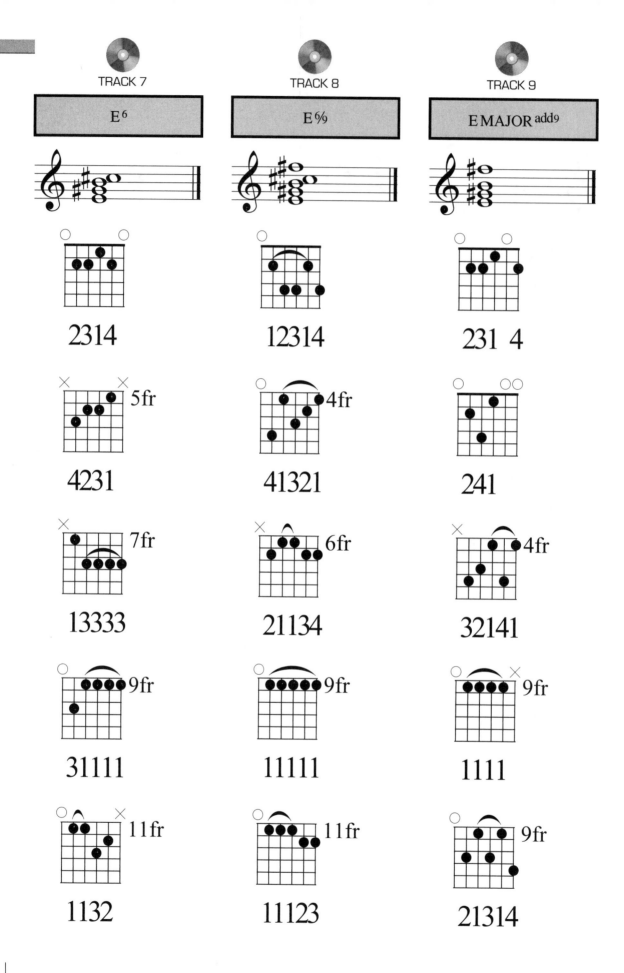

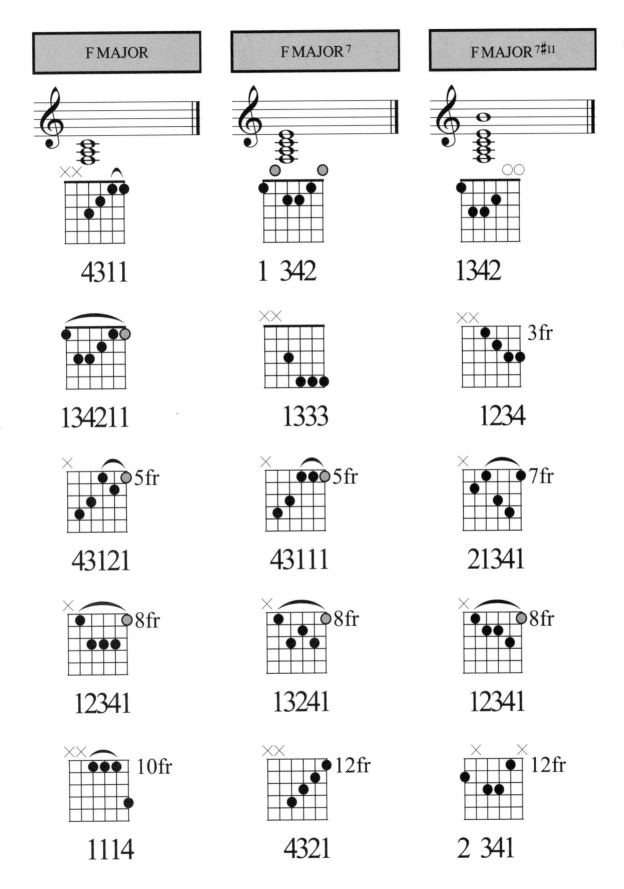

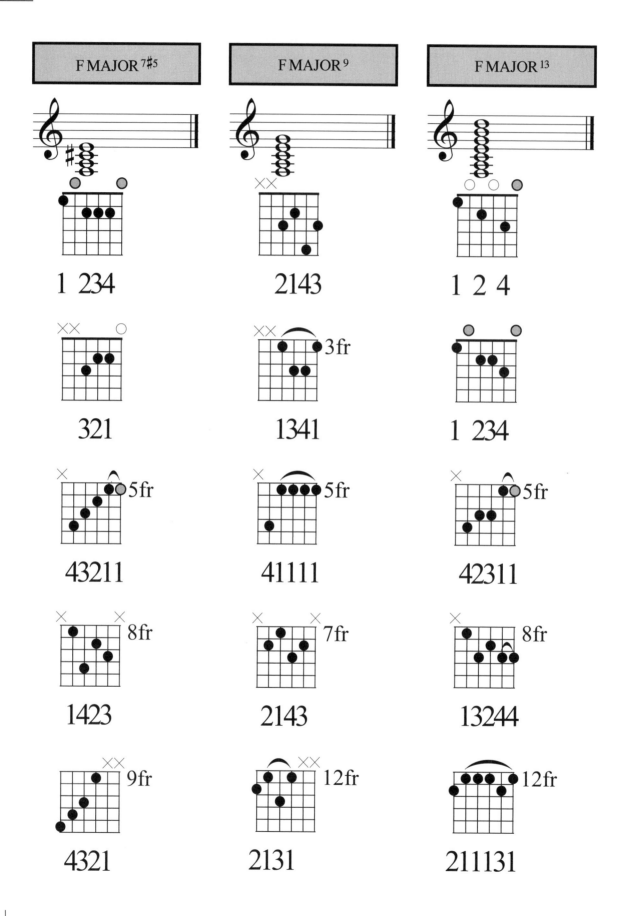

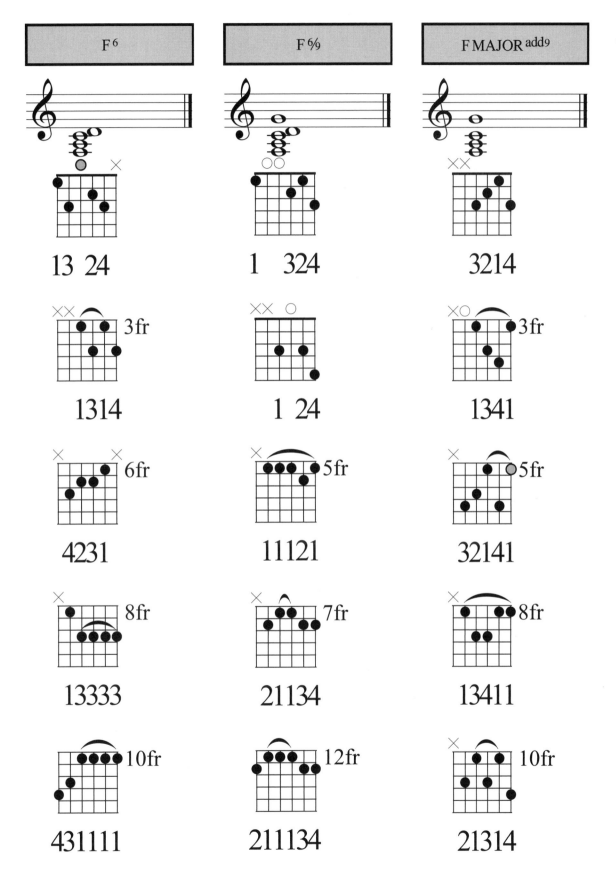

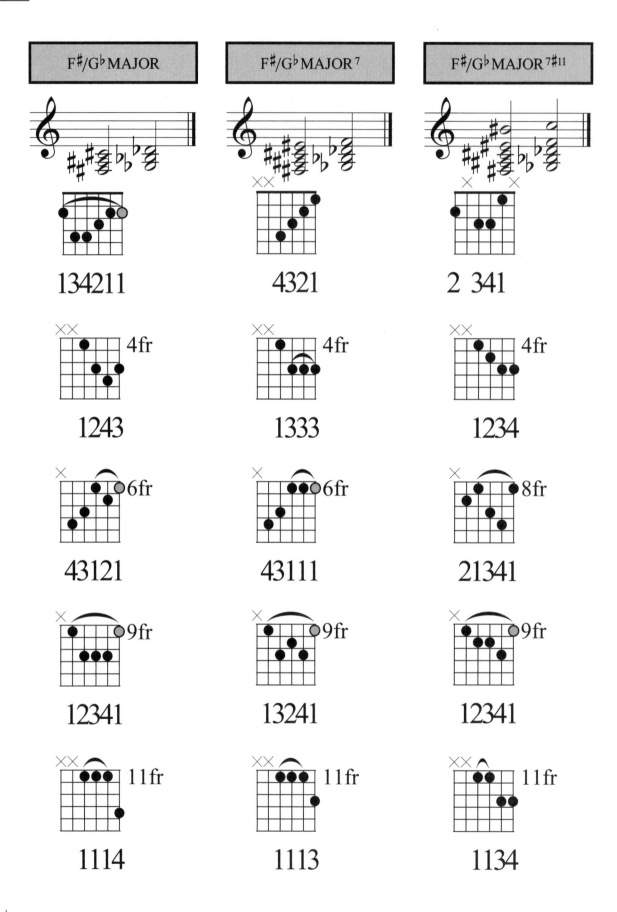

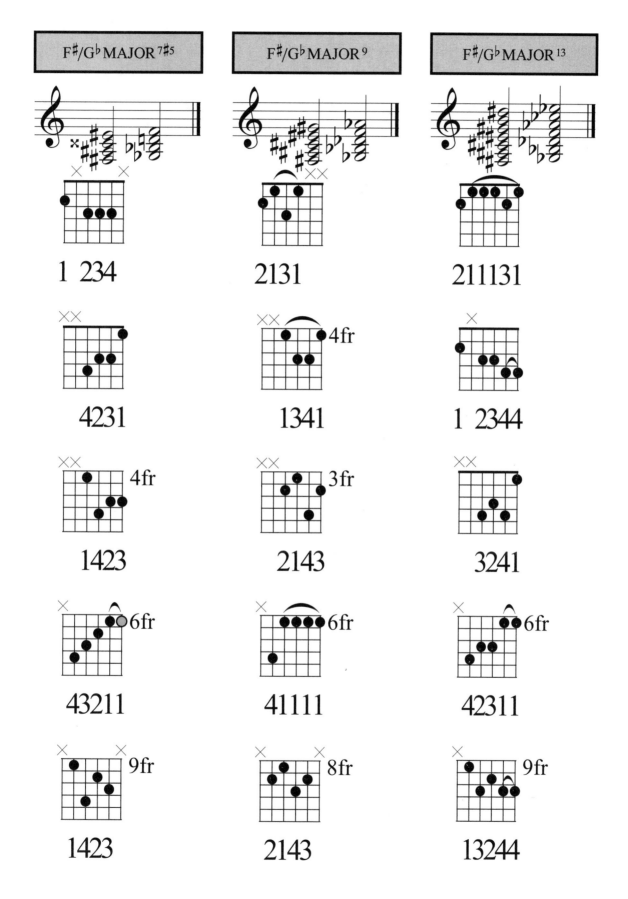

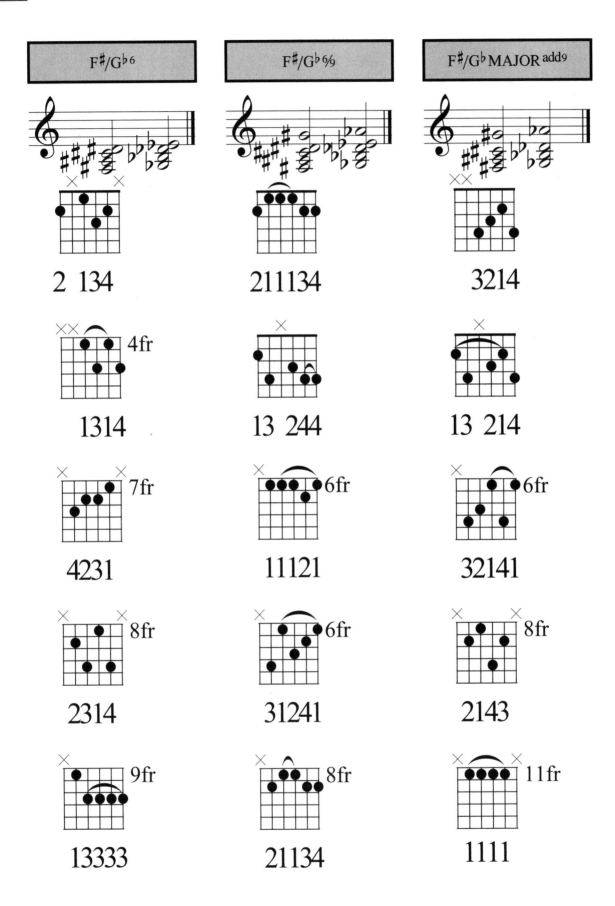

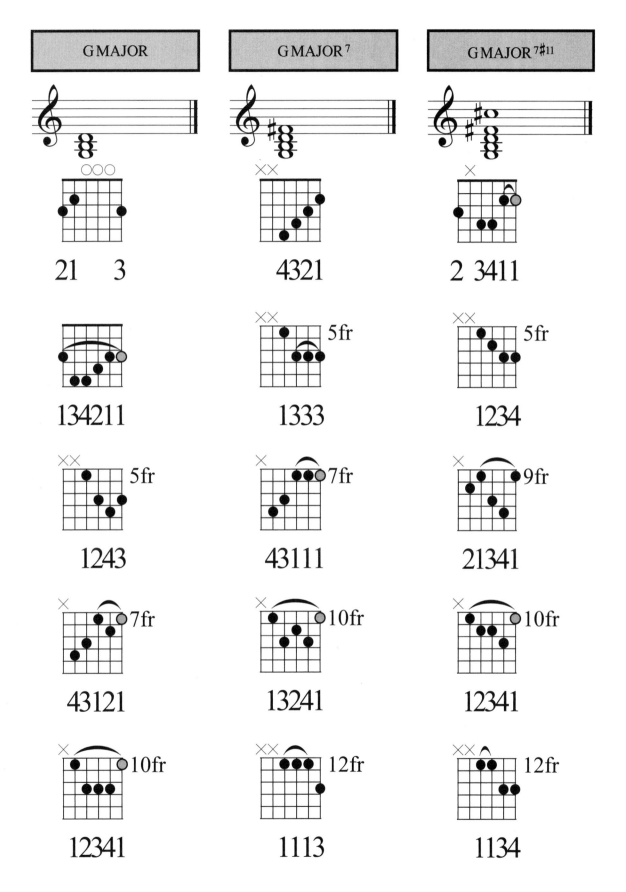

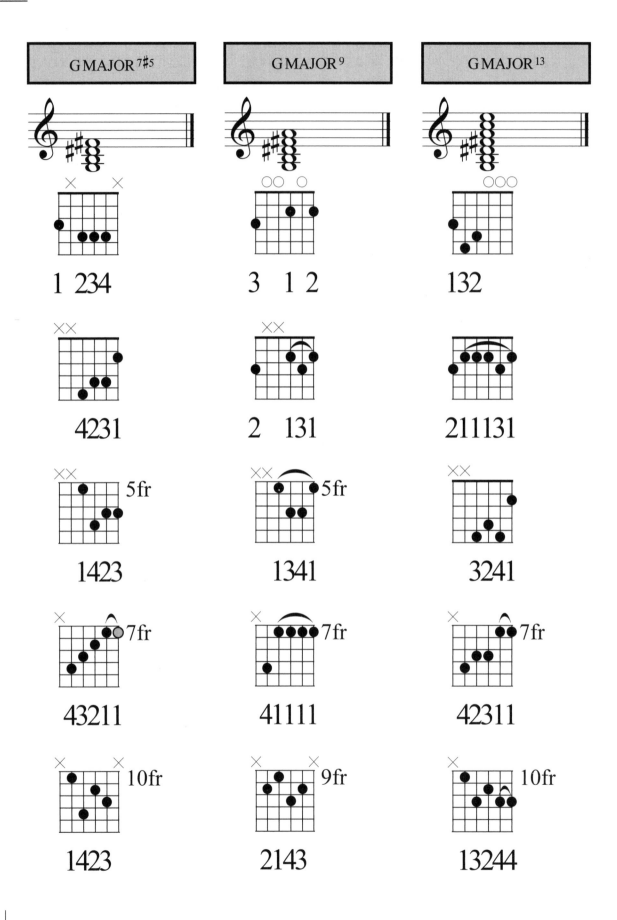

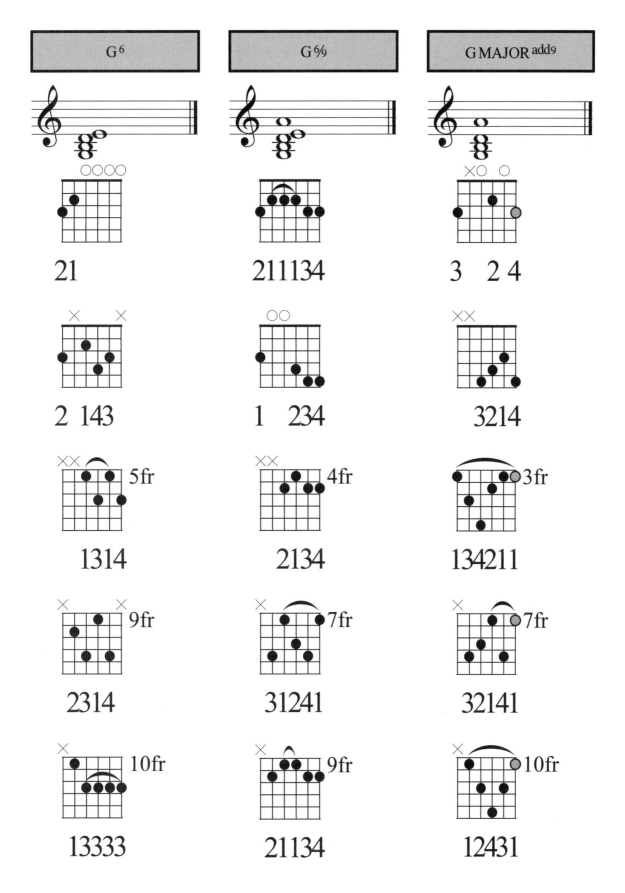

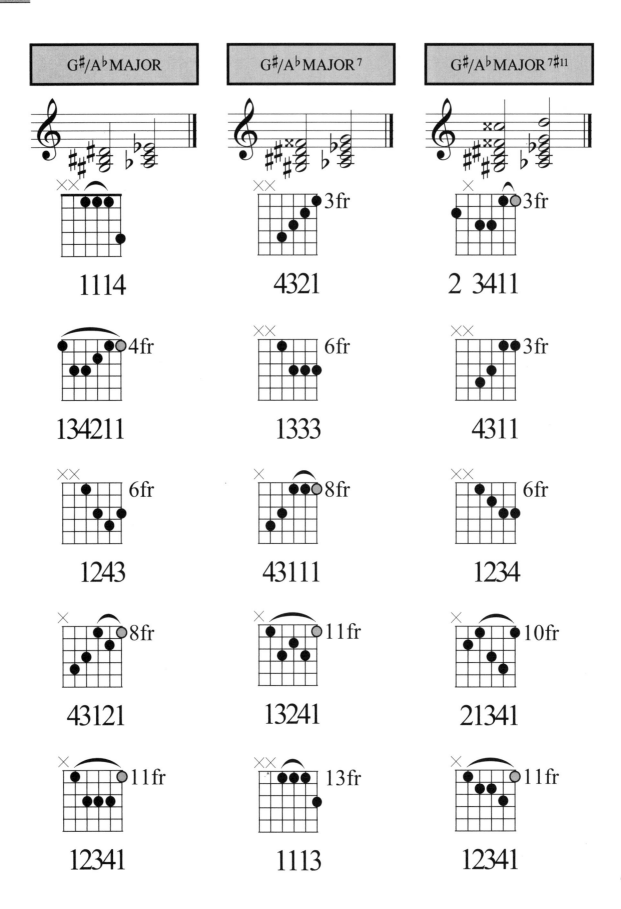

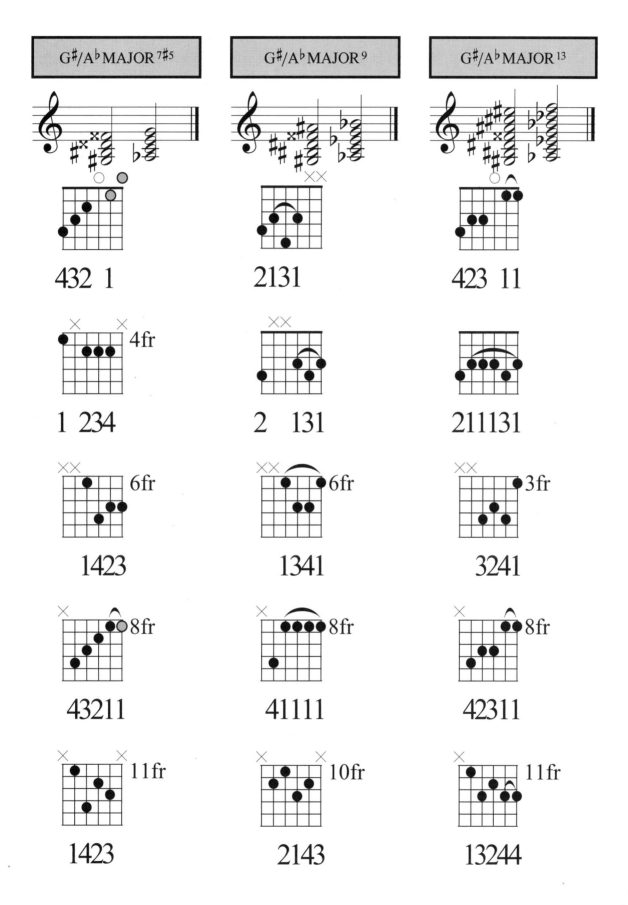

G#/Ab MAJOR 7#5	G#/Ab MAJOR 9	G#/Ab MAJOR 13
432 1	2131	423 11
1 234 4fr	2 131	211131
1423 6fr	1341 6fr	3241 3fr
43211 8fr	41111 8fr	42311 8fr
1423 11fr	2143 10fr	13244 11fr

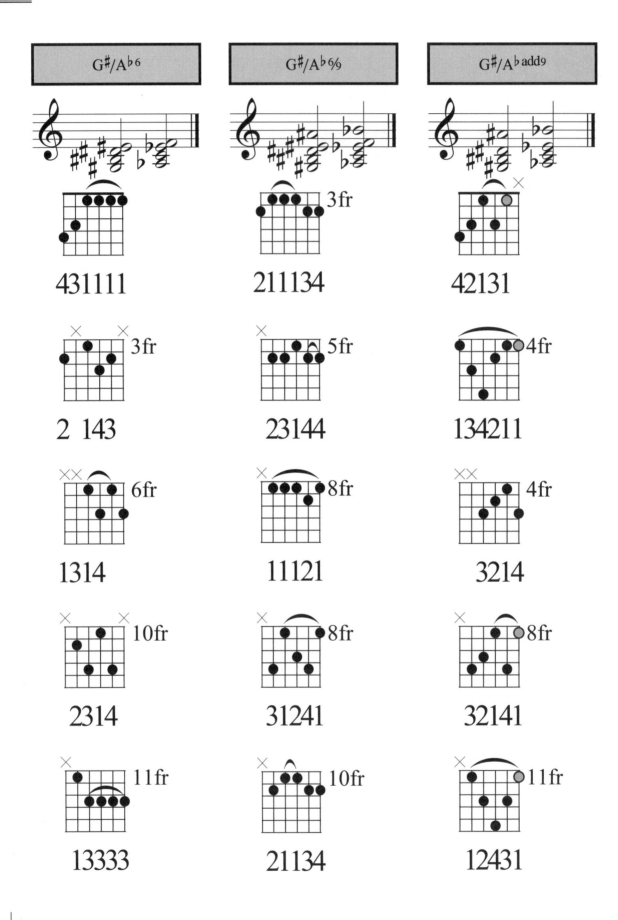

A MAJOR	A MAJOR ^{7}	A MAJOR $^{7\sharp 11}$

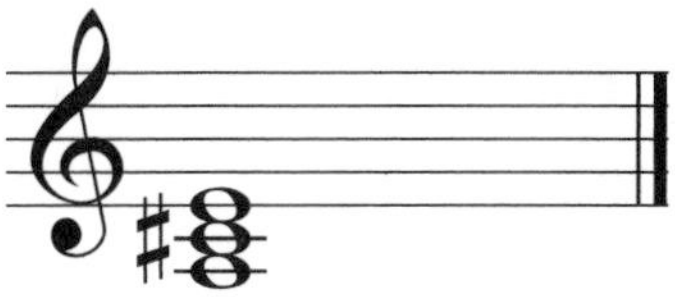

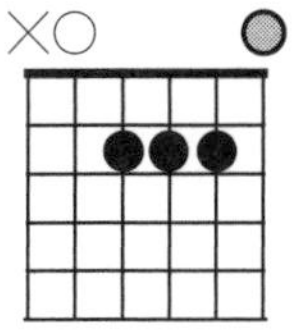

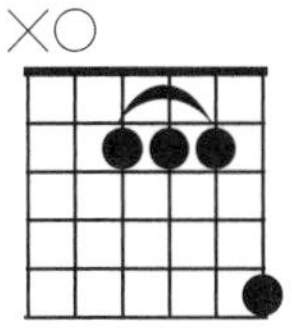

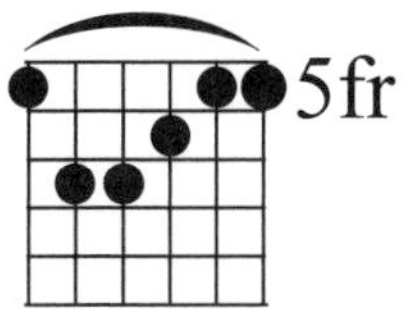

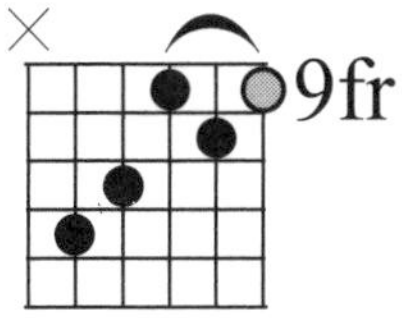

123

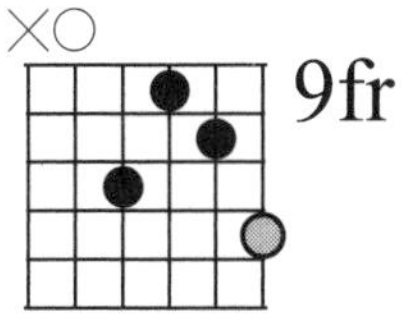

213

214

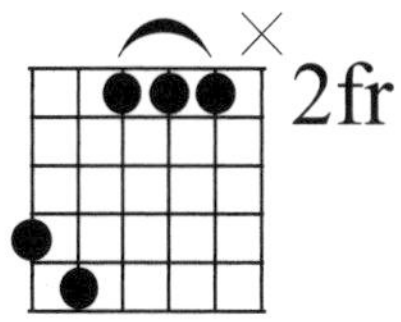

1114

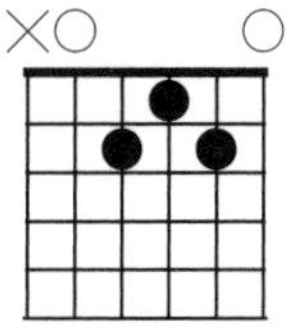

4321

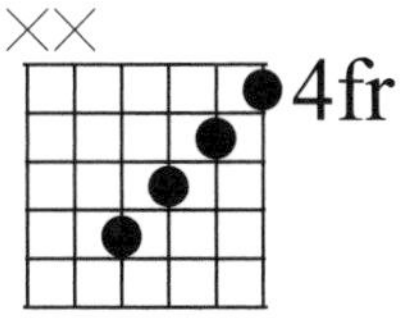

34111

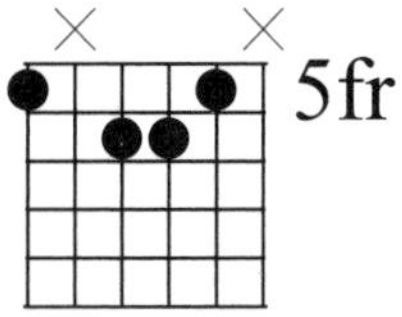

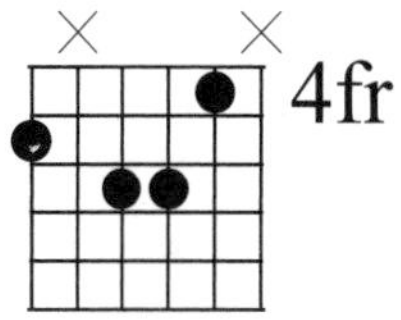

134211

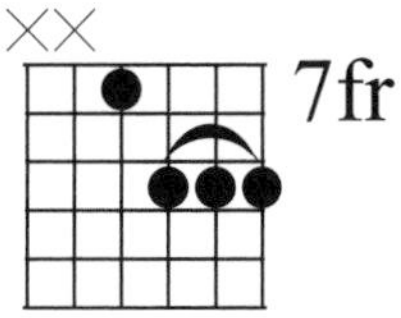

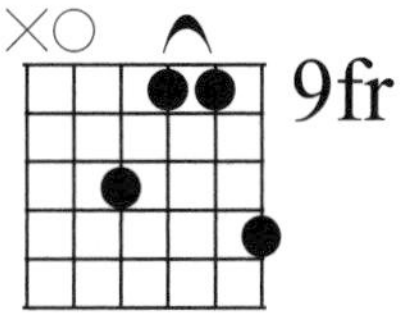

1 342

2 341

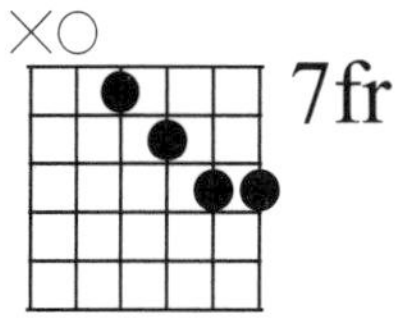

43121

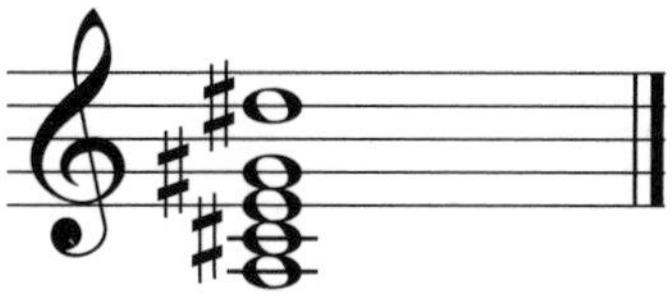

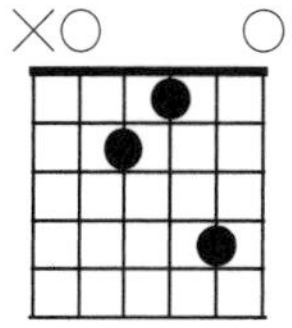

1333

1234

3124

3114

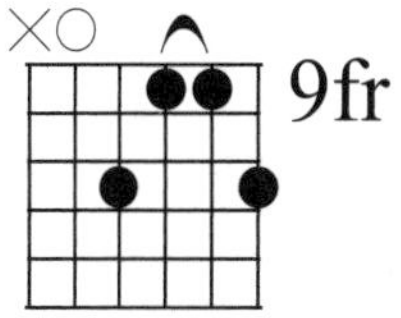

3114

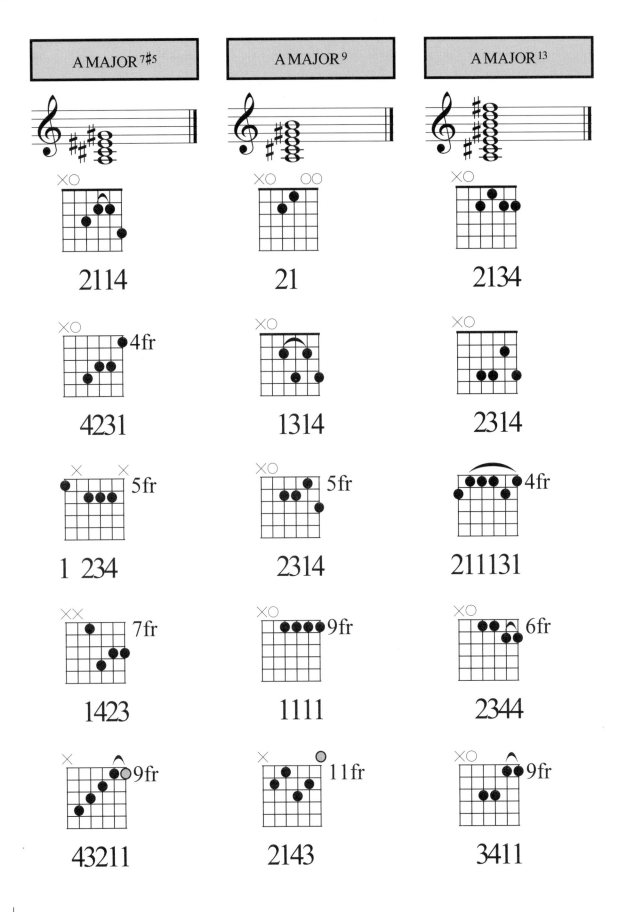

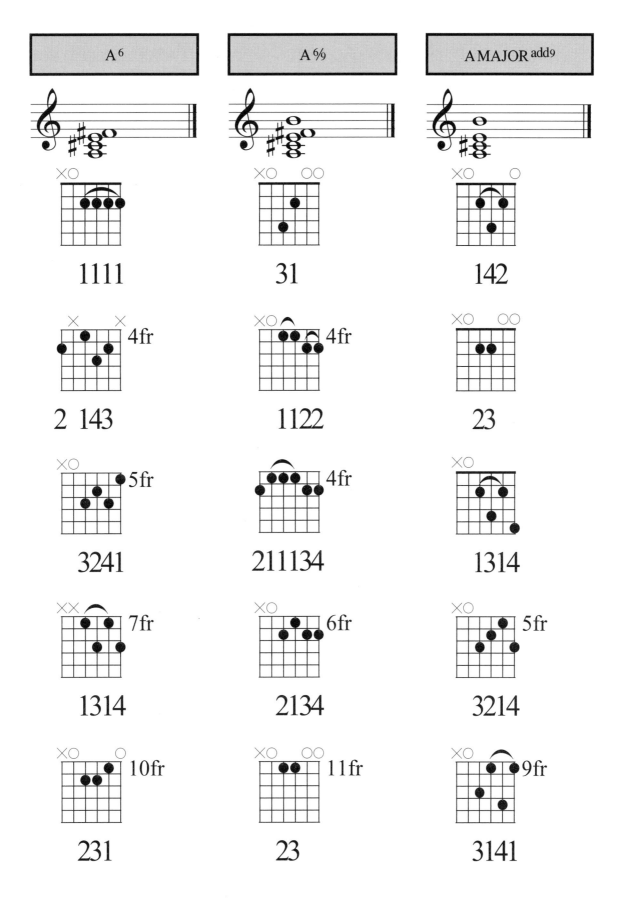

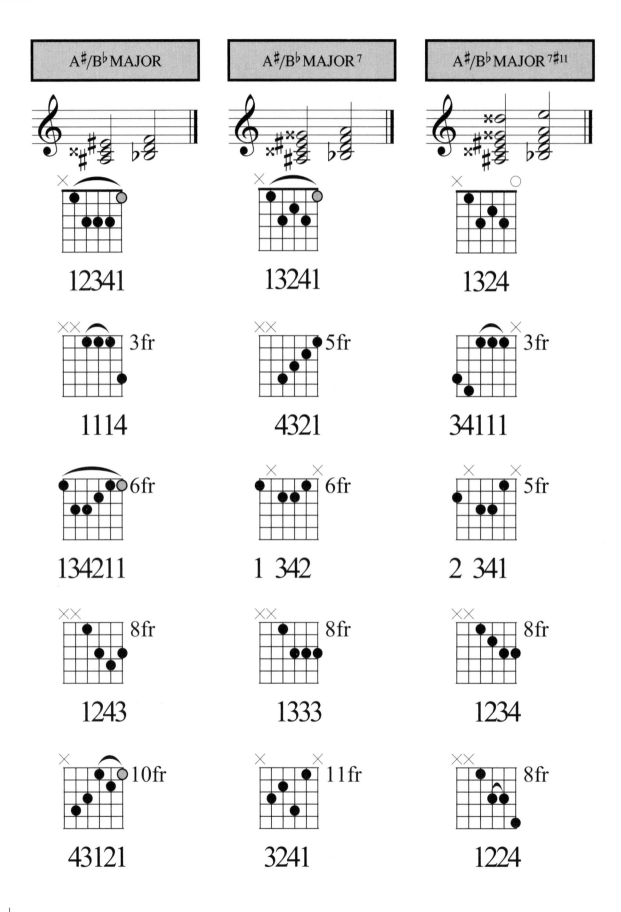

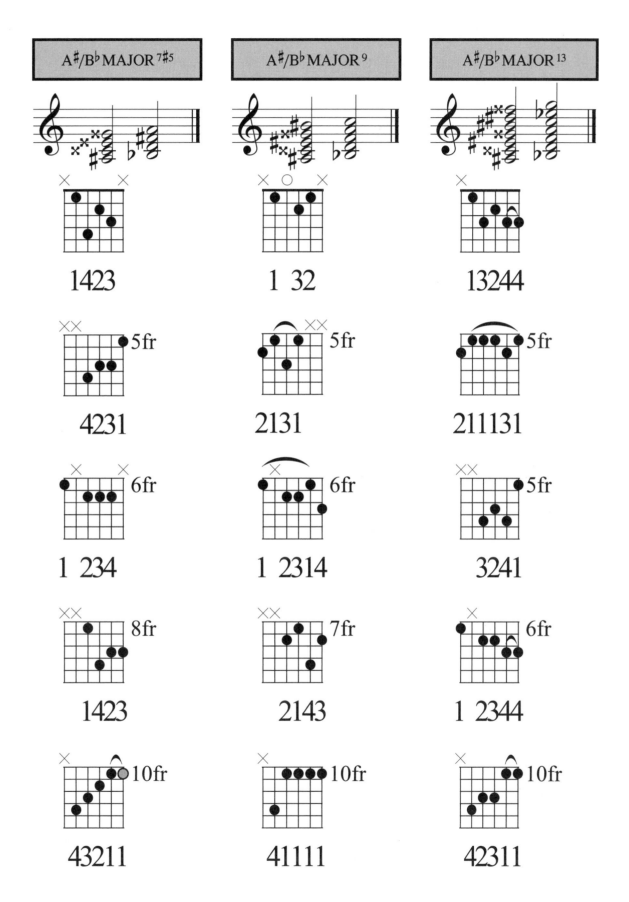

A#/Bb MAJOR 7#5

A#/Bb MAJOR 9

A#/Bb MAJOR 13

1423

1 32

13244

4231

2131

211131

1 234

1 2314

3241

1423

2143

1 2344

43211

41111

42311

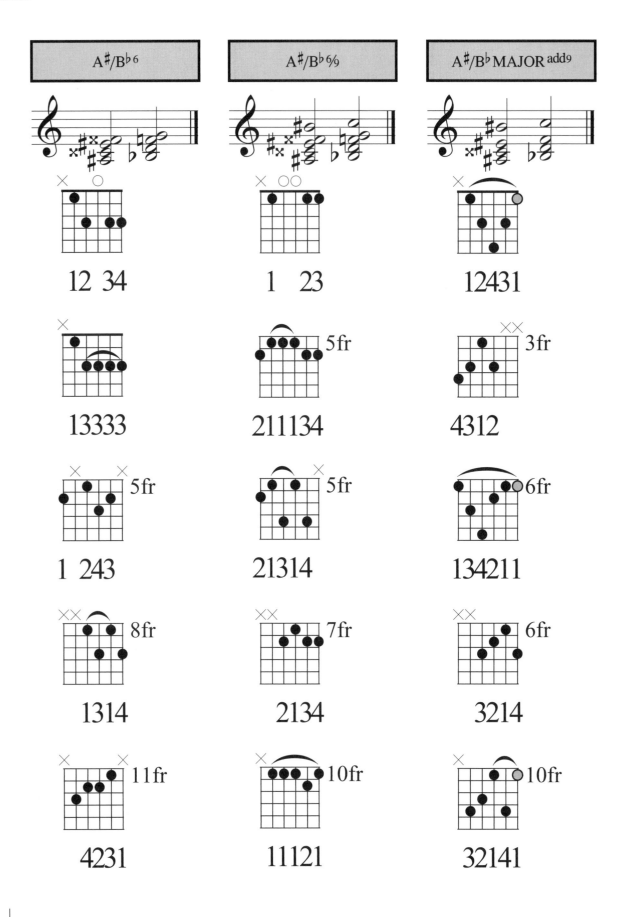

B MAJOR	B MAJOR⁷	B MAJOR ^{7#11}

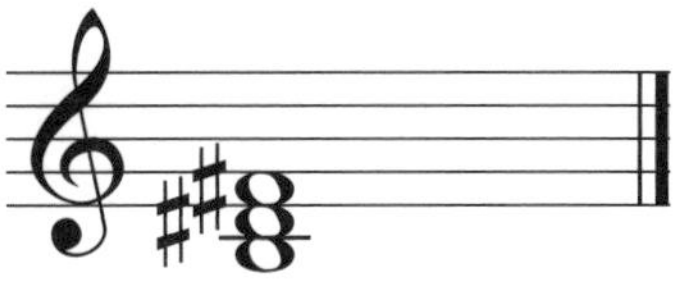

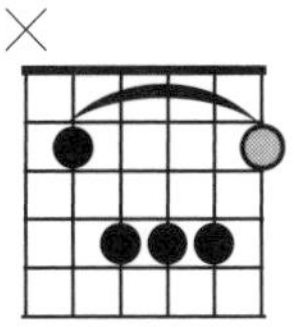

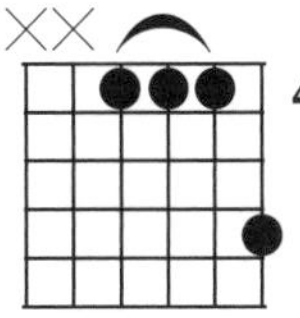

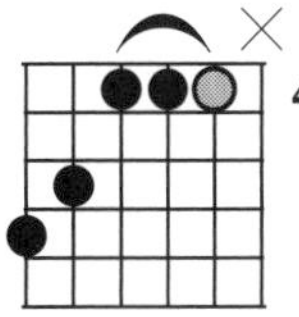

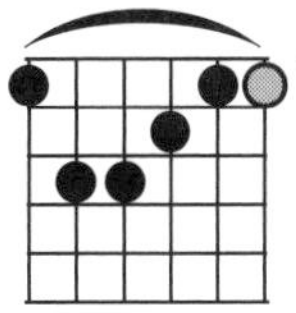

12341   214 3   21341

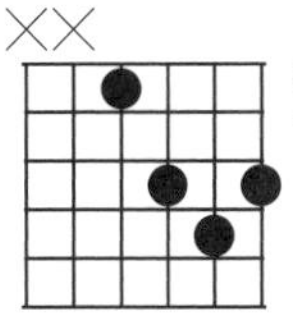

1114   13241   34111

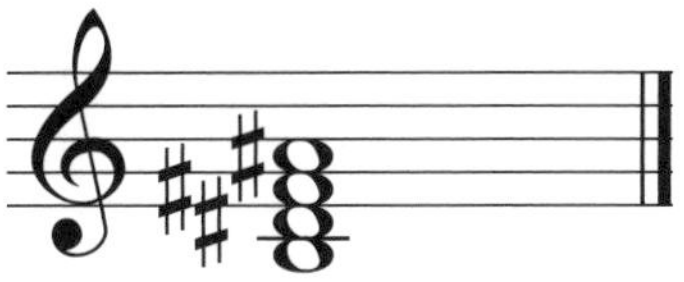

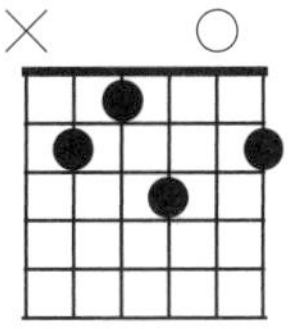

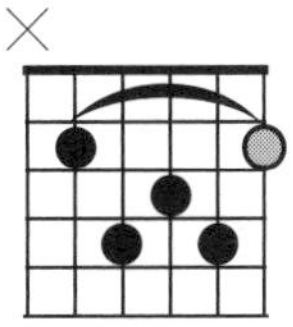

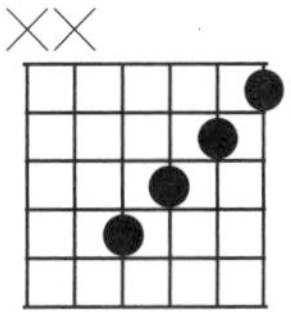

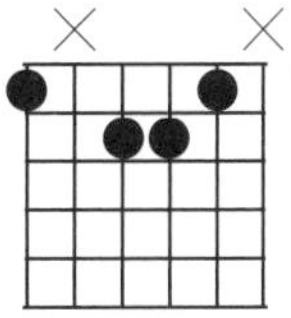

43111   4321   2 341

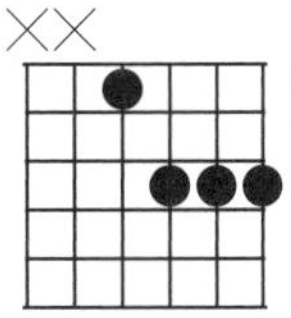

134211   1 342   1234

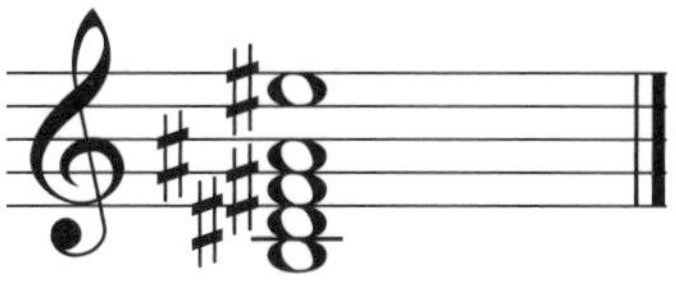

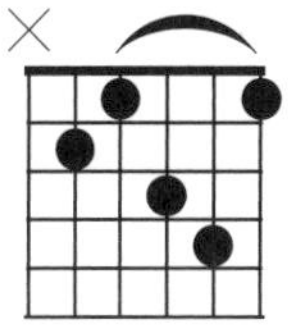

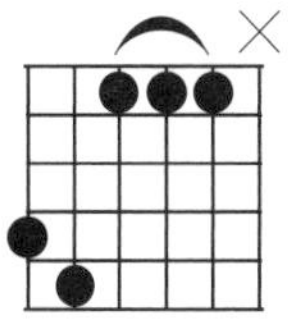

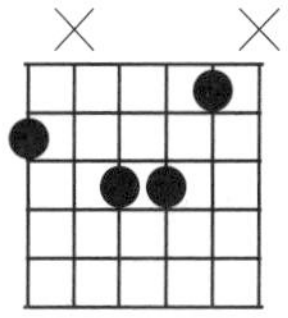

1243   1333   1224

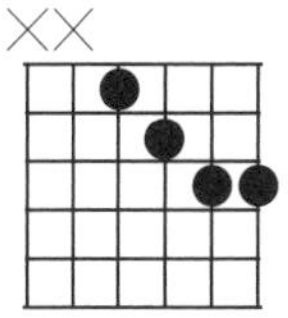

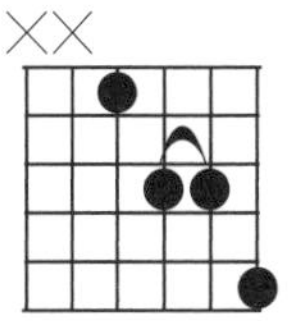

B MAJOR 7#5	B MAJOR 9	B MAJOR 13

213 4

2143

21344

1423

2131

13244

1 234

1 2314

211131

4231

2143

3241

1423

41111

1 2344

B^6	B$^{6}_{9}$	B MAJOR^{add9}

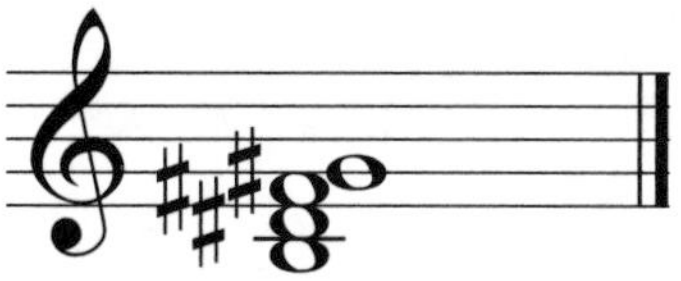

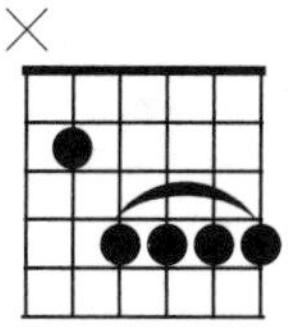

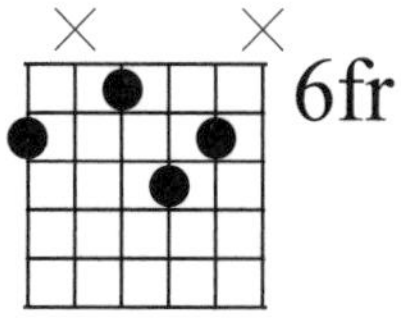

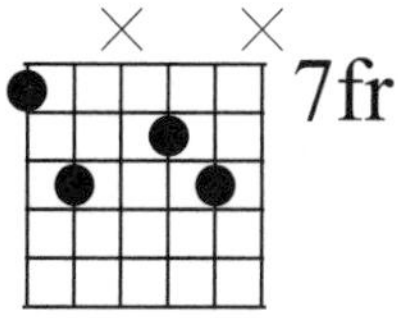

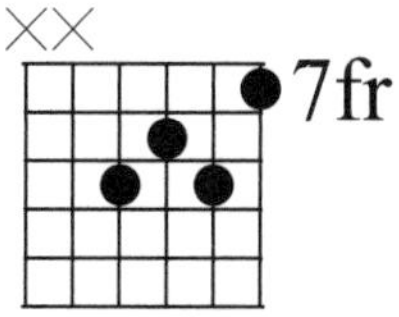

13333   21134   12431

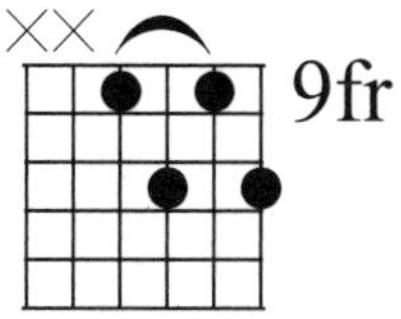

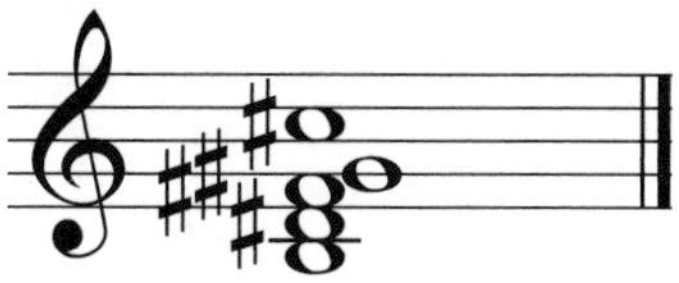

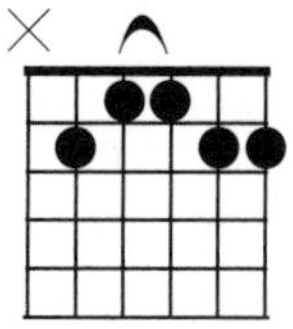

2 143   21314   4213

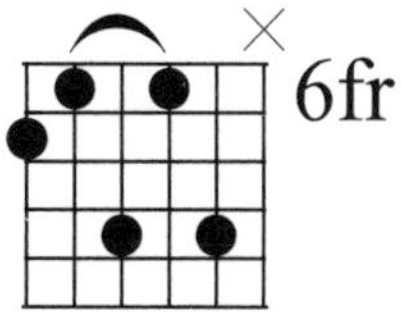

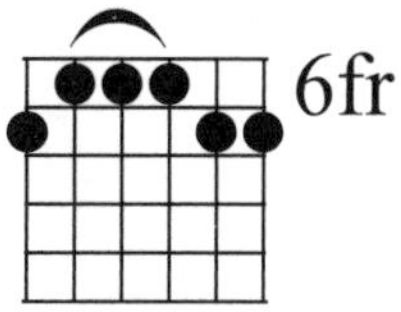

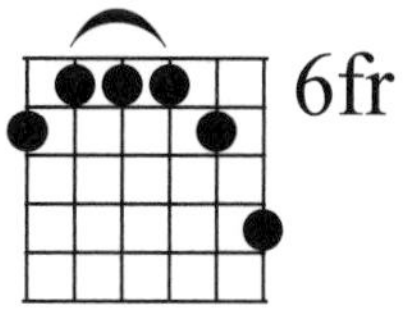

13 24   211134   3214

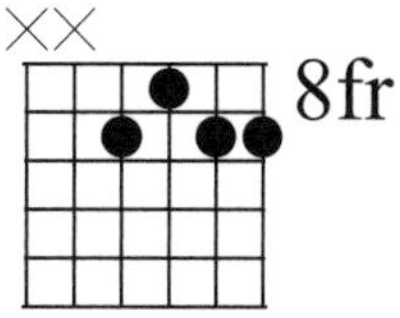

3241   211134   134211

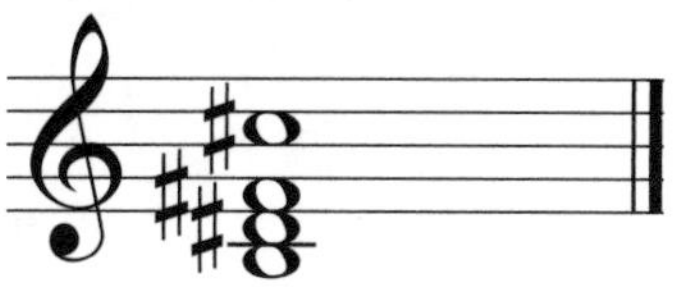

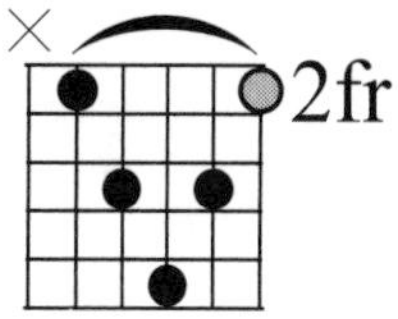

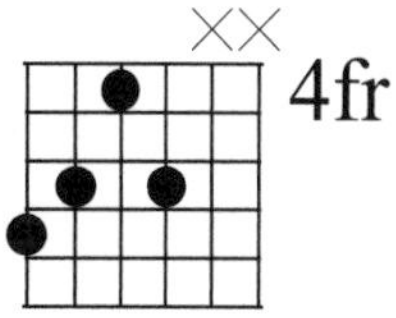

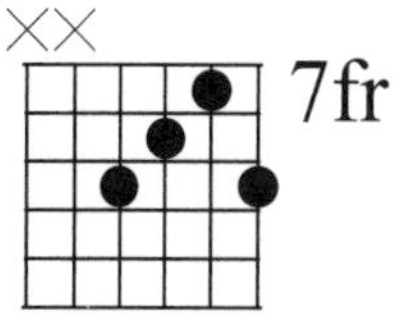

1314   2134   42 1

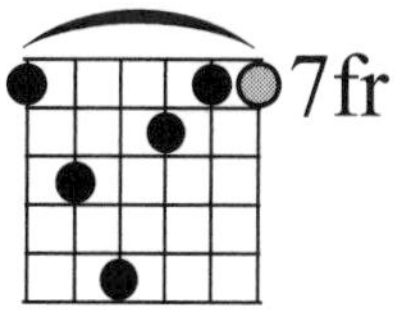

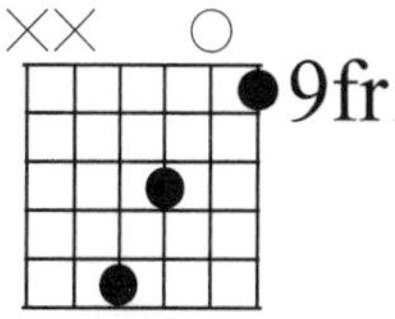

Chapter 4

Minor Chords

Minor chords are the darker and sadder cousins to the perky major chords. Their place in music is long settled and their use is widespread. Along with major, minor makes up the widest variety of sounds most guitar players explore.

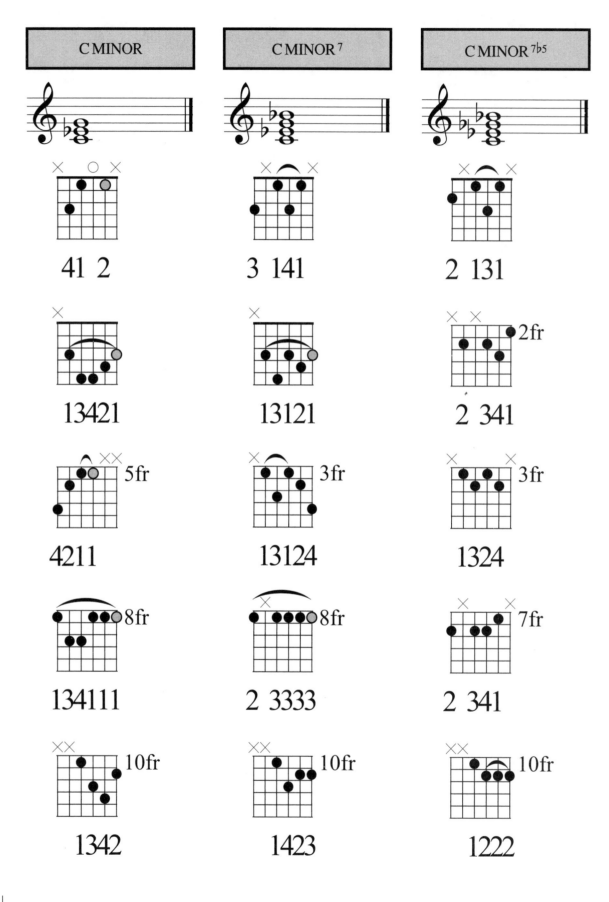

C MINOR (Maj⁷)	C MINOR ⁹	C MINOR ⁹ (Maj⁷)

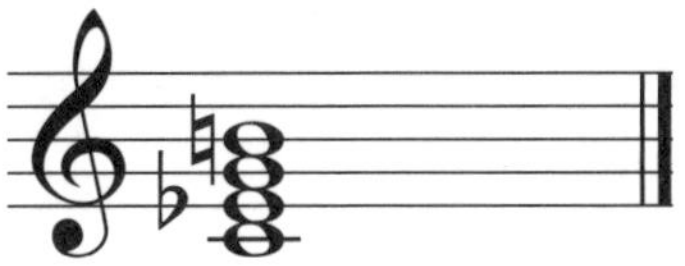

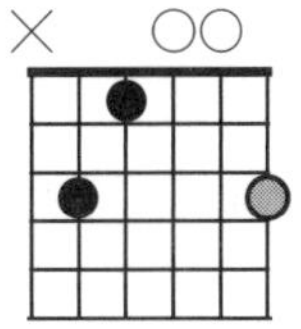

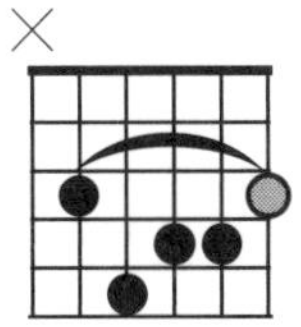

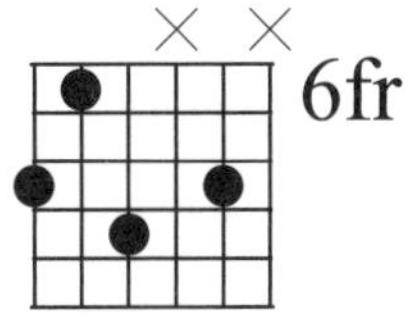

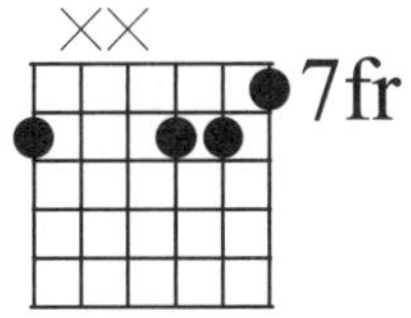

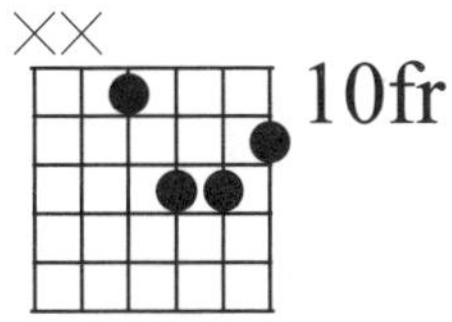

31 4

21333

2143

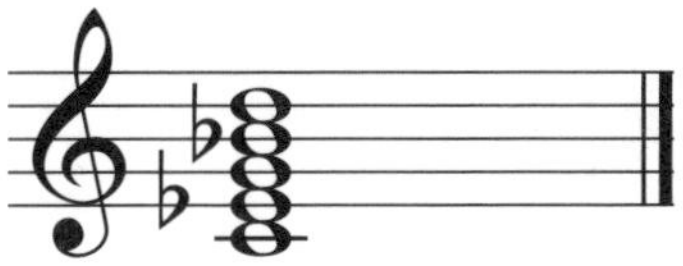

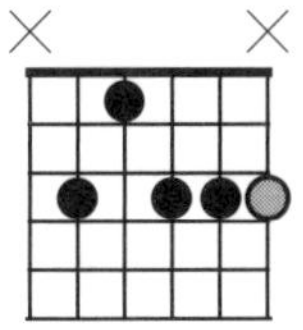

14231

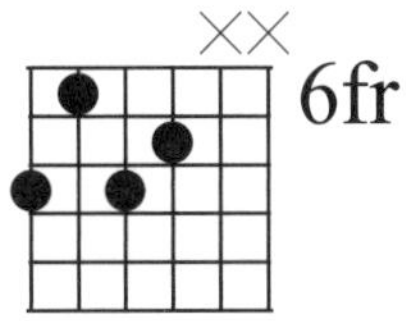

3142

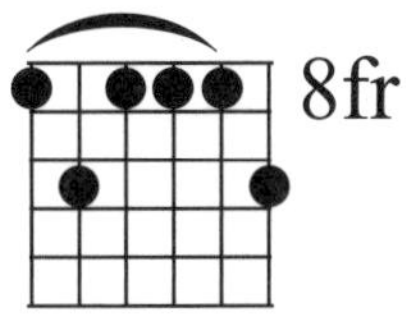

43211

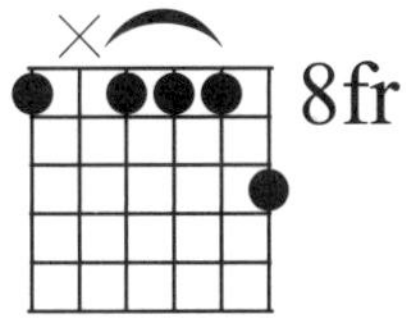

214 3

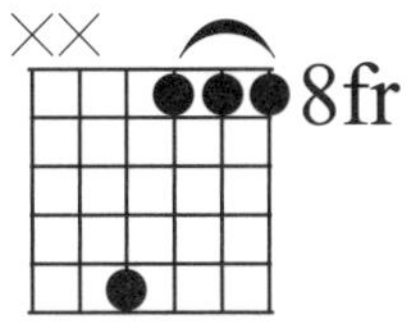

131114

3142

2 341

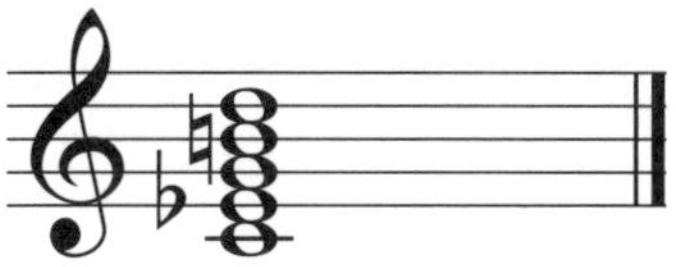

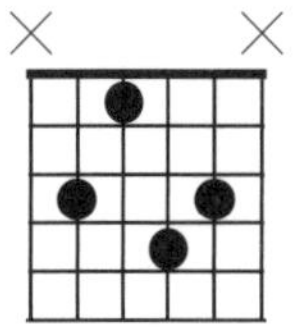

2 3334

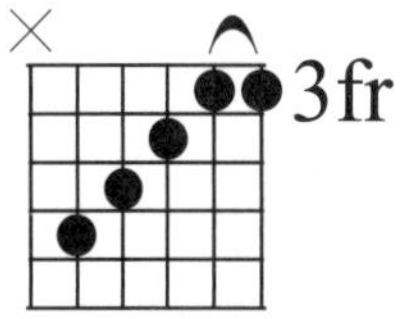

132114

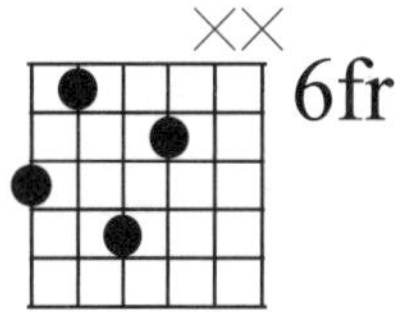

1342

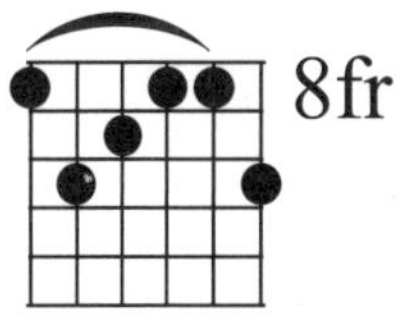

4111

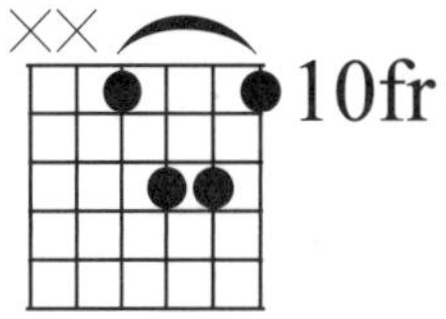

1341

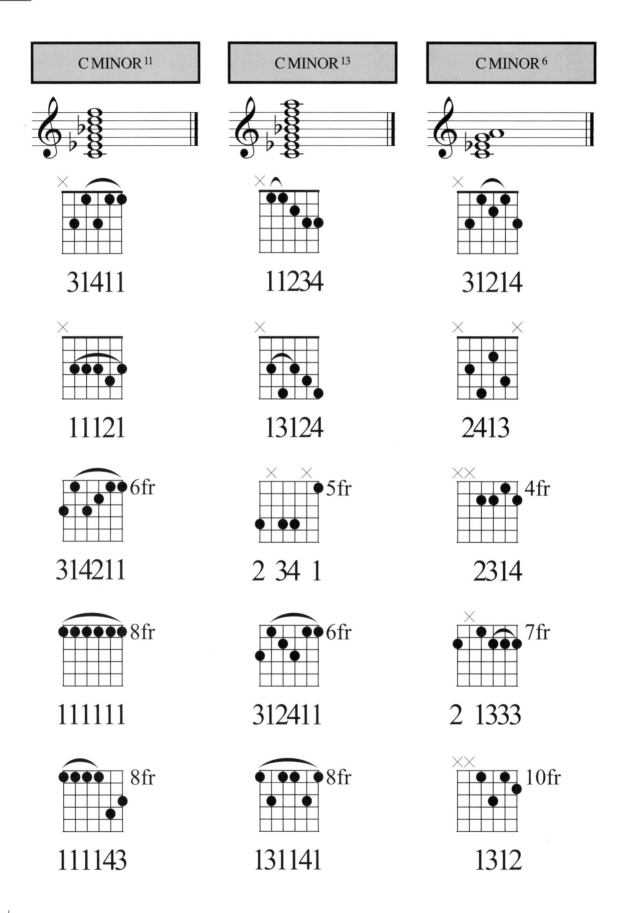

C MINOR b6

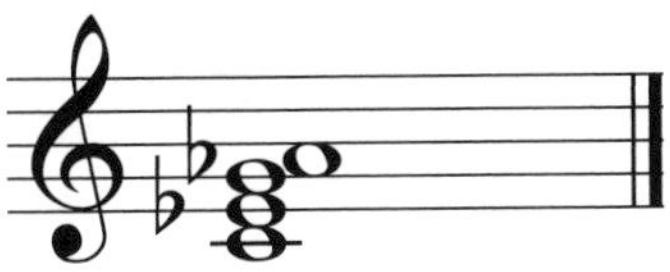

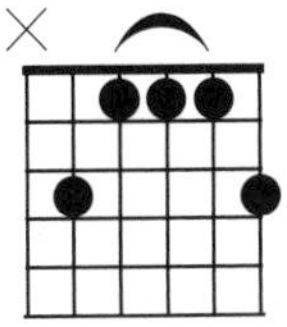

31114

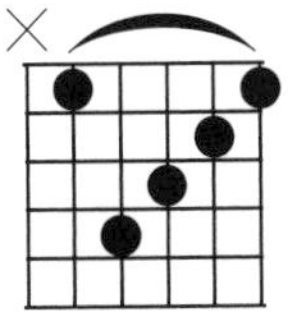

14321

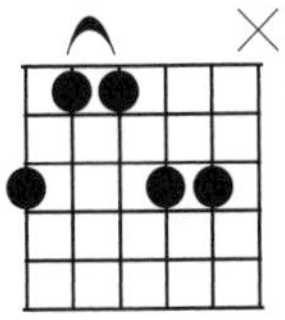

21134

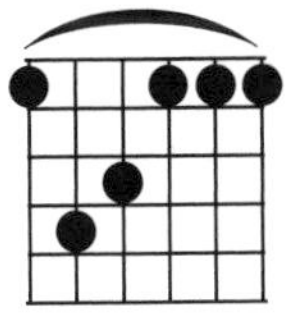

143111

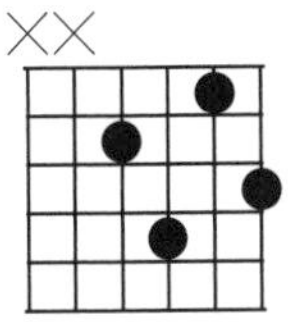

2413

C MINOR 6/9

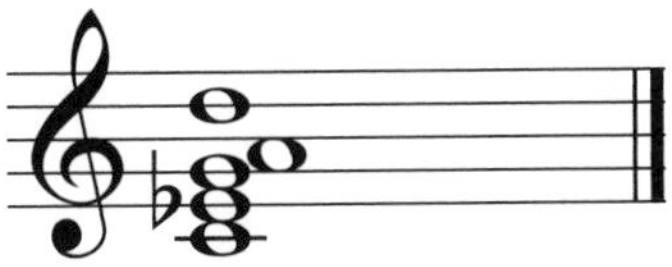

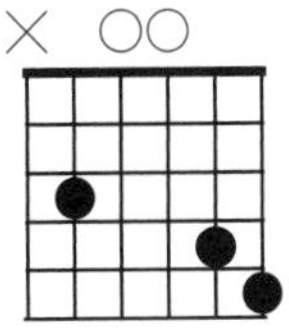

1　23

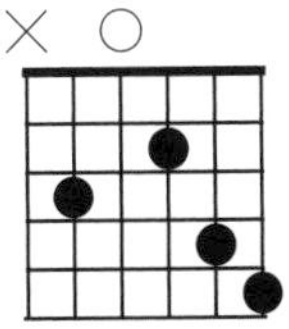

2　134

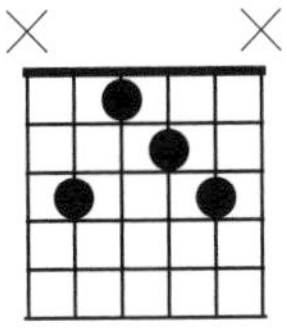

3124

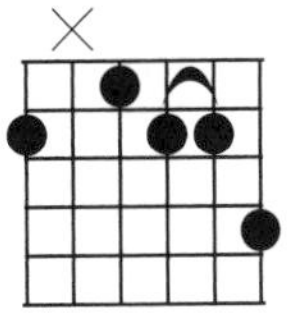

2　1334

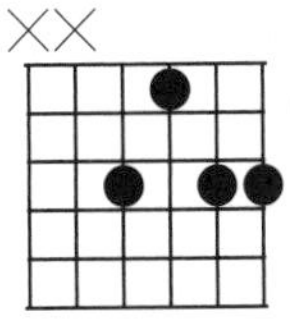

2134

C MINOR add9

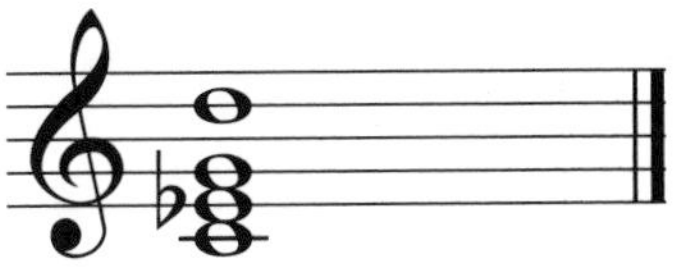

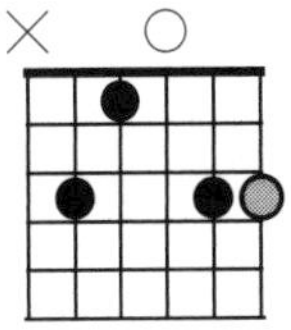

21　34

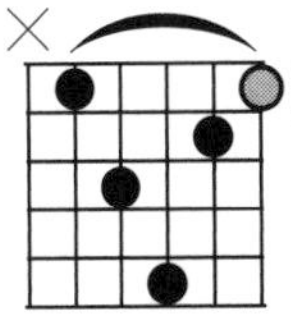

13421

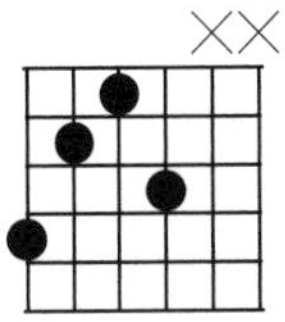

1243

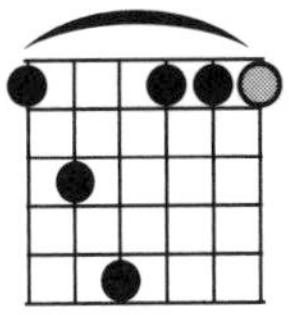

134111

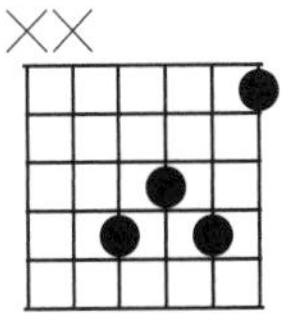

3241

4213

421

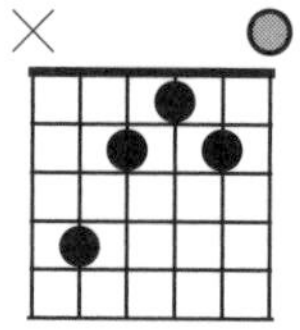

31

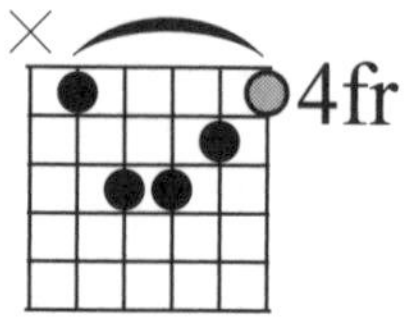

13421

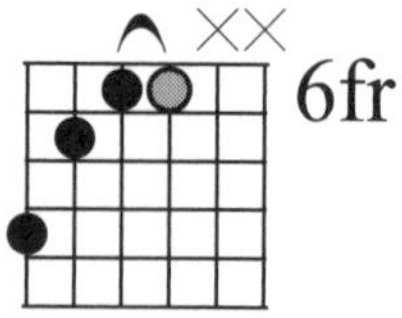

13121

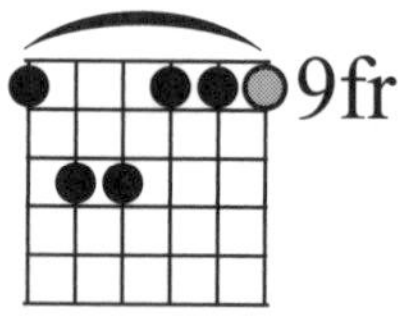

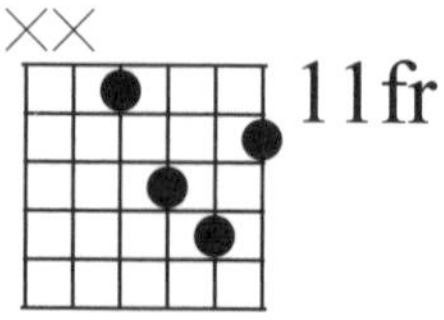

2 341

4211

2314

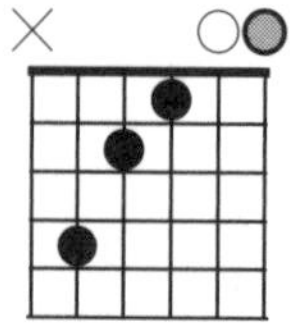

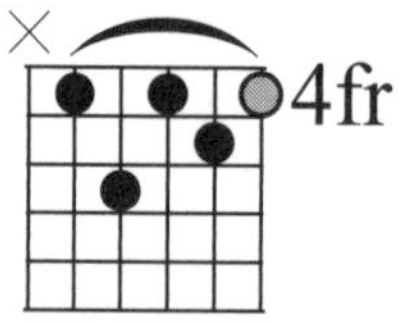

1324

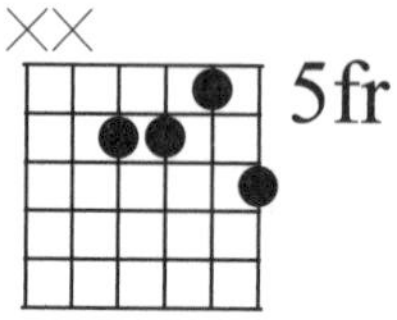

134111

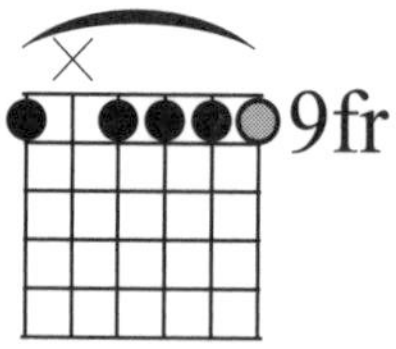

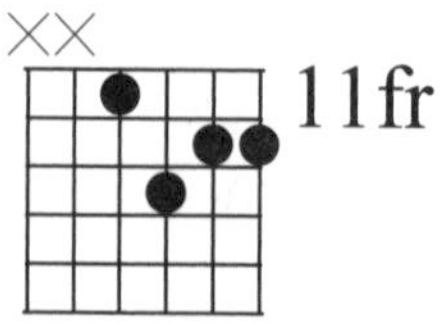

2 3333

2 341

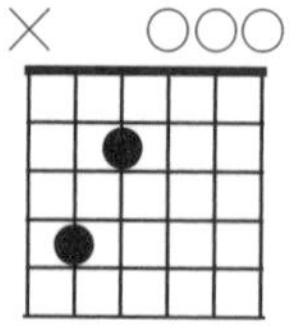

1342

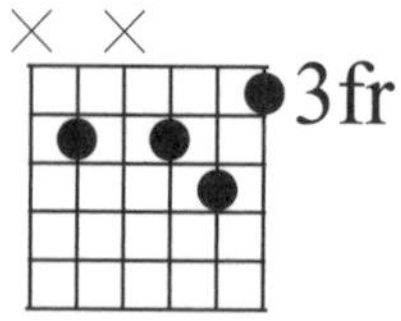

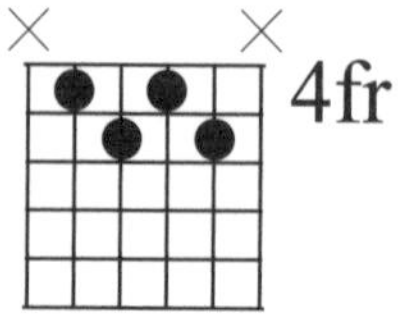

1423

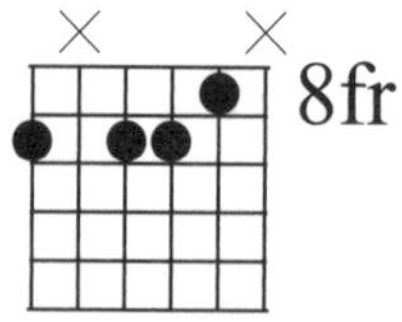

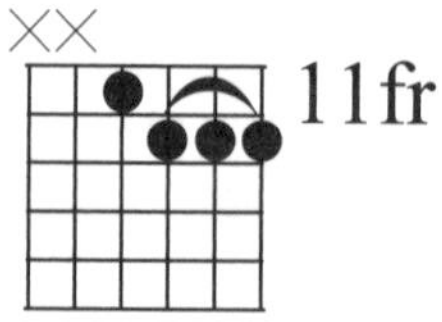

1222

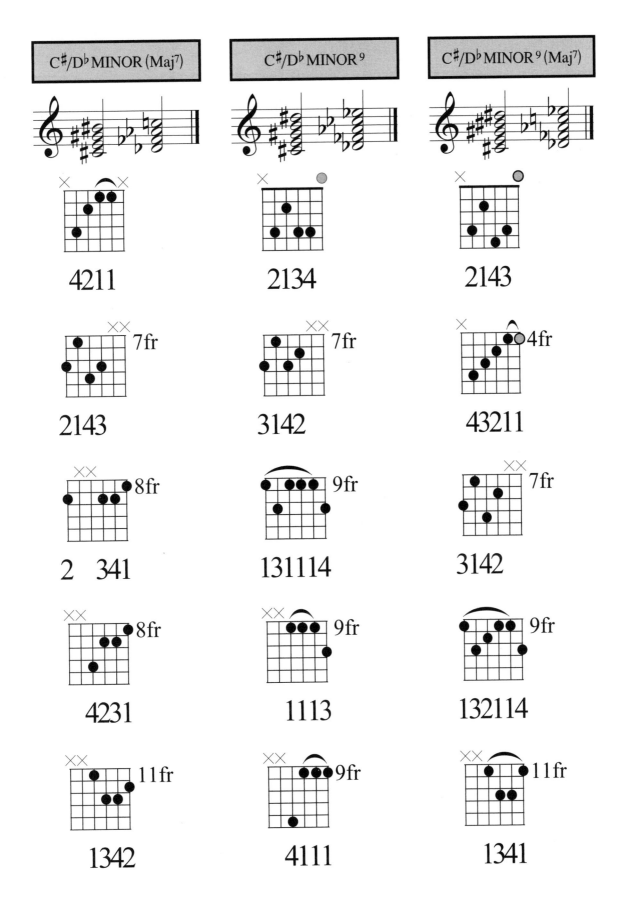

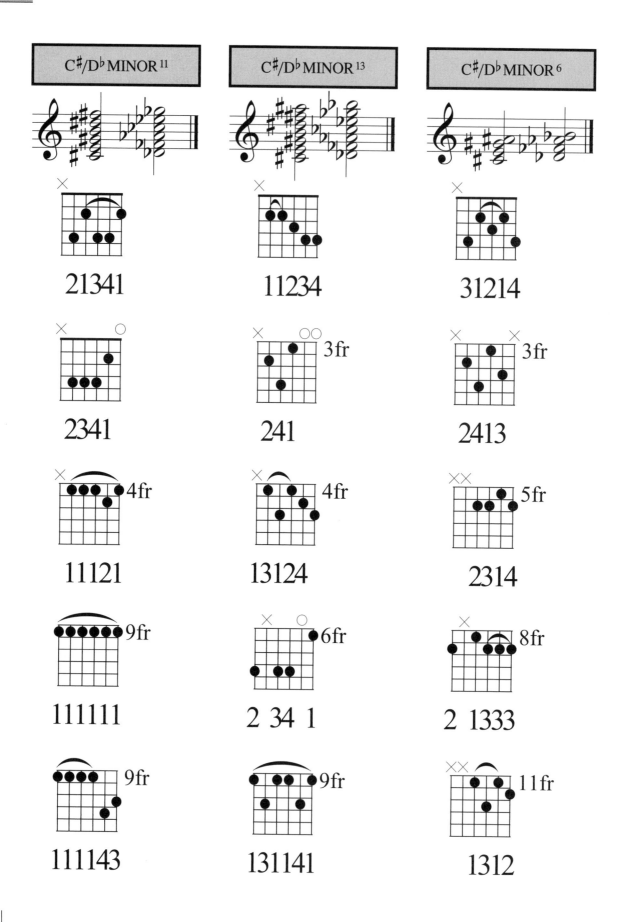

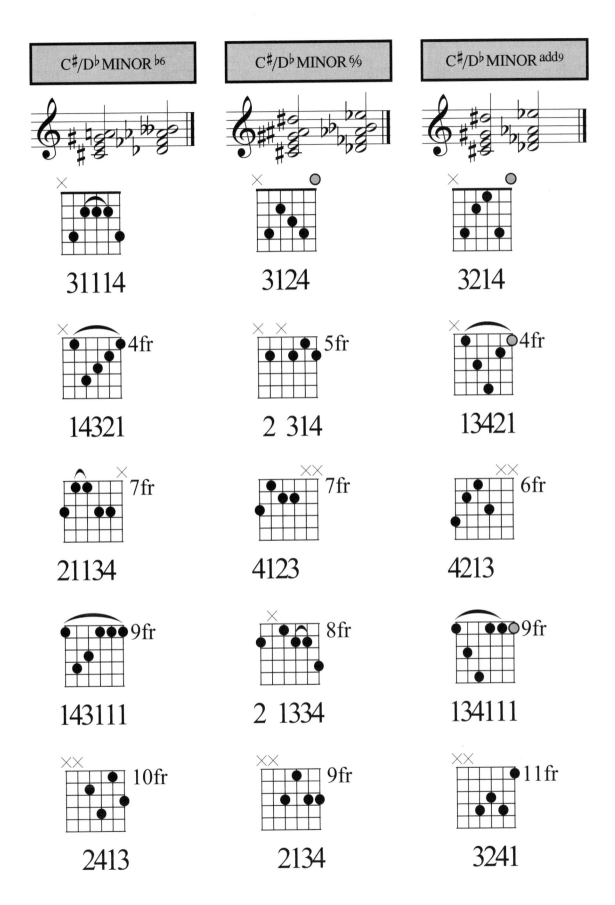

C#/D♭ MINOR ♭6	C#/D♭ MINOR 6/9	C#/D♭ MINOR add9
31114	3124	3214
14321 (4fr)	2 314 (5fr)	13421 (4fr)
21134 (7fr)	4123 (7fr)	4213 (6fr)
143111 (9fr)	2 1334 (8fr)	134111 (9fr)
2413 (10fr)	2134 (9fr)	3241 (11fr)

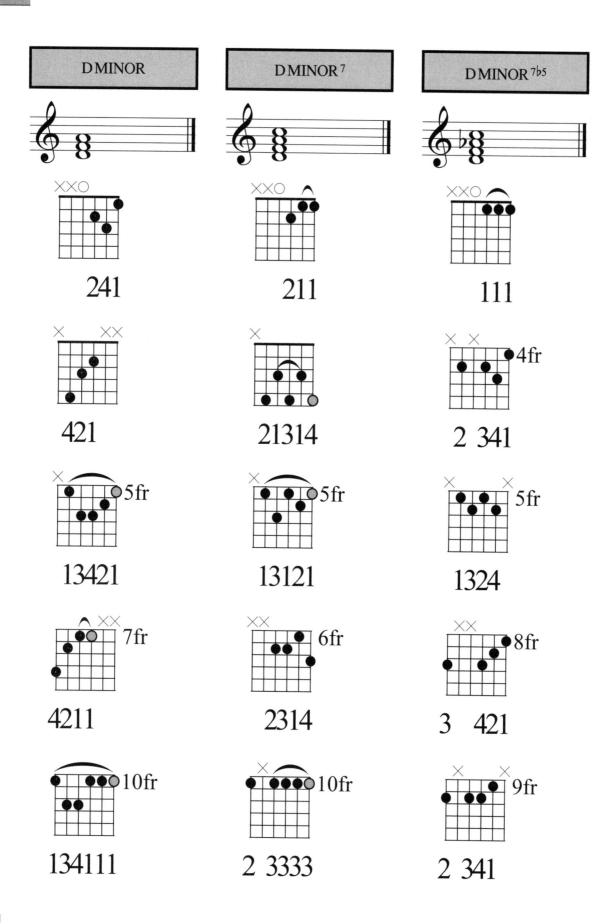

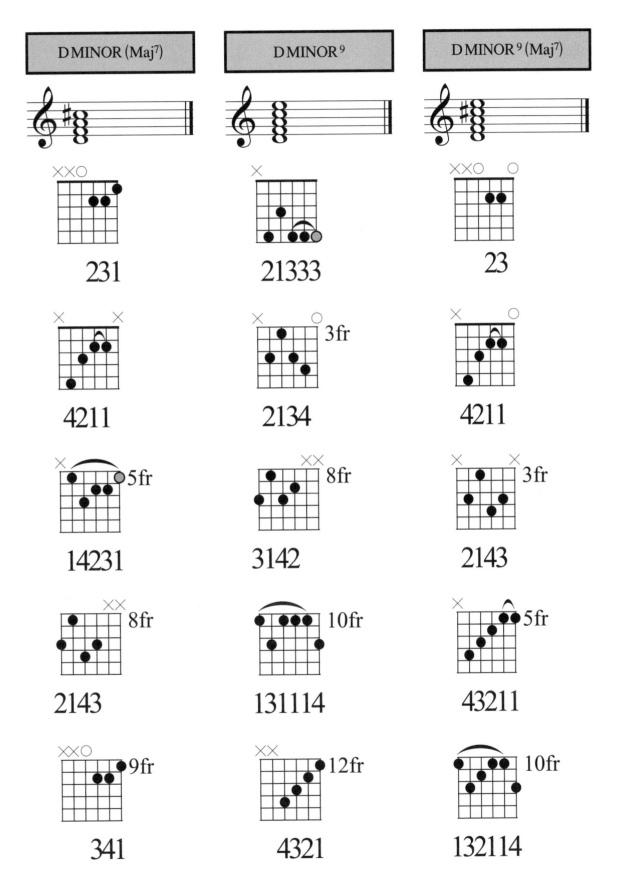

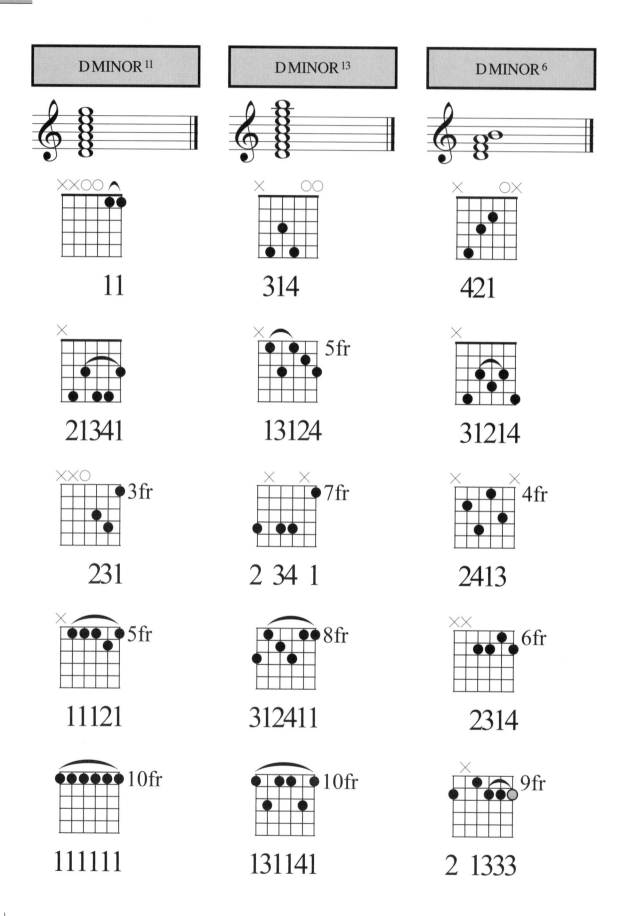

D MINOR $^{\flat 6}$

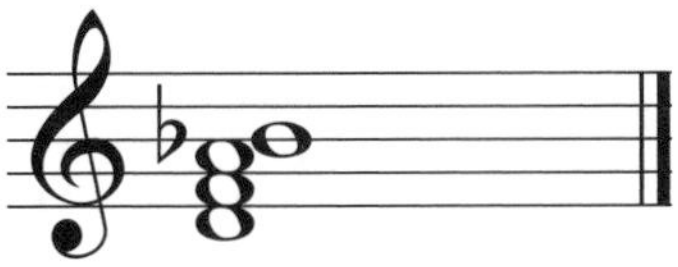

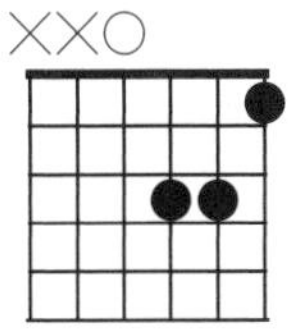

341

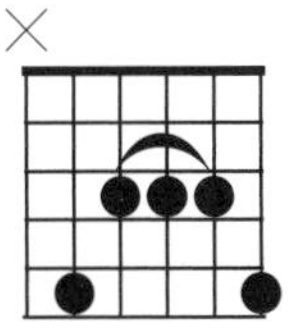

31114

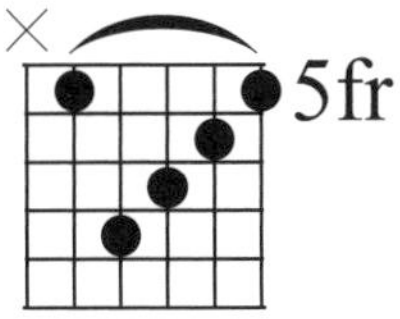

14321

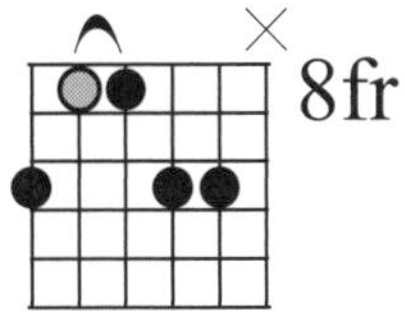

21134

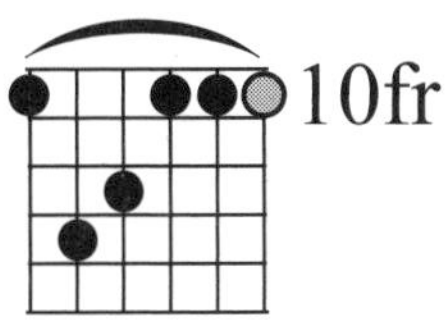

143111

D MINOR $^{6/9}$

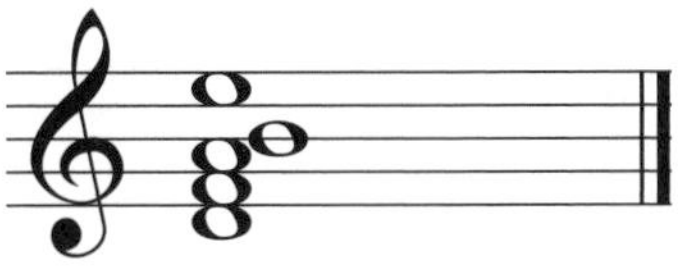

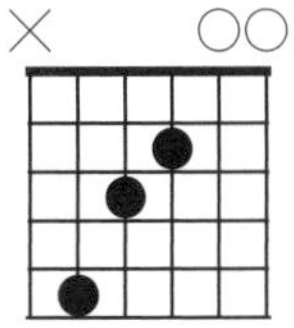

421

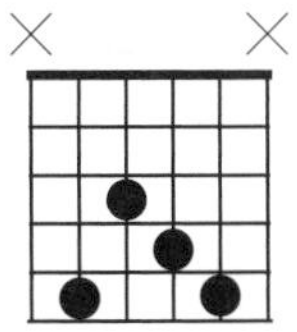

3124

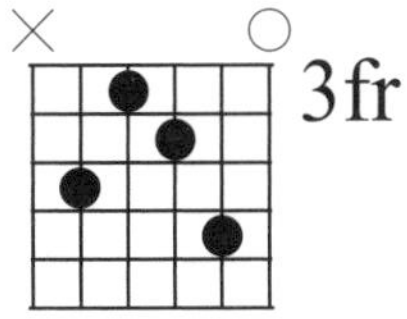

3124

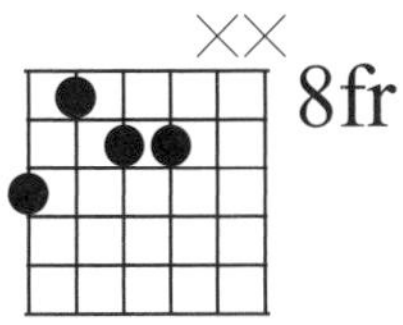

4123

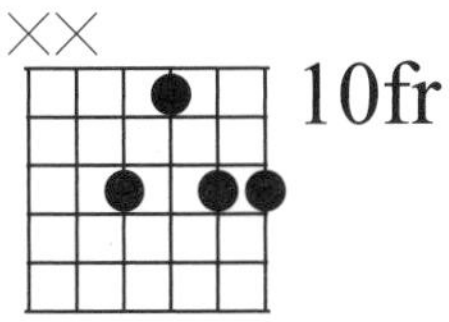

2134

D MINOR ^{add9}

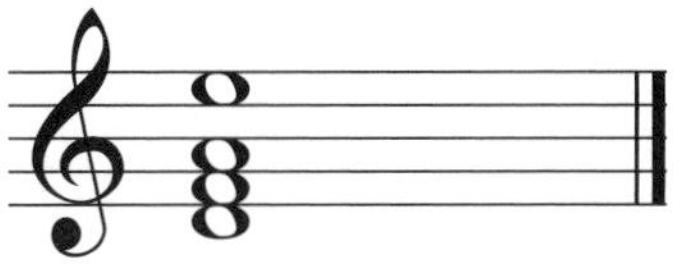

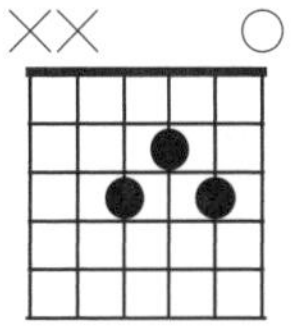

213

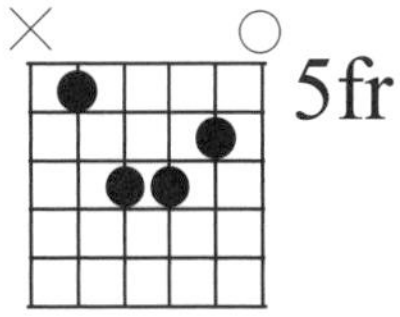

1342

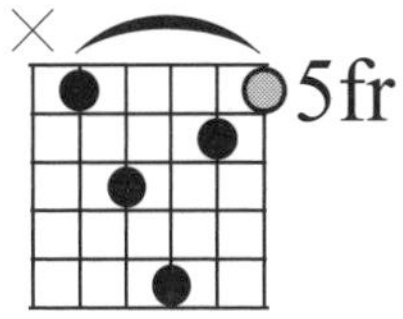

13421

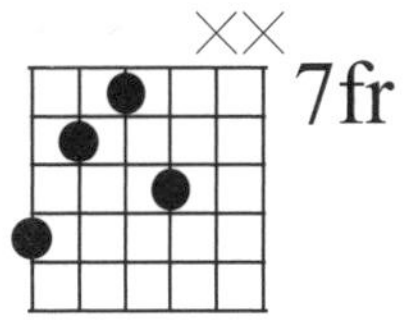

1243

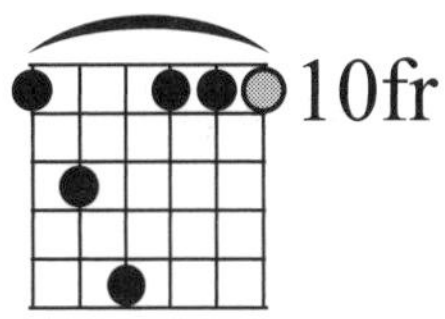

134111

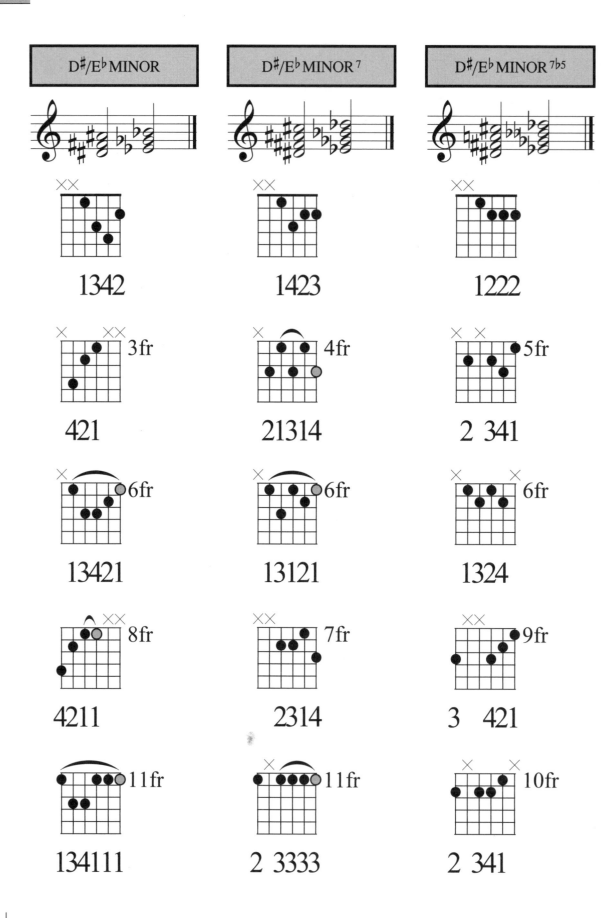

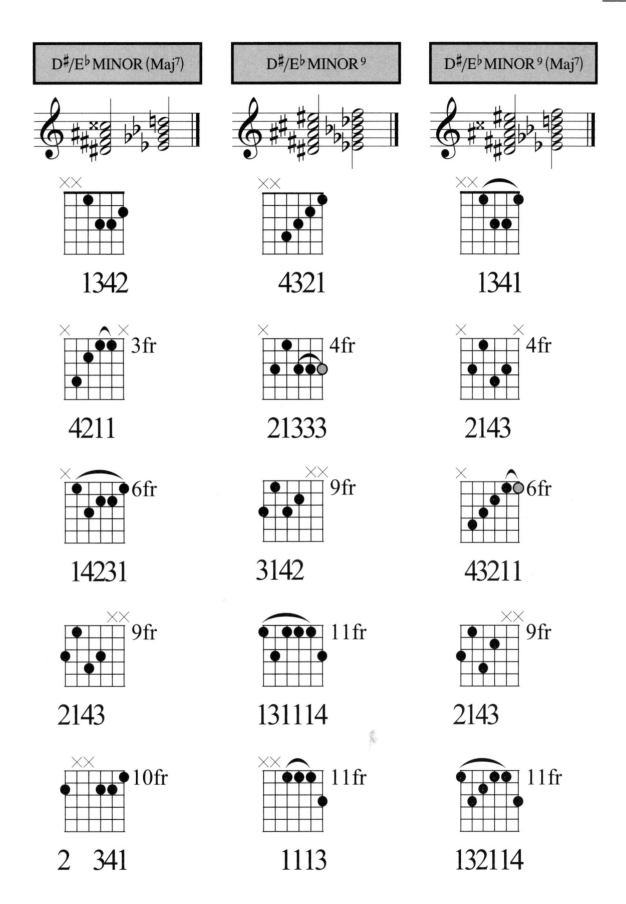

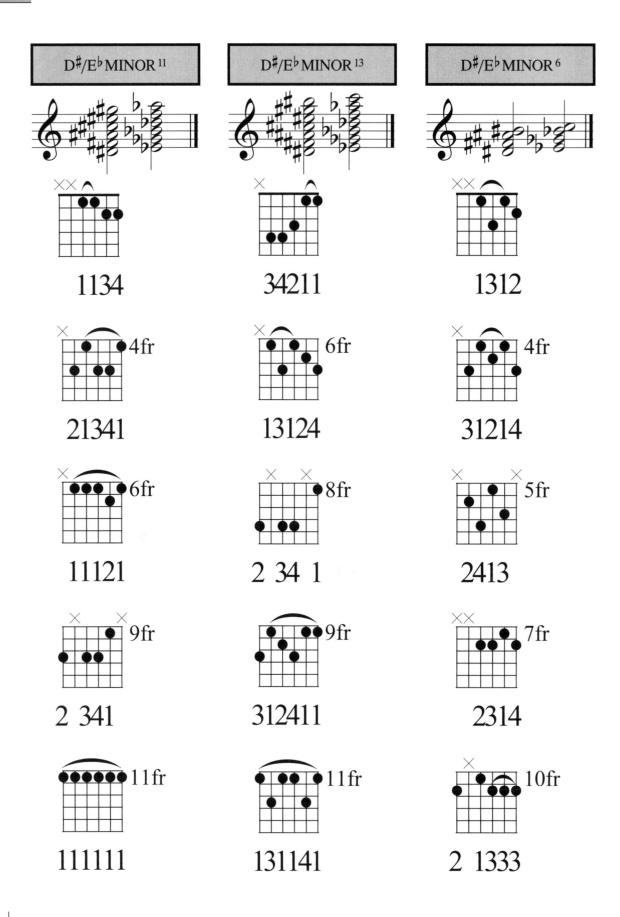

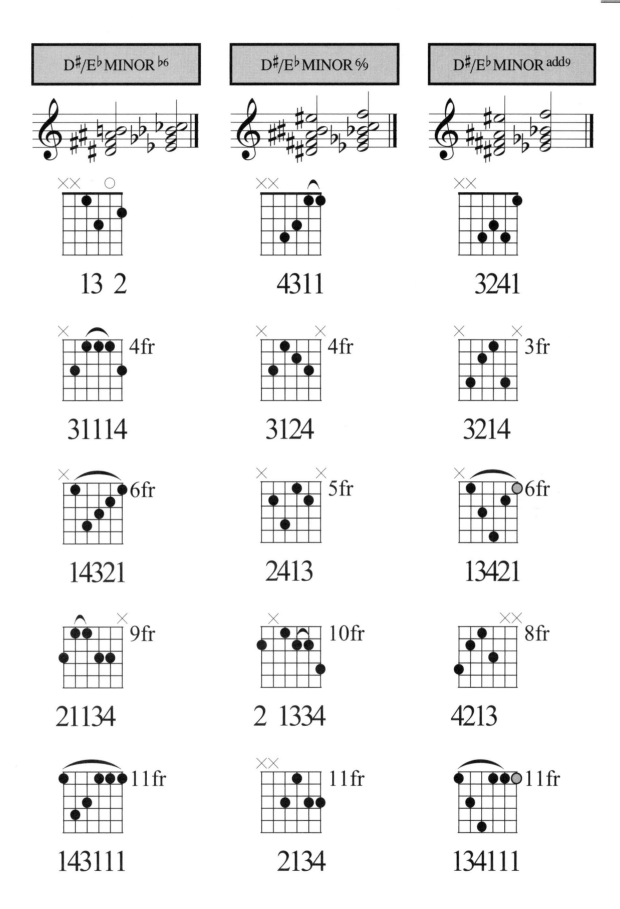

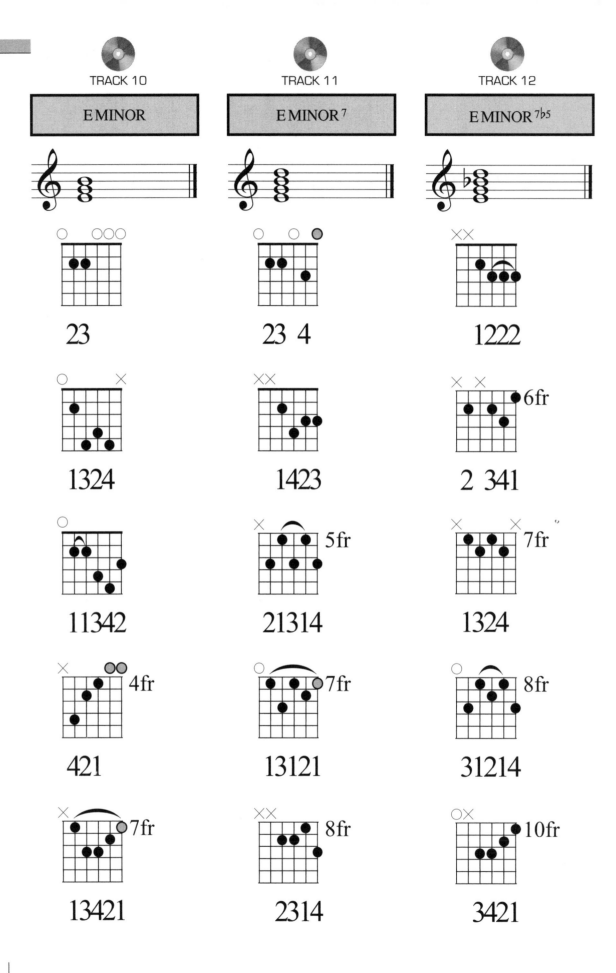

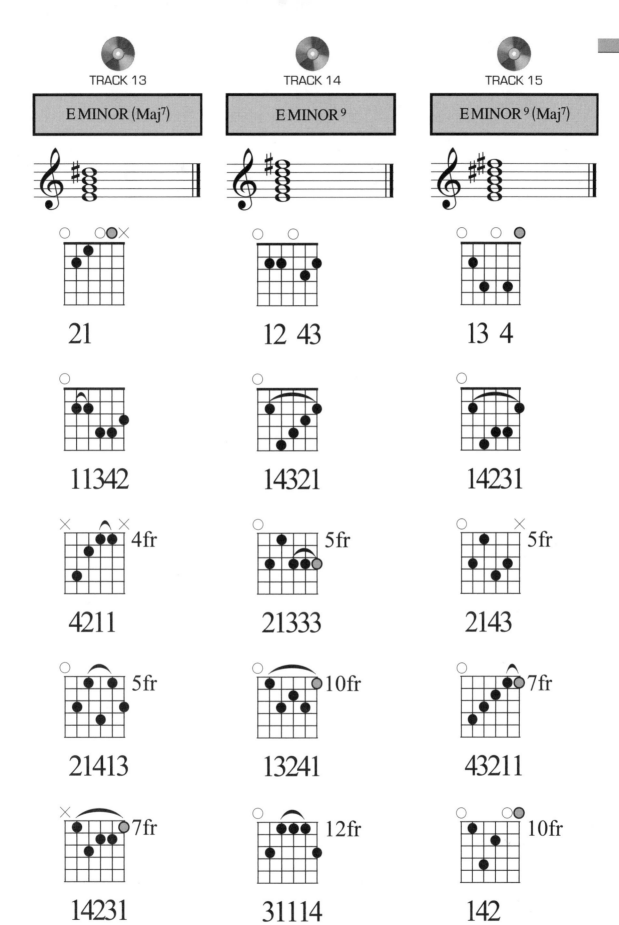

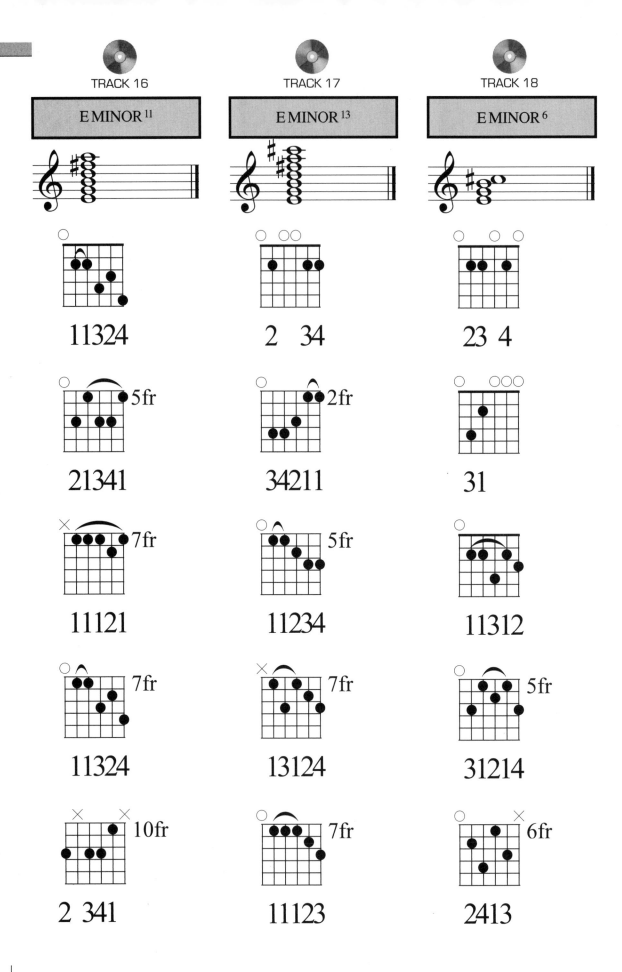

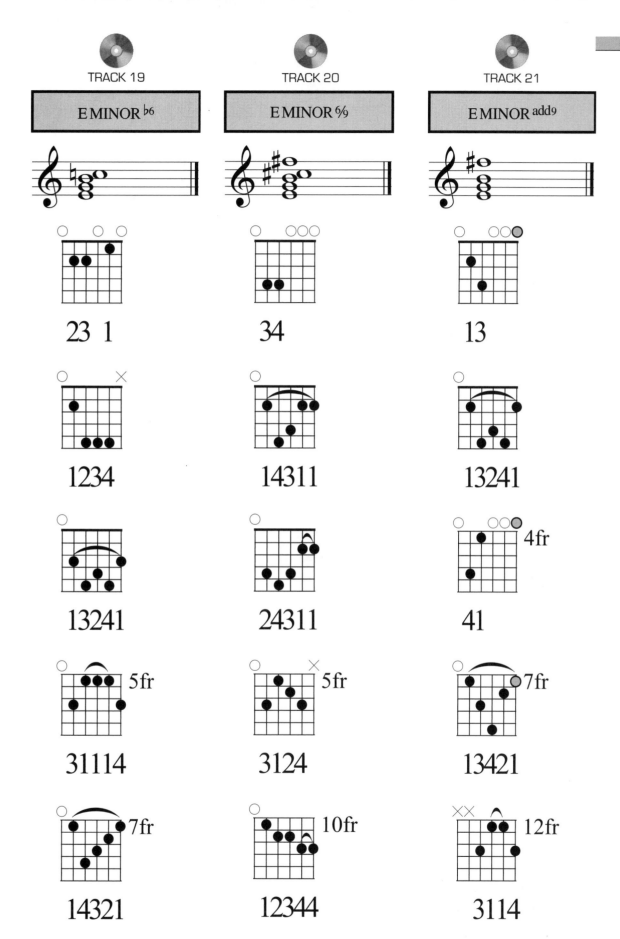

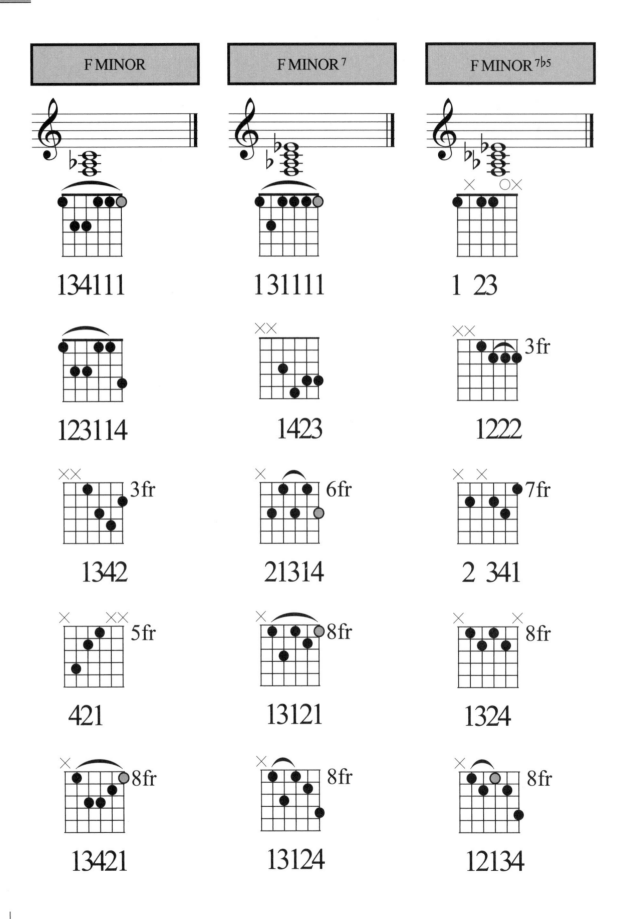

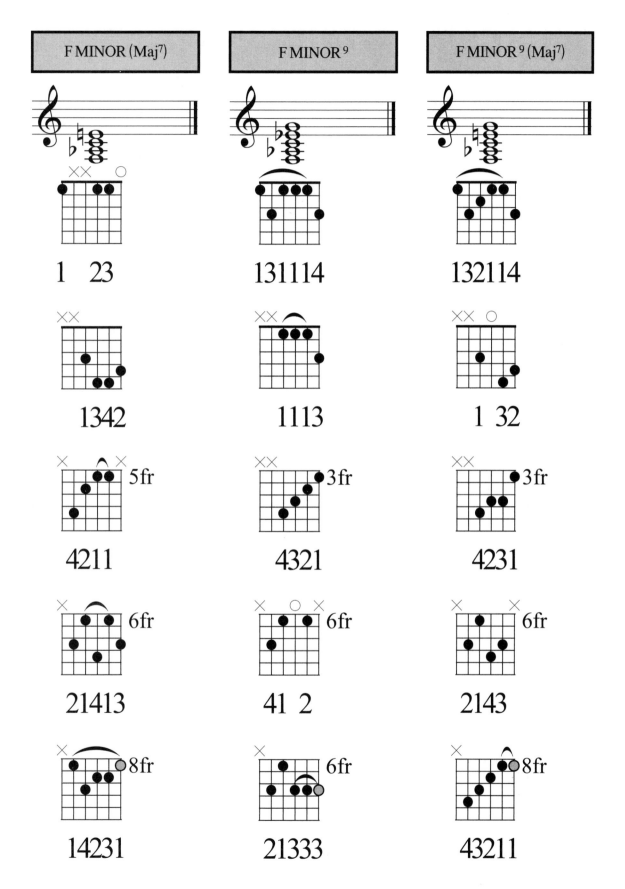

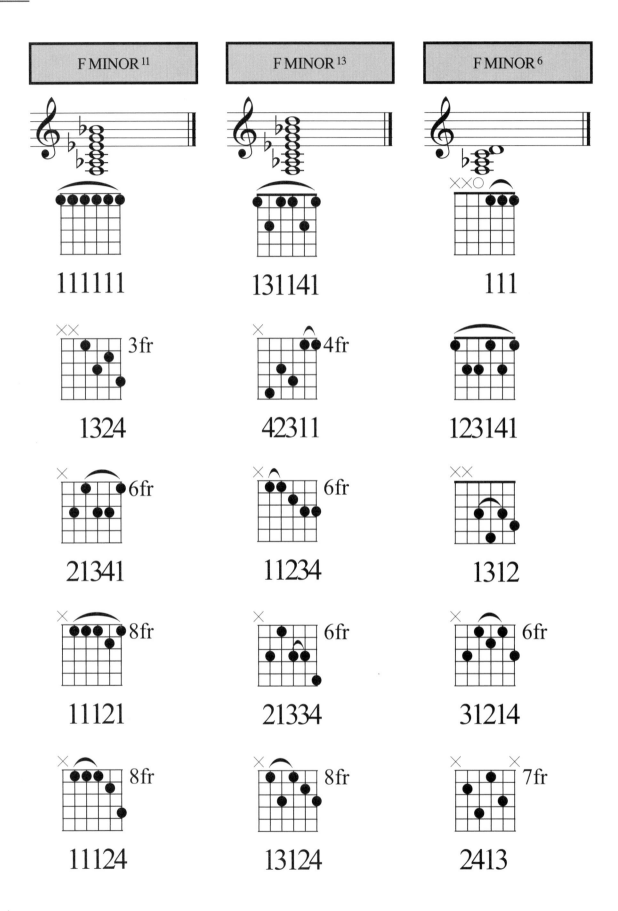

F MINOR b6	F MINOR 6/9	F MINOR add9

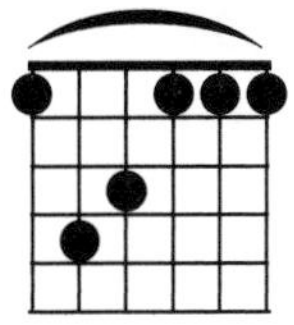

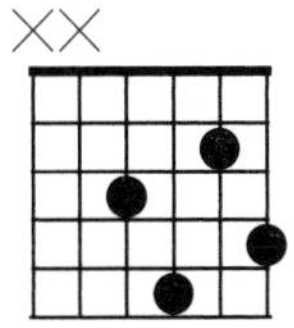

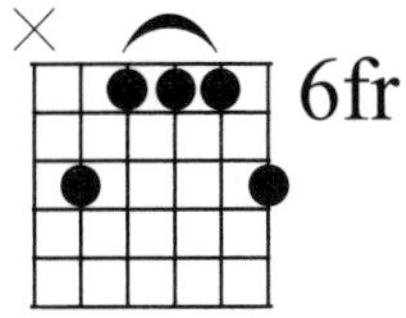

143111 · 113 · 134111

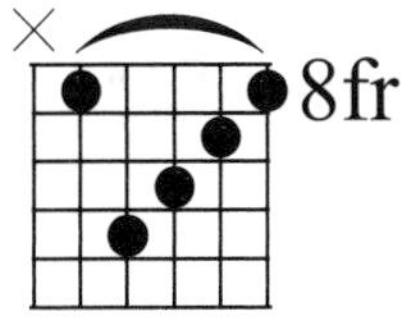

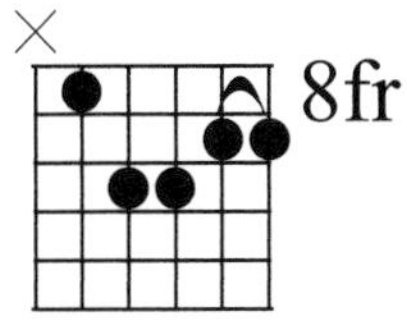

2413 · 1 224 · 2 14

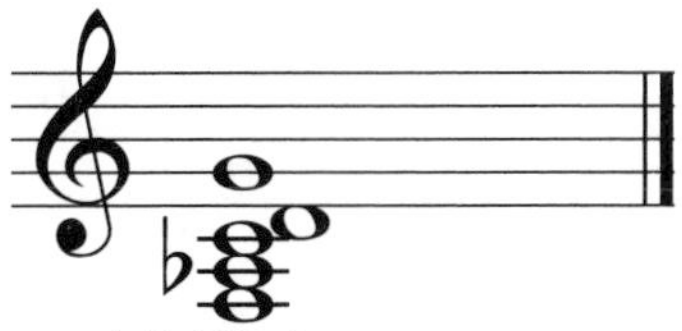

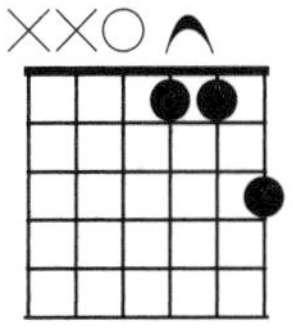

31114 6fr · 3124 6fr · 4111

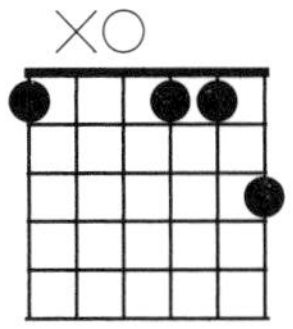

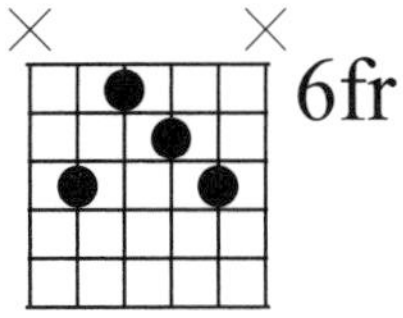

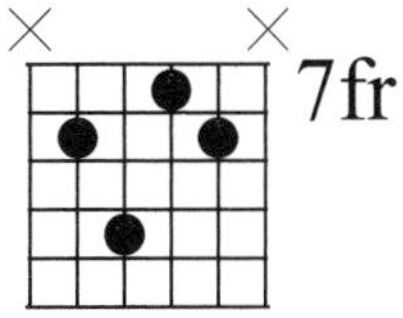

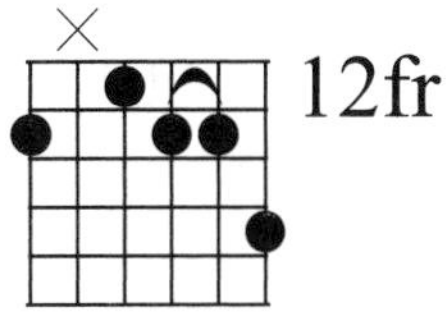

14321 8fr · 2413 7fr · 3214 5fr

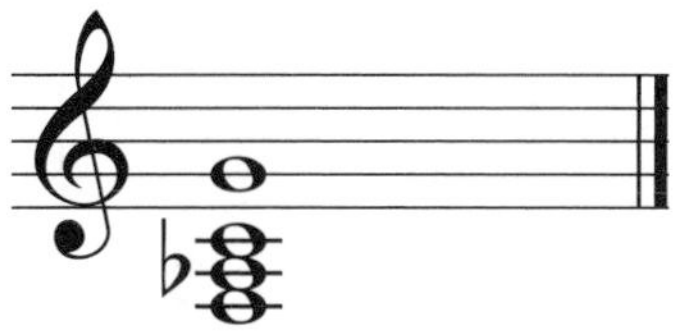

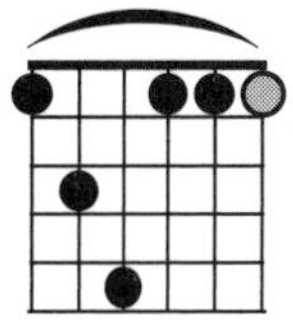

13422 8fr · 2 1334 12fr · 13421 8fr

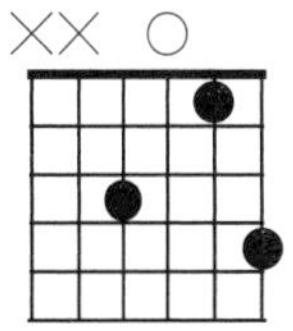

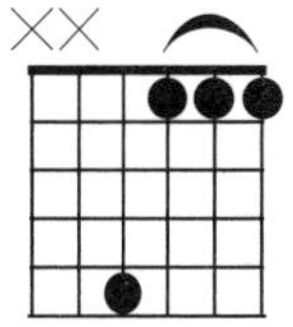

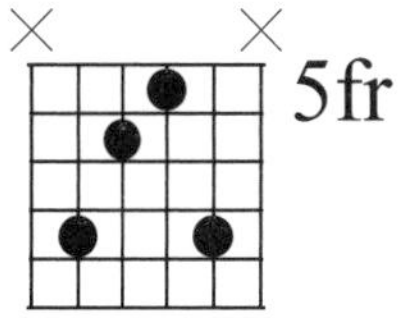

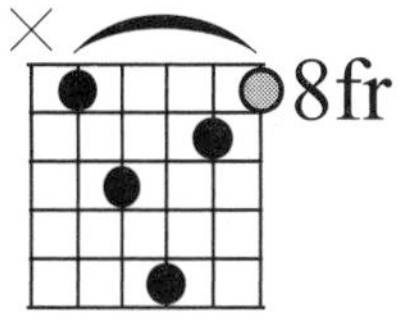

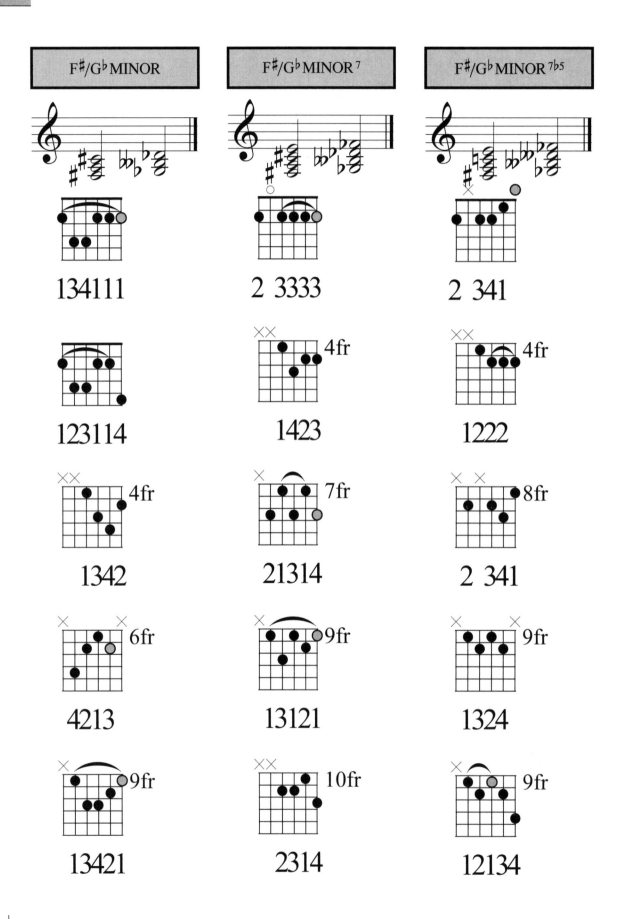

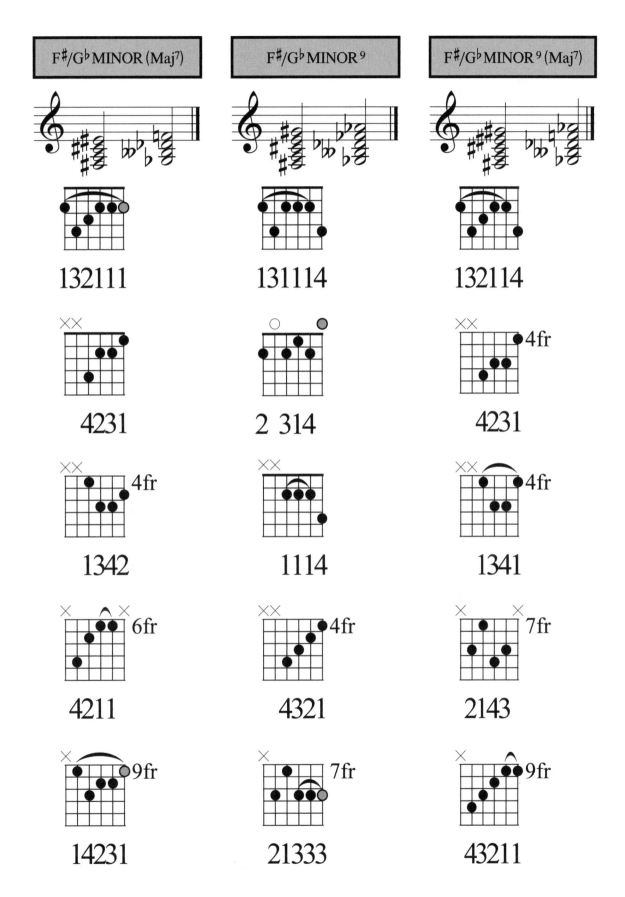

F#/G♭ MINOR (Maj7)   F#/G♭ MINOR 9   F#/G♭ MINOR 9 (Maj7)

132111   131114   132114

4231   2 314   4231

1342   1114   1341

4211   4321   2143

14231   21333   43211

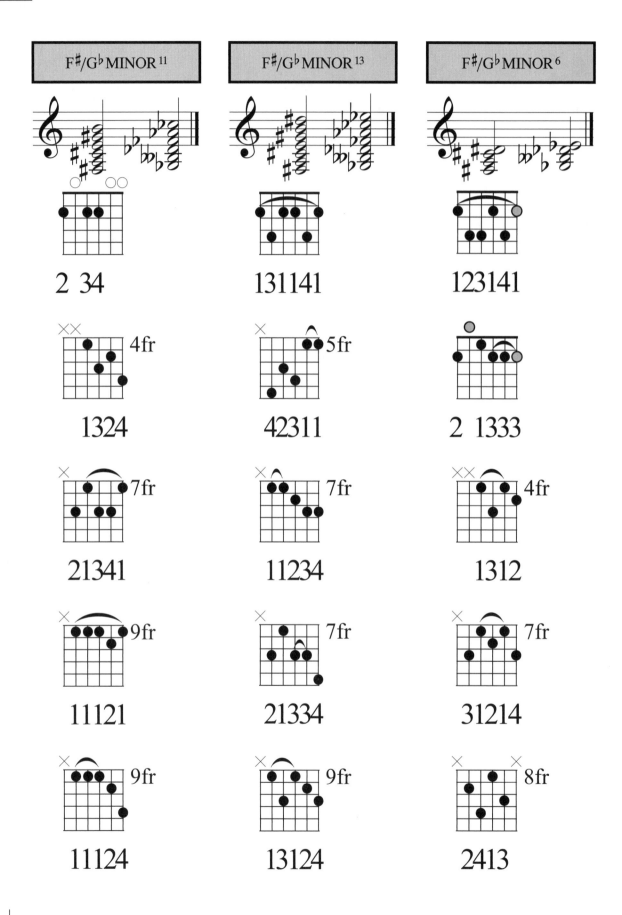

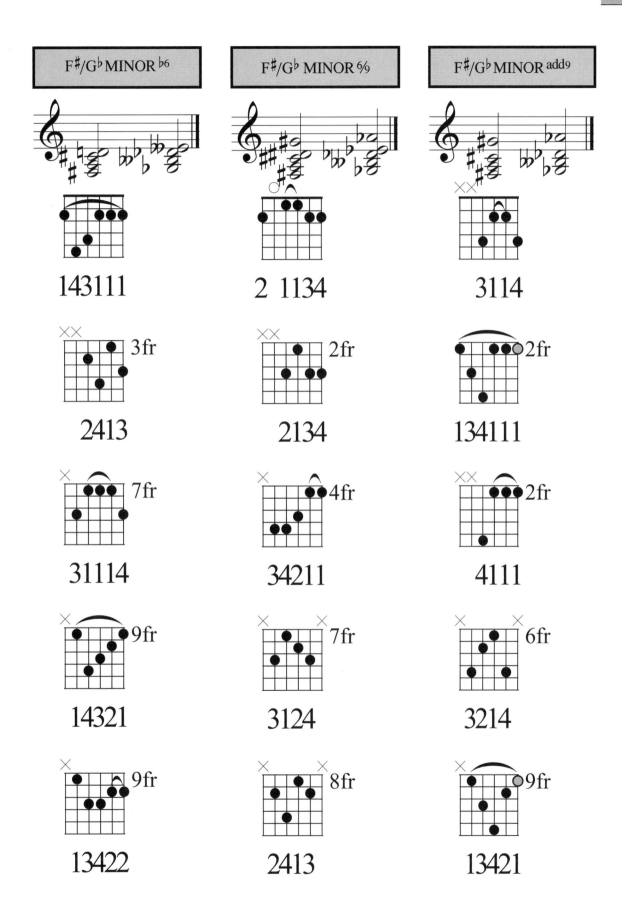

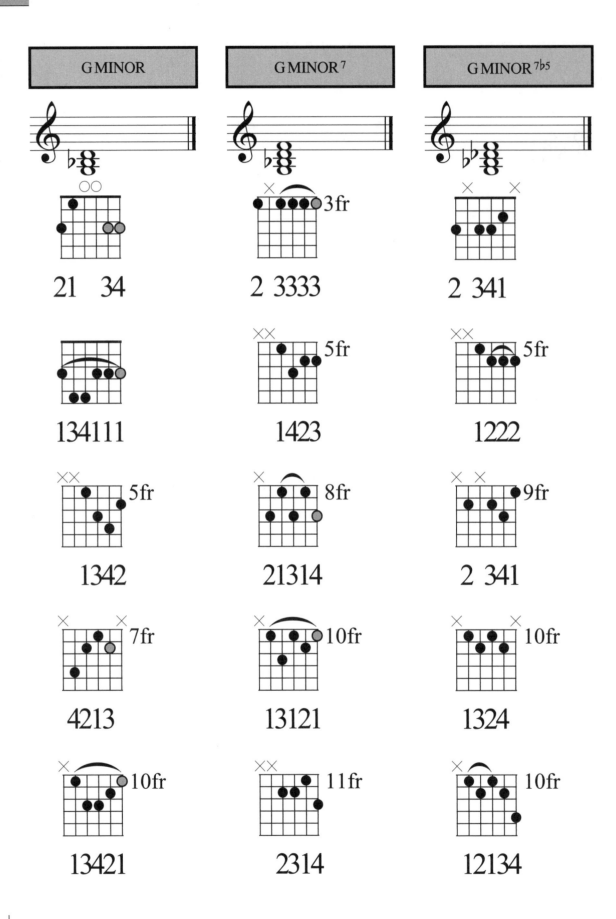

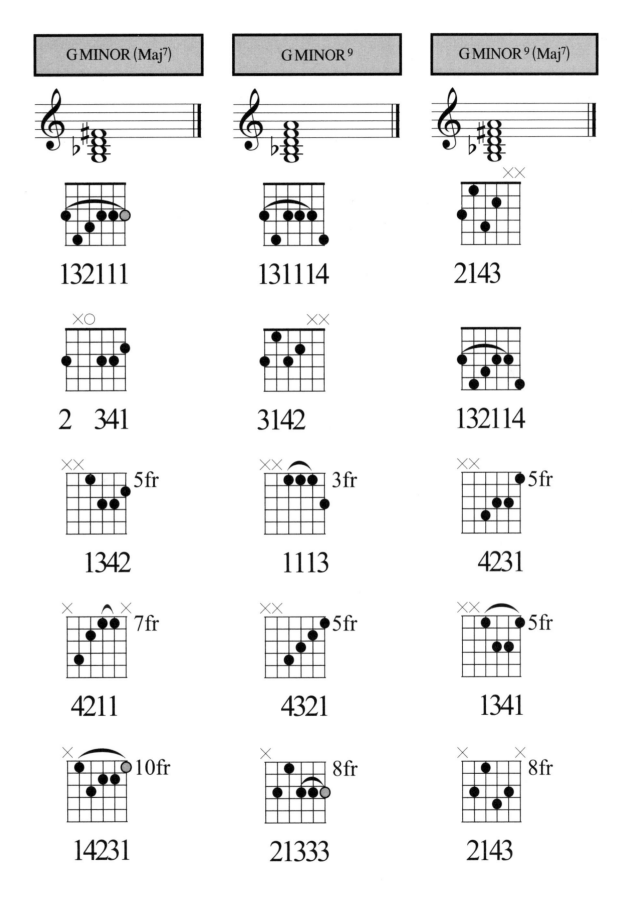

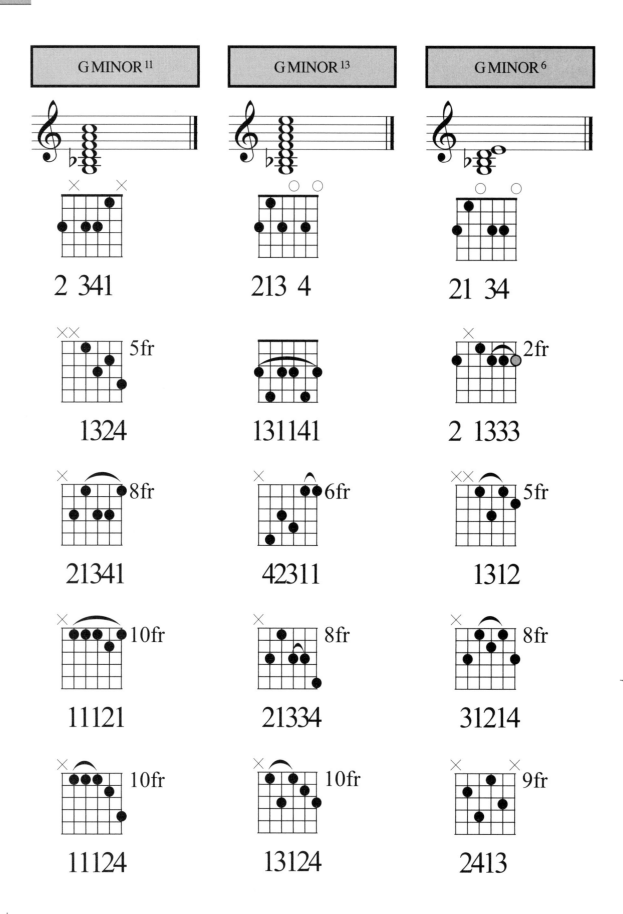

G MINOR 11

2 341

1324

21341

11121

11124

G MINOR 13

213 4

131141

42311

21334

13124

G MINOR 6

21 34

2 1333

1312

31214

2413

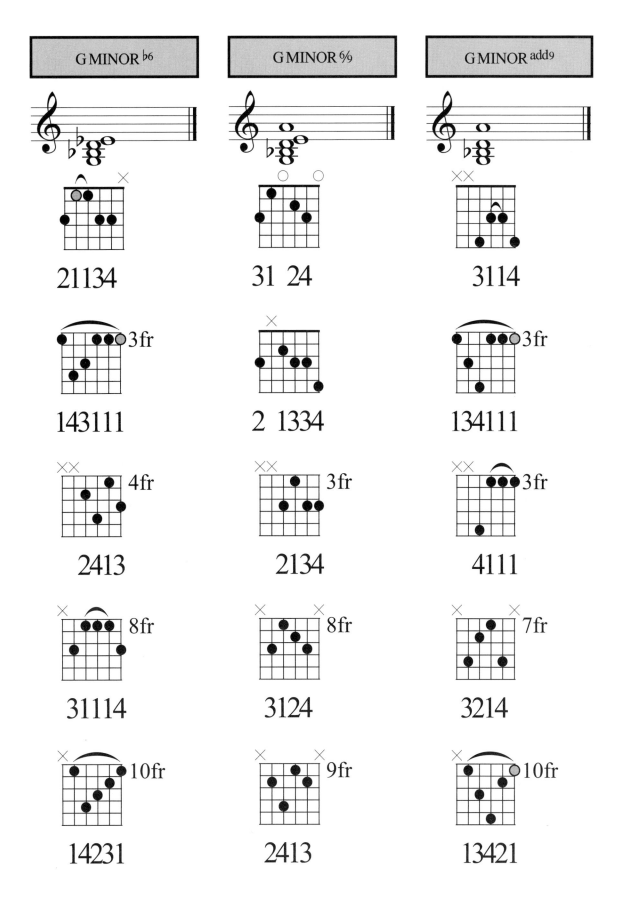

G MINOR ♭6	G MINOR 6/9	G MINOR add9
21134	31 24	3114
143111	2 1334	134111
2413	2134	4111
31114	3124	3214
14231	2413	13421

G#/A♭ MINOR

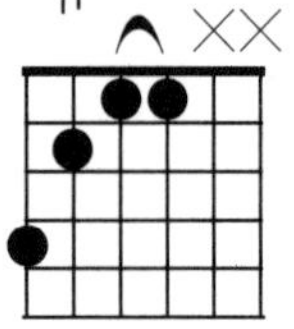

4211

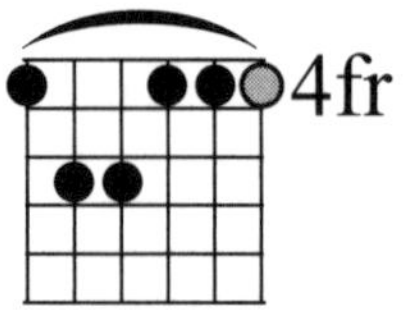

134111   4fr

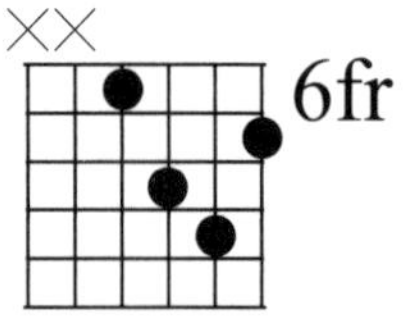

1342   6fr

4213   8fr

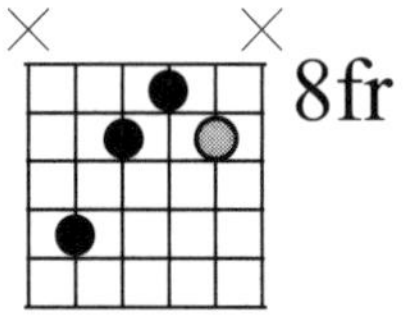

13421   11fr

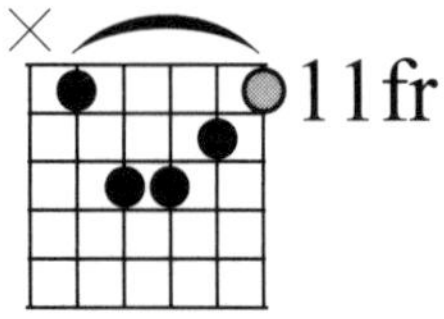

G#/A♭ MINOR⁷

2 3333   4fr

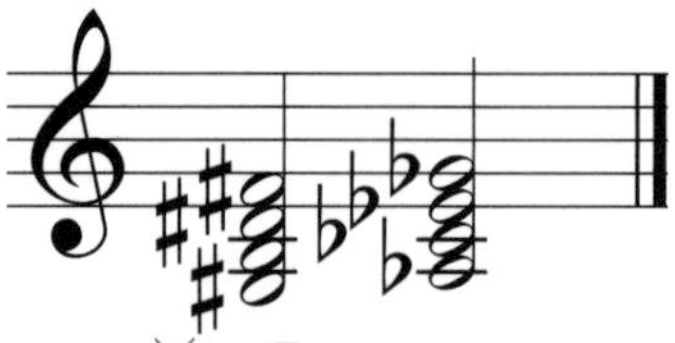

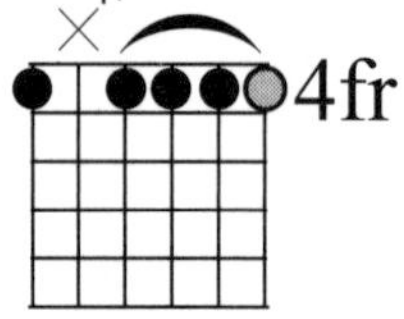

1423   6fr

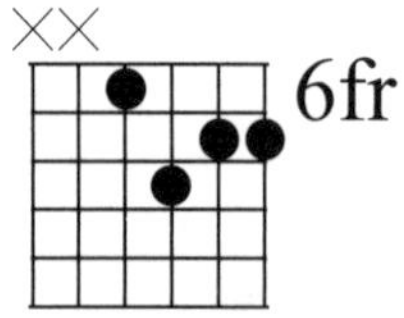

21314   9fr

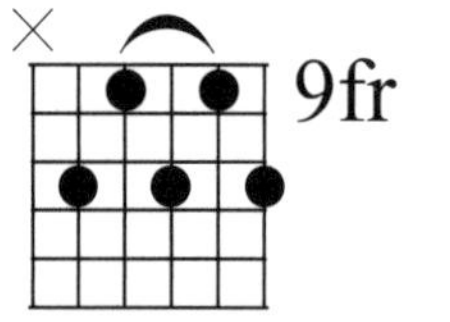

13121   11fr

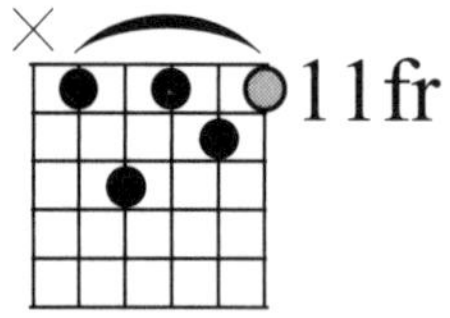

13124   11fr

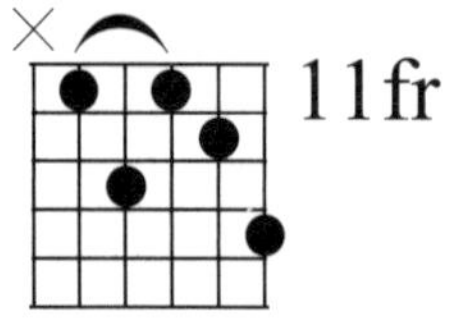

G#/A♭ MINOR⁷♭⁵

2 341

1222   6fr

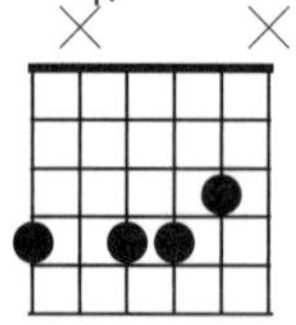

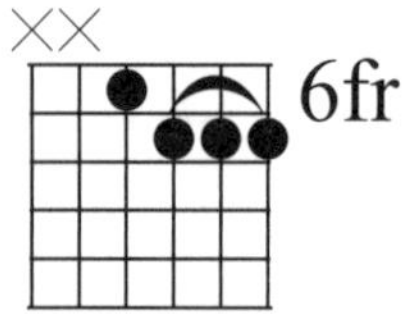

2 341   10fr

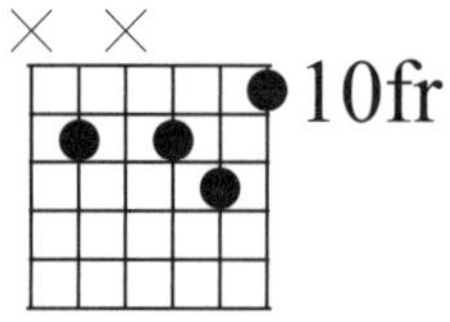

1324   11fr

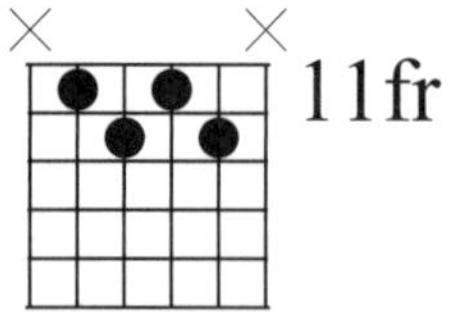

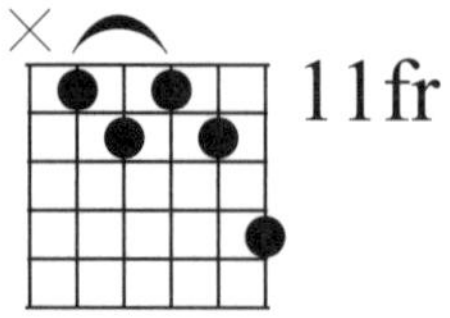

12134   11fr

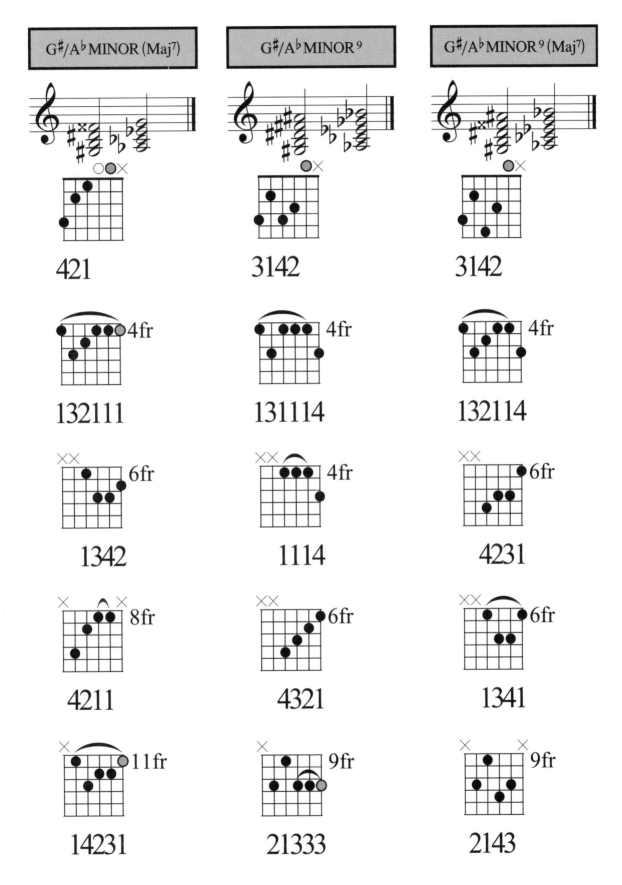

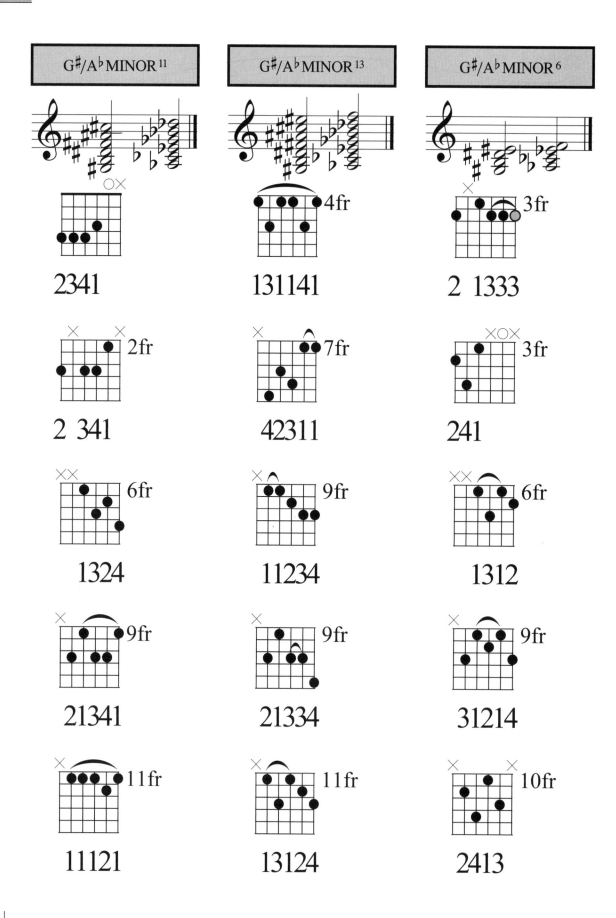

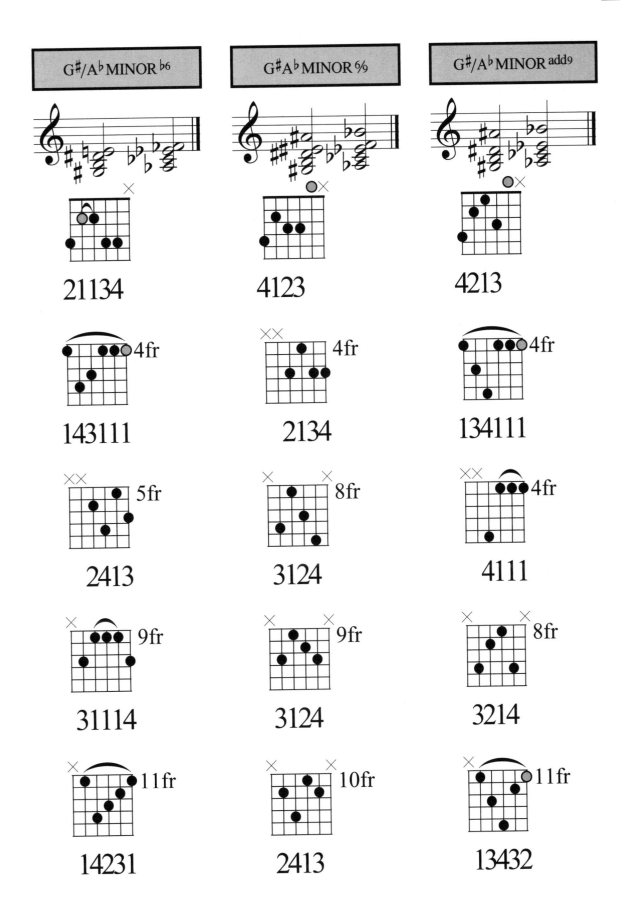

A MINOR

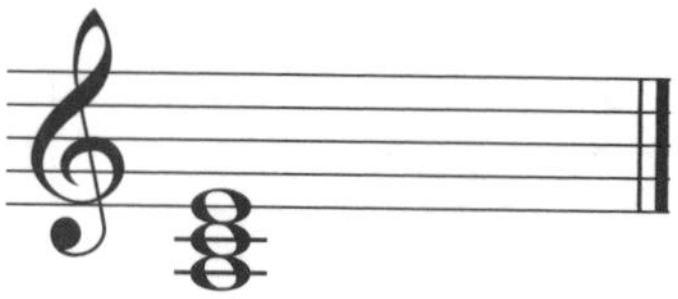

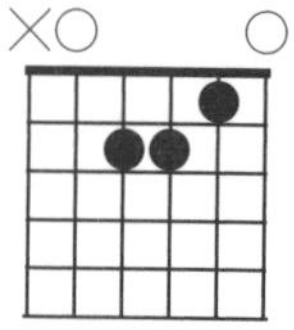

231

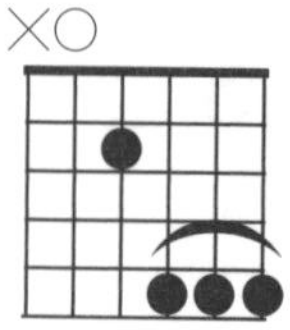

1444

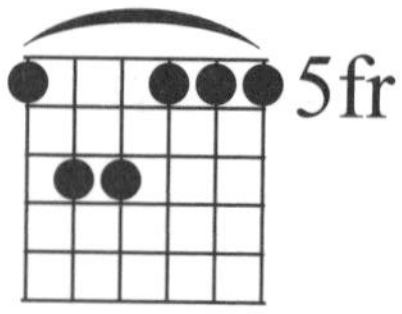

134111

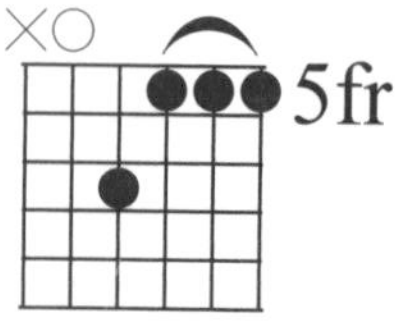

3111

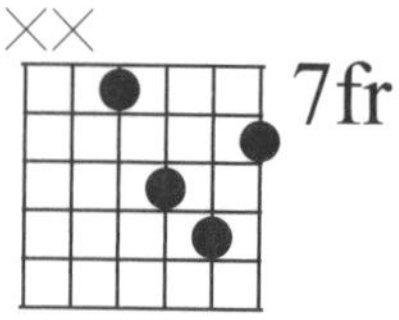

1342

A MINOR^{7}

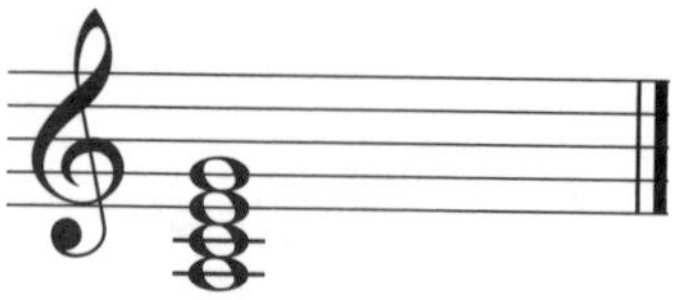

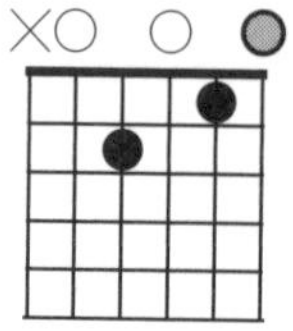

2 1

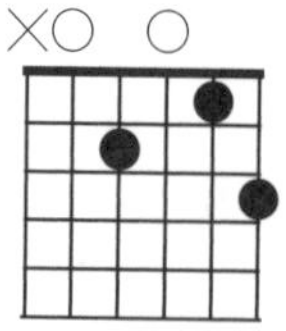

2 14

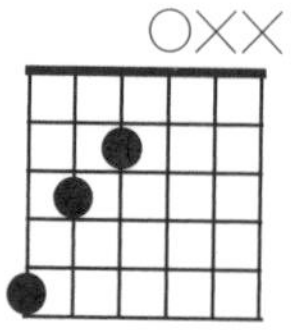

421

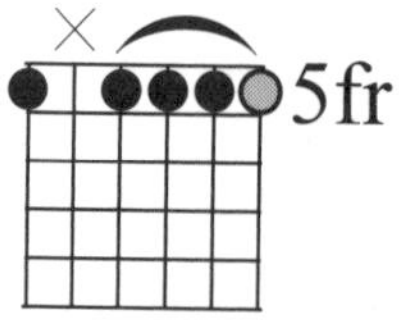

2 3333

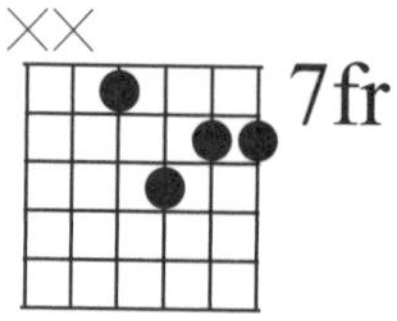

1423

A MINOR$^{7\flat5}$

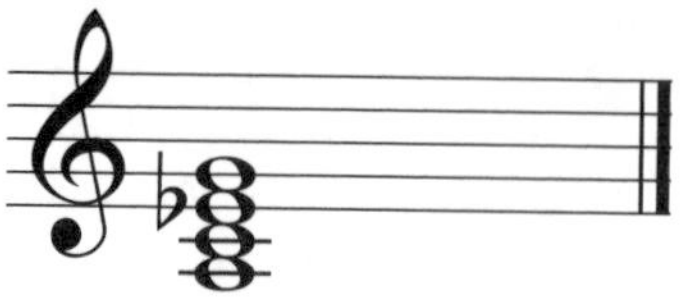

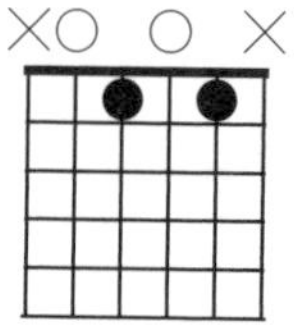

1 2

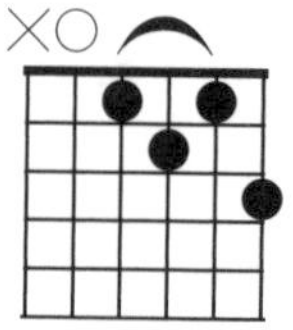

1214

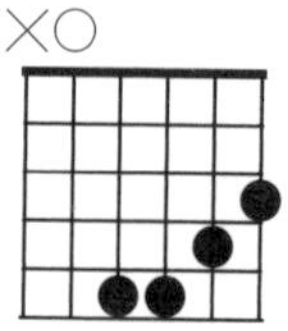

3421

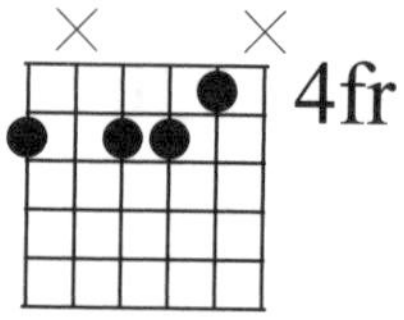

2 341

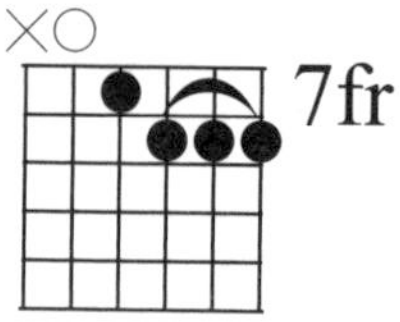

1222

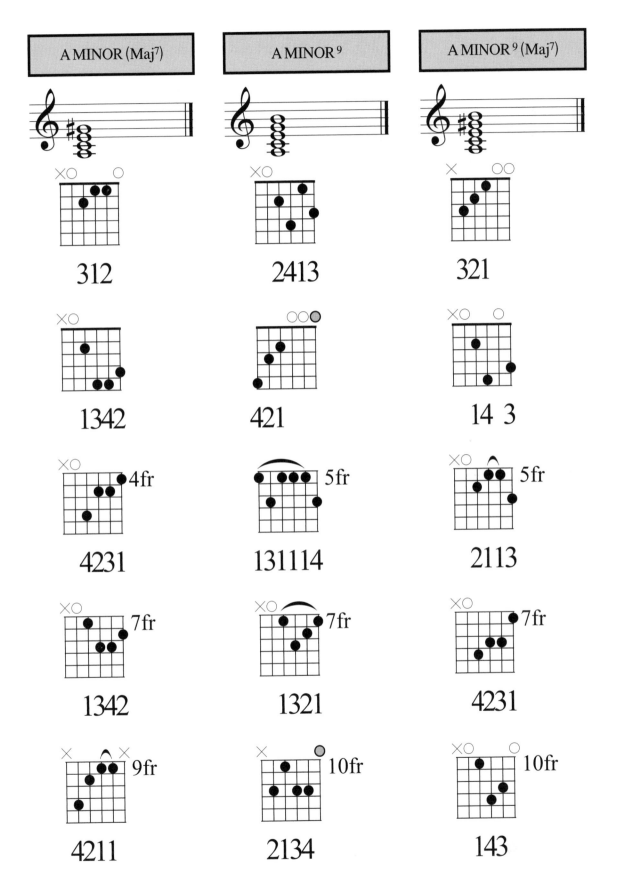

A MINOR 11	A MINOR 13	A MINOR 6

1

2 13

2314

341

4 1

421

314211

2341

123141

111114

3241

1312

3214

131141

132

A MINOR ♭6

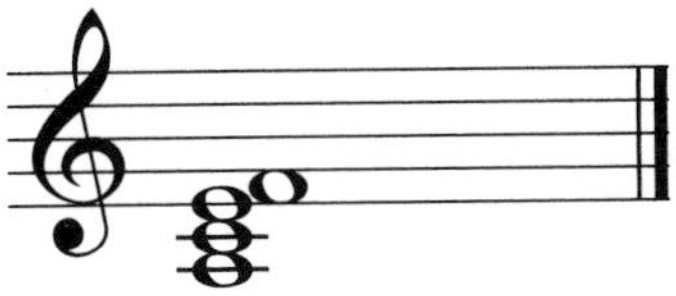

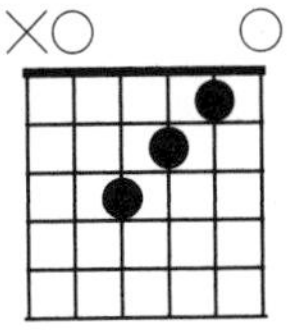

321

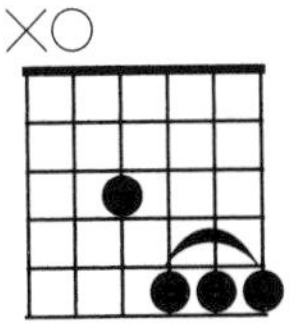

1333

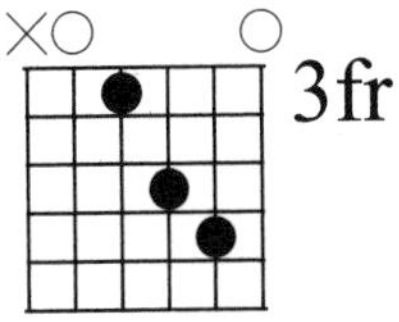

134

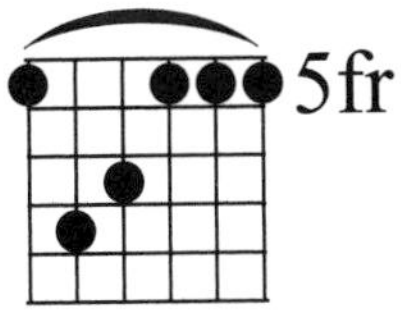

143111

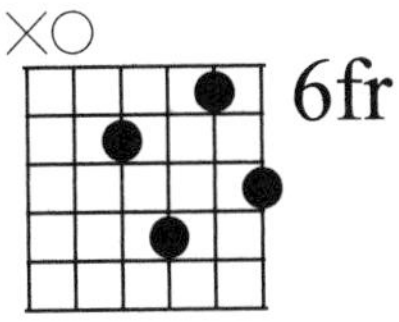

2413

A MINOR 6/9

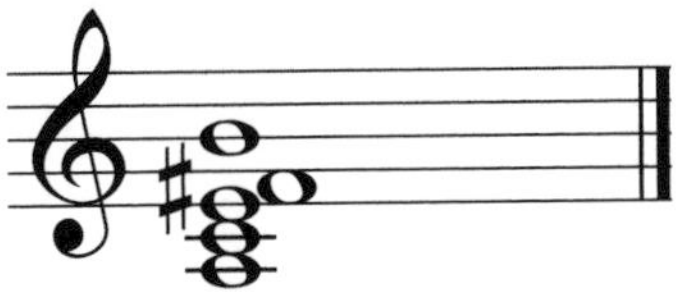

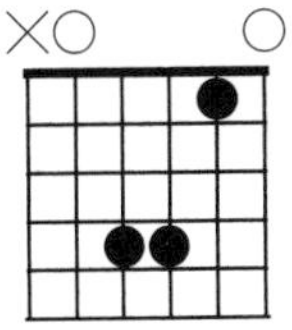

341

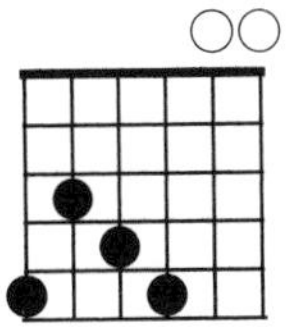

3124

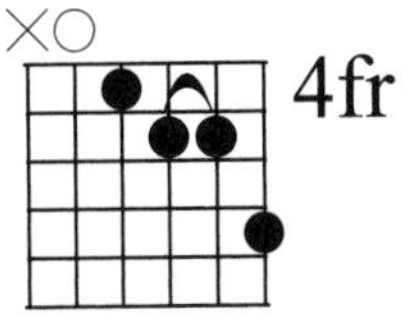

1224

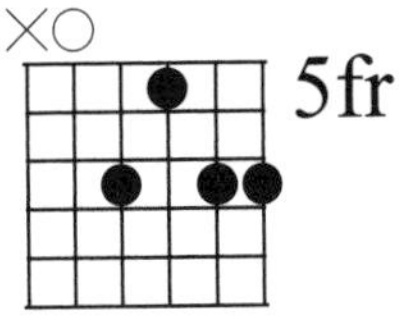

2134

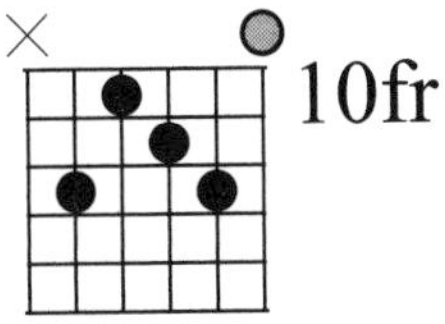

3124

A MINOR add9

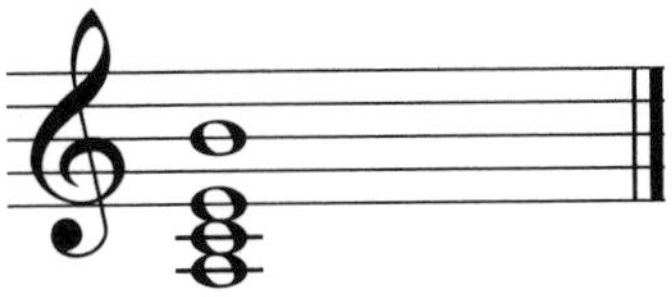

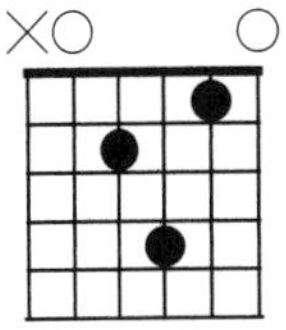

241

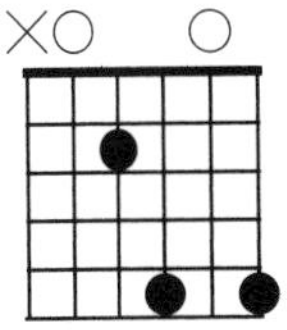

13 4

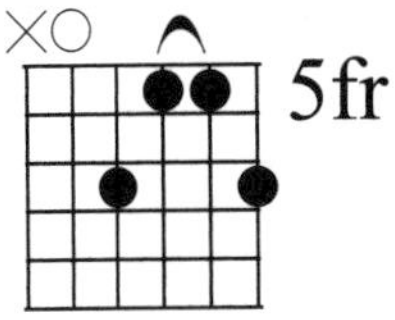

3114

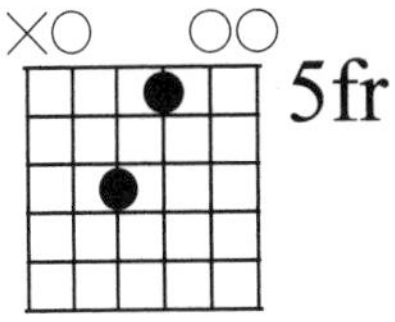

31

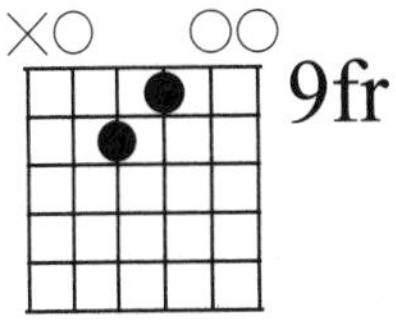

21

13421

13121

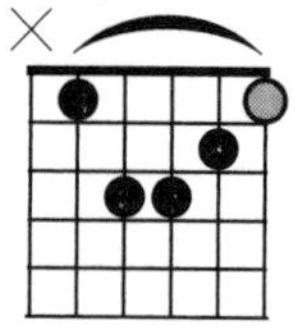

1324

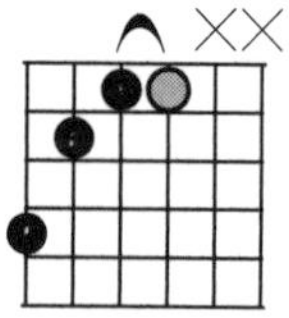

4211   3fr

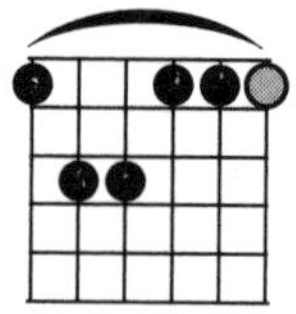

2314

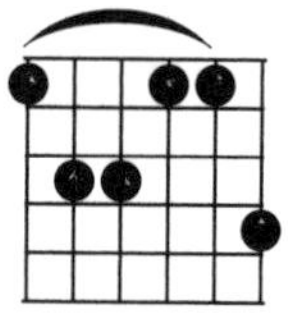

1324

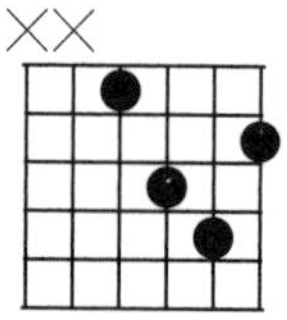

134111   6fr

2 3333   6fr

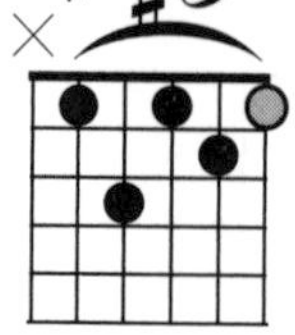

12134

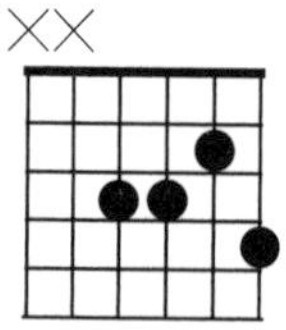

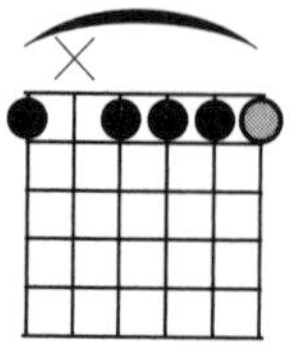

123114   6fr

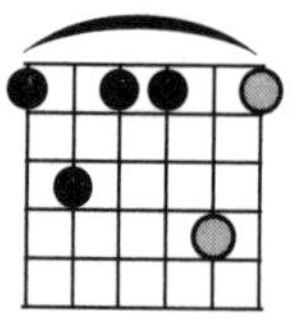

131141   6fr

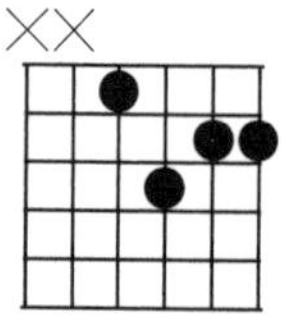

2 341   5fr

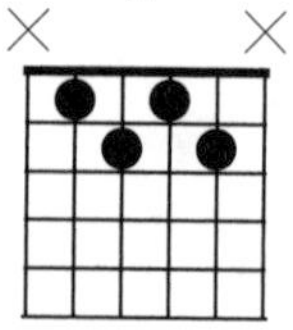

1342   8fr

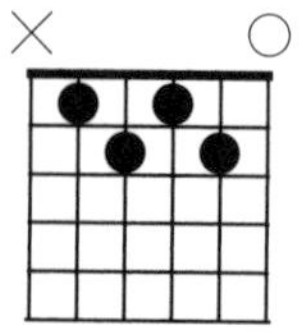

1423   8fr

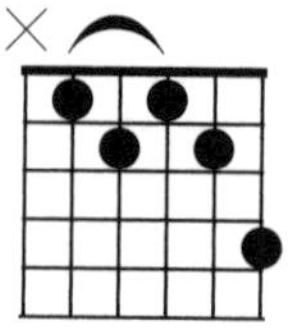

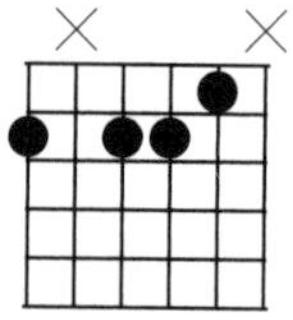

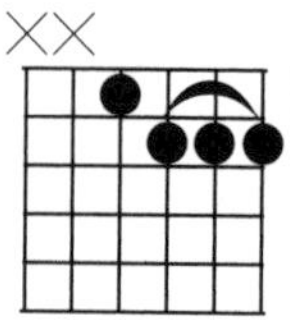

1222   8fr

A#/B♭ MINOR (Maj7)	A#/B♭ MINOR 9	A#/B♭ MINOR 9 (Maj7)

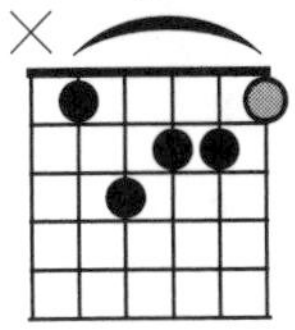

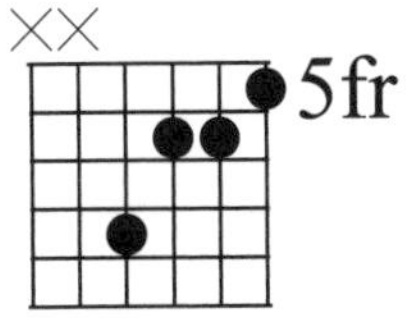

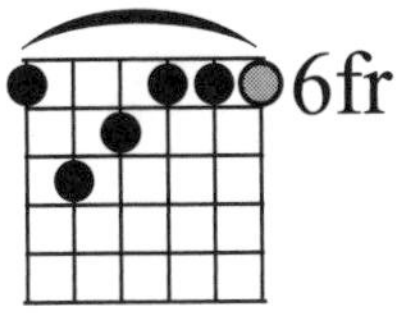

14231 · 43111 · 43211

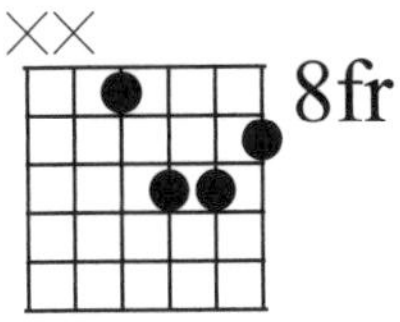

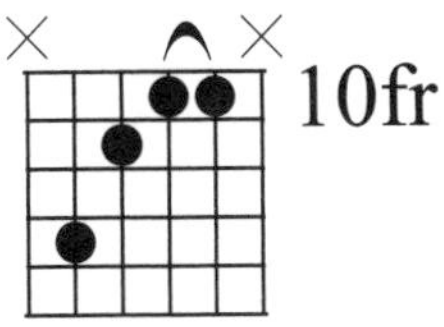

4231 (5fr) · 2143 (4fr) · 3142 (4fr)

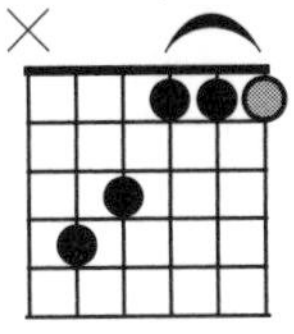

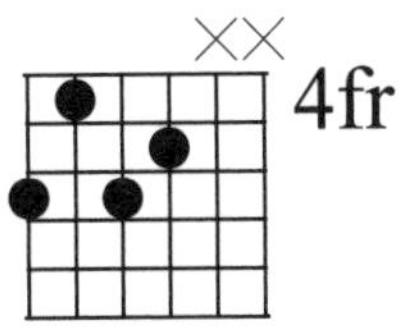

132111 (6fr) · 131114 (6fr) · 132114 (6fr)

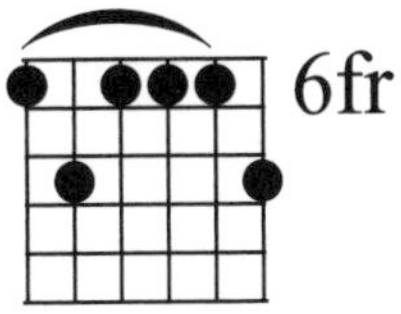

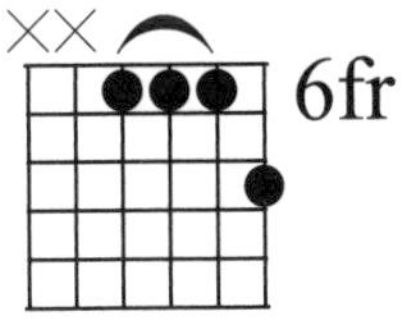

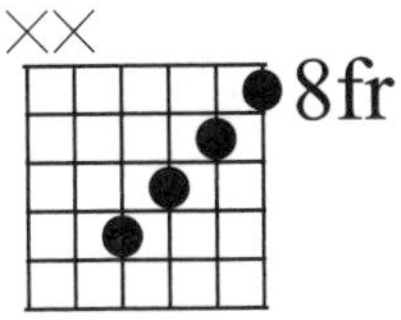

1342 (8fr) · 1114 (6fr) · 4231 (8fr)

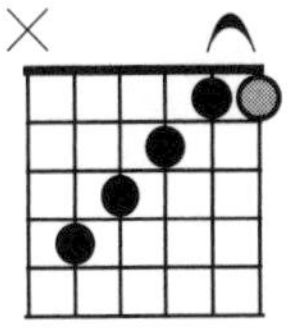

4211 (10fr) · 4321 (8fr) · 2143 (11fr)

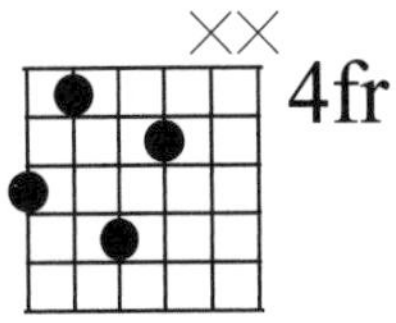

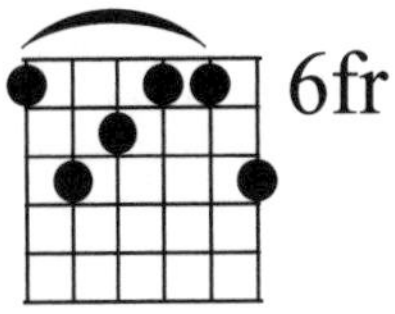

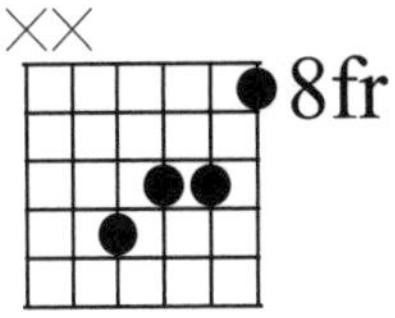

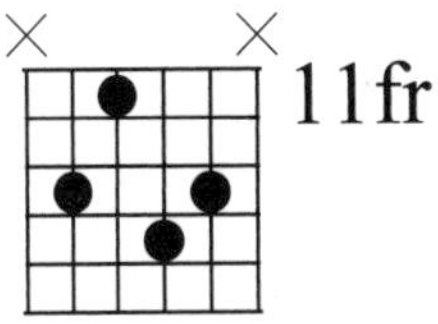

107

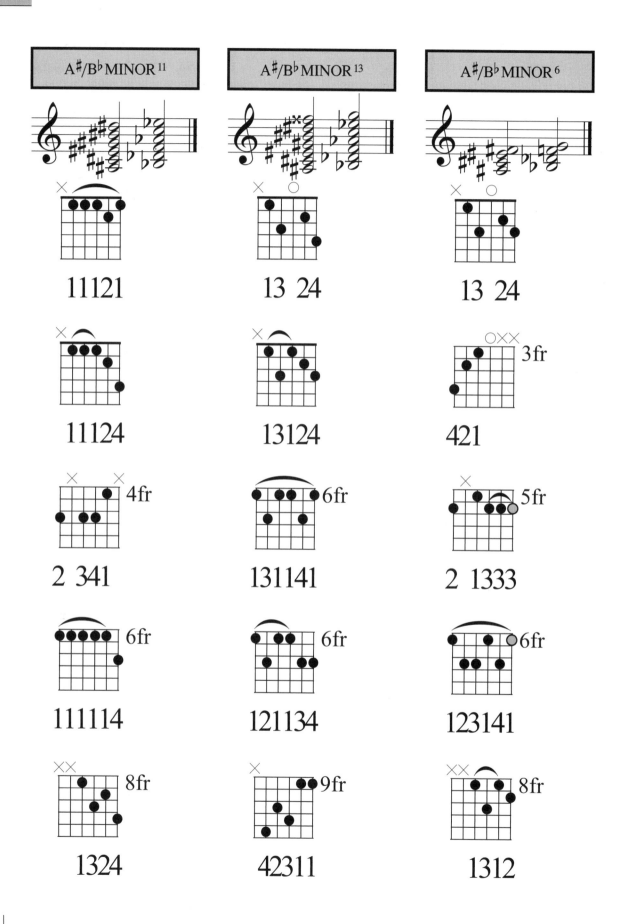

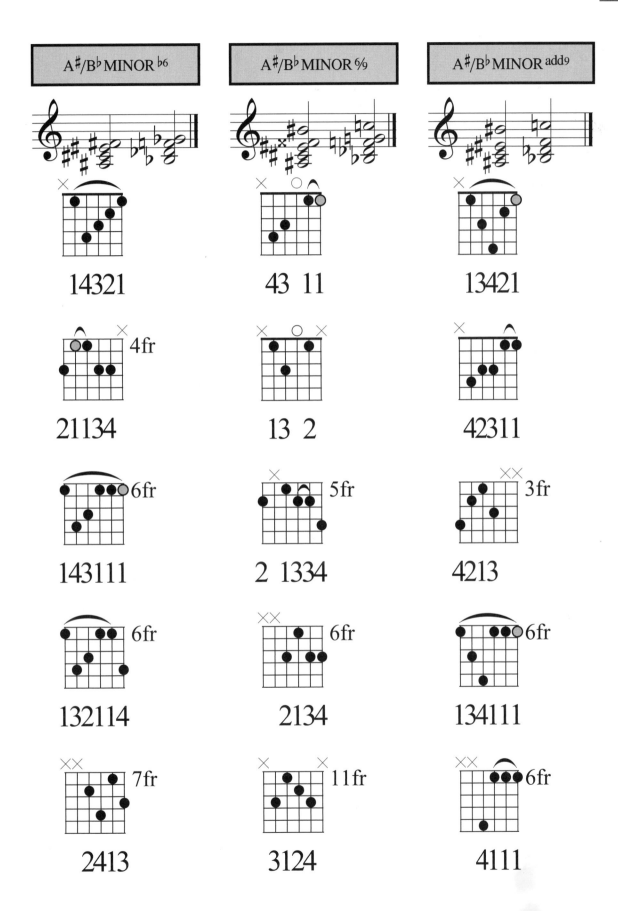

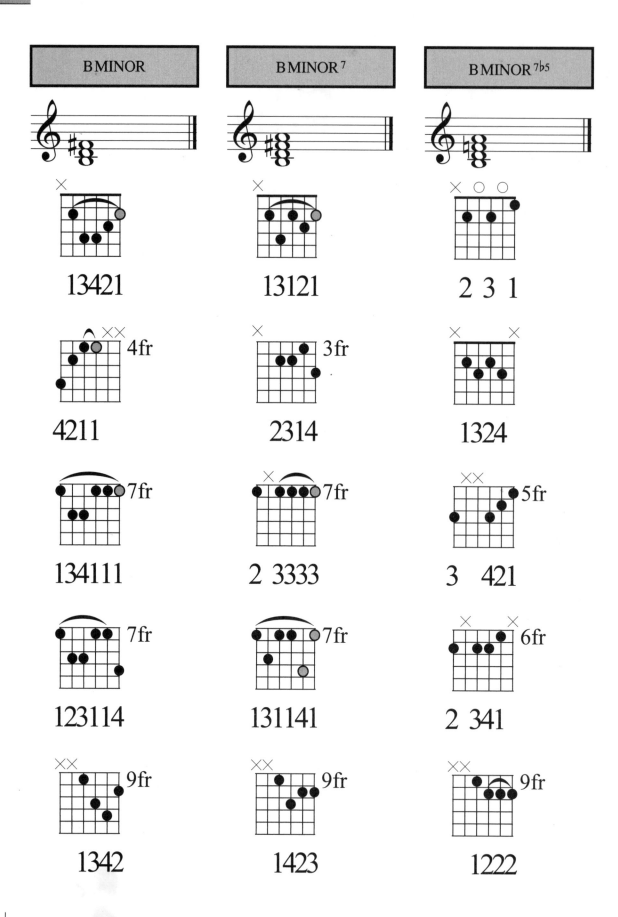

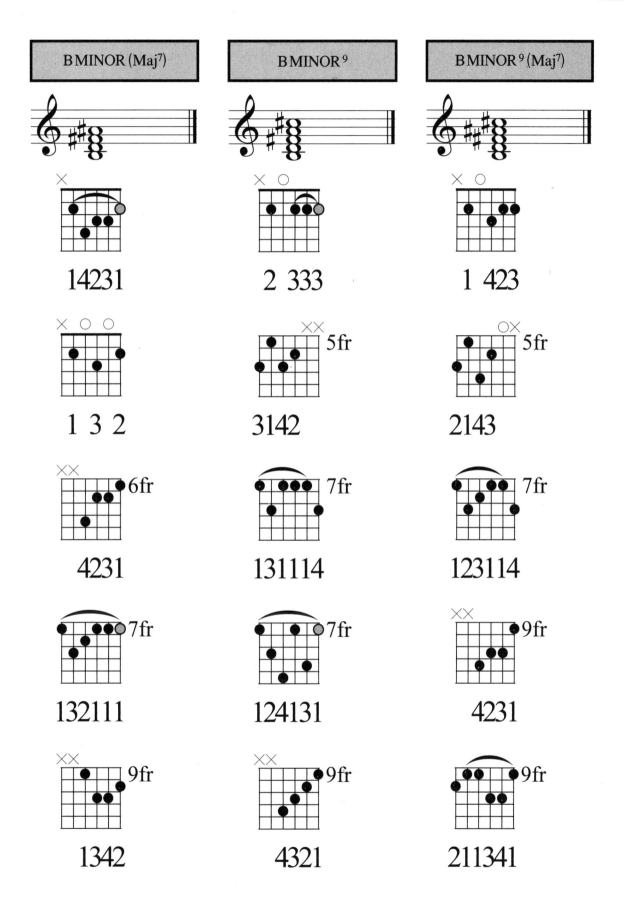

B MINOR 11	B MINOR 13	B MINOR 6
2 34	1 2 4	2 143
1423	13124	2413
11124	2 34 1	2 1333
2 3411	131141	123141
1324	42311	1312

B MINOR ♭6

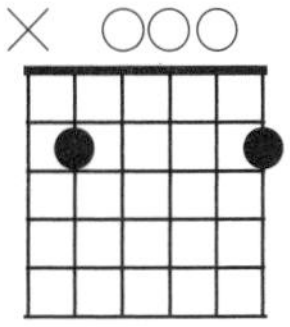

× ○○○

1   2

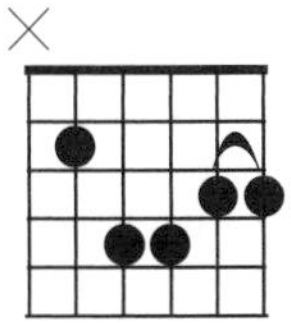

×

13422

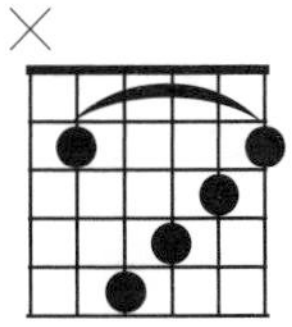

×

14321

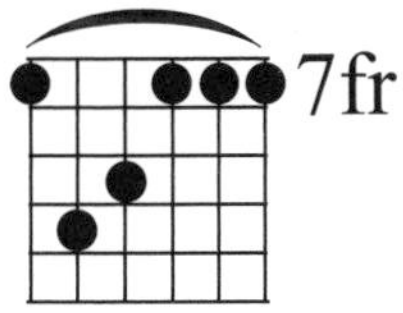

7fr

143111

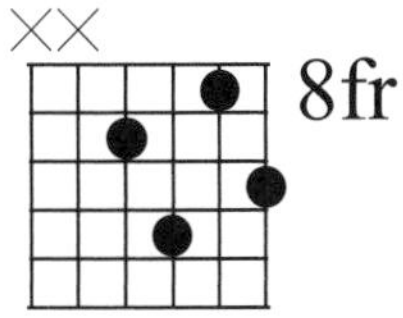

××   8fr

2413

B MINOR 6/9

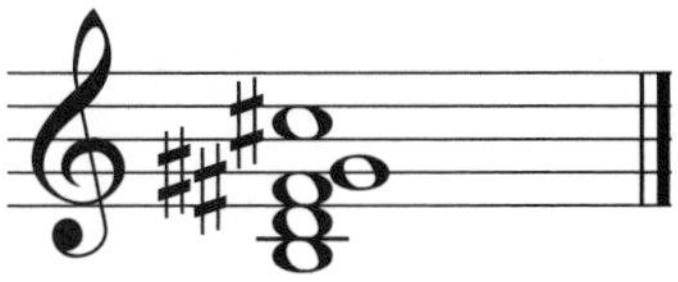

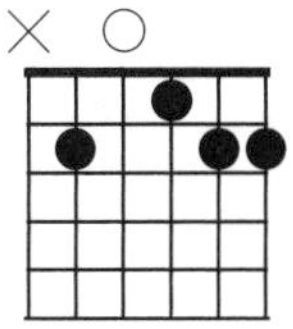

× ○

2 134

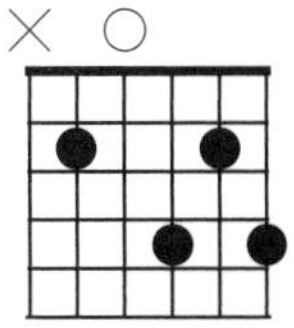

× ○

1 324

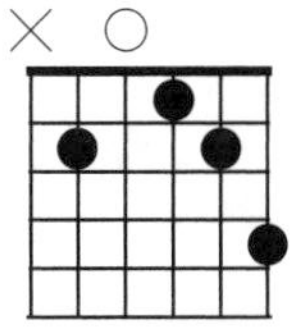

× ○

2 134

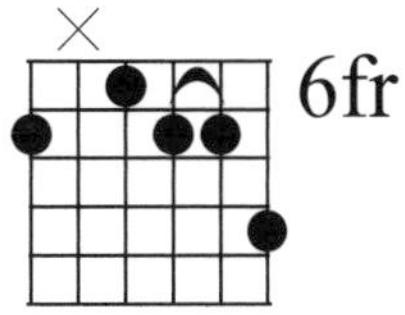

×   6fr

2 1334

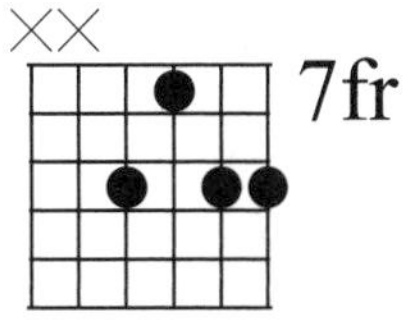

××   7fr

2134

B MINOR add9

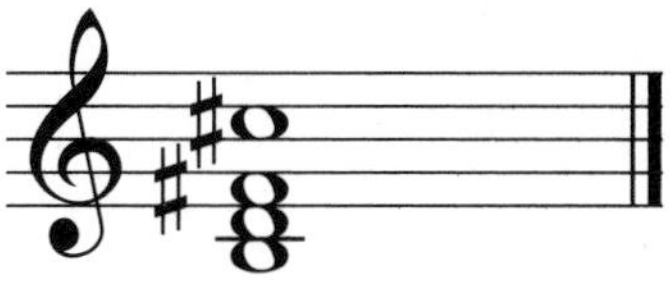

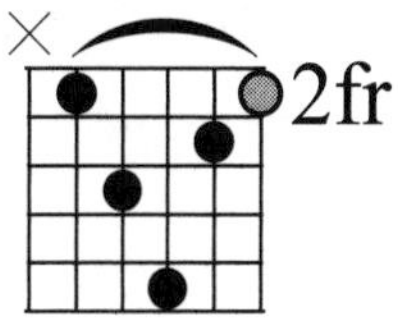

×   2fr

13421

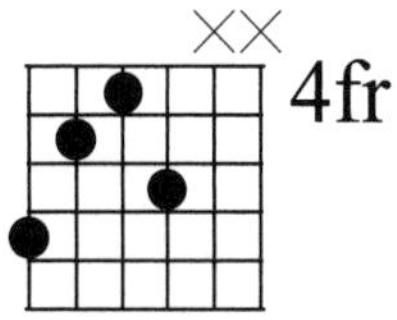

××   4fr

4213

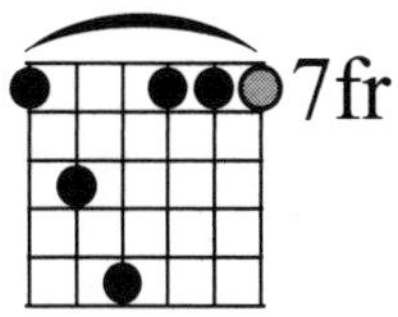

7fr

134111

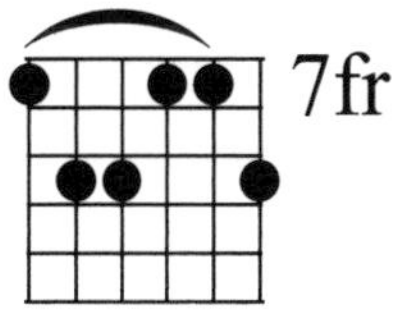

7fr

123114

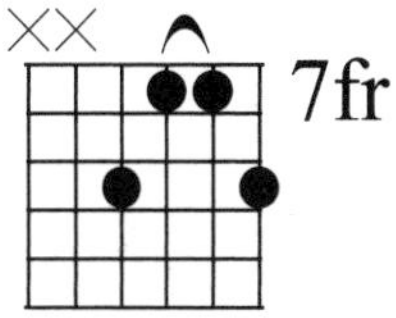

××   7fr

3114

5

Chapter 5

Dominant Chords

In its simplest form, the dominant chord, also referred to simply as the "seventh chord," is commonly used in modern music. As the chords get more elaborate and altered, you start moving into the realm of jazz and its particular use of these colorful chords. Here you will find some unique and unusual sounds.

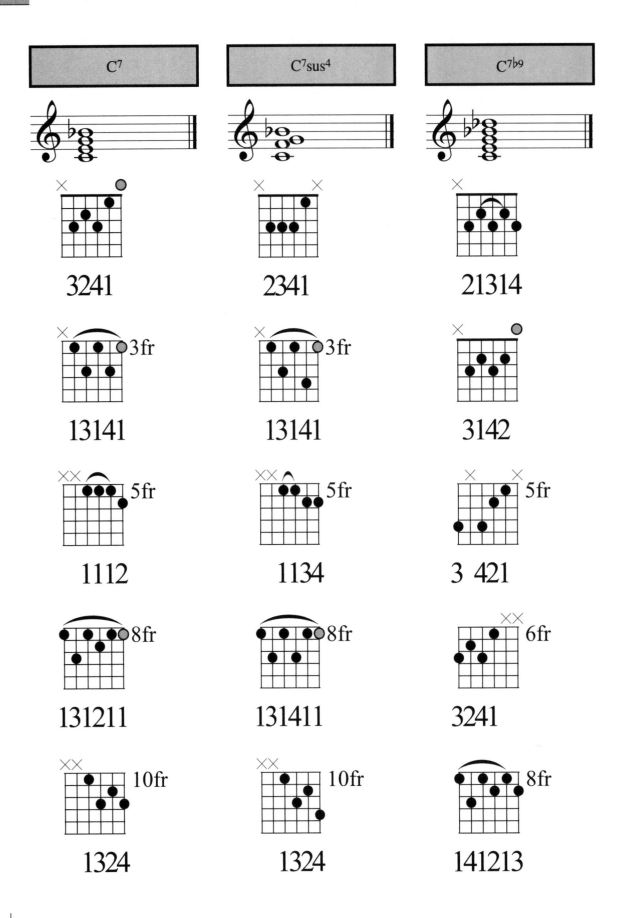

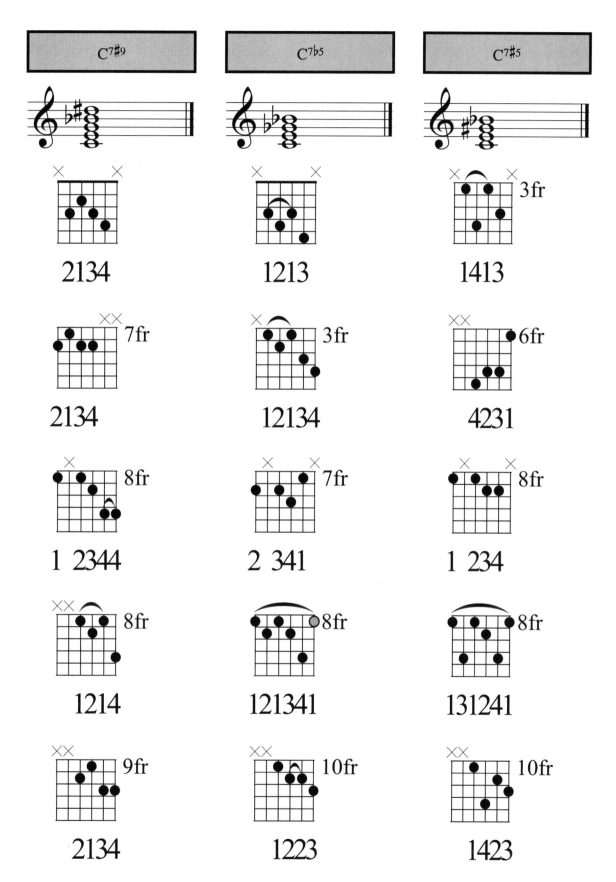

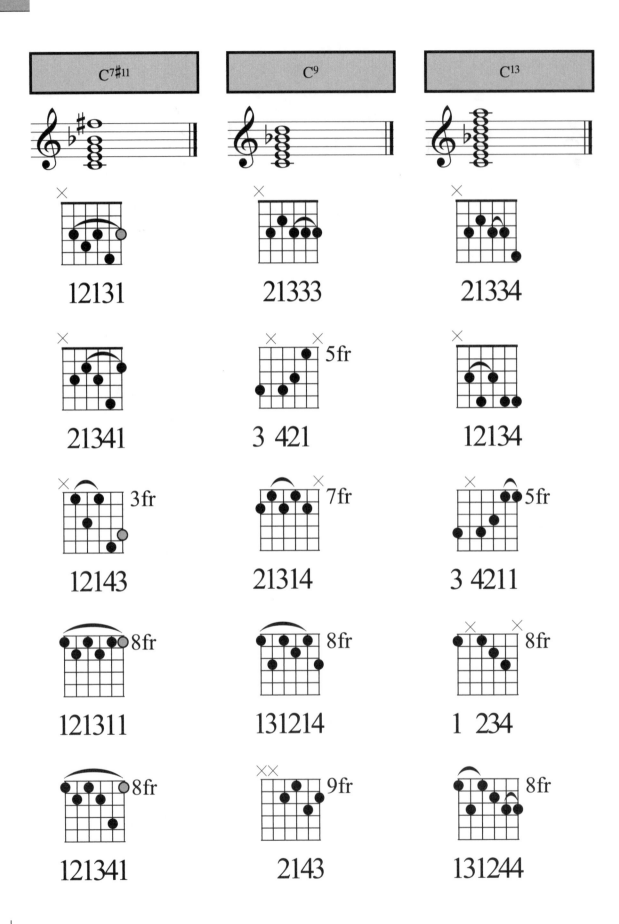

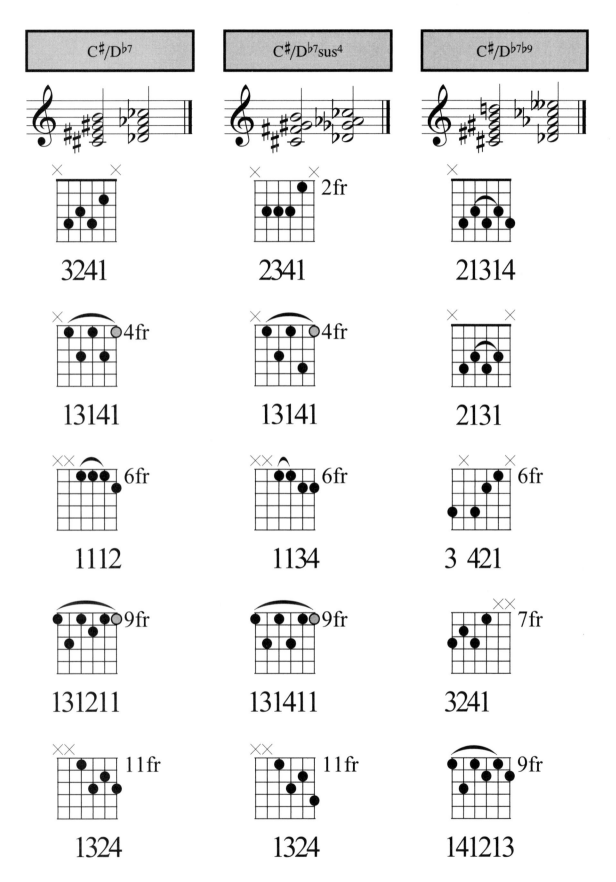

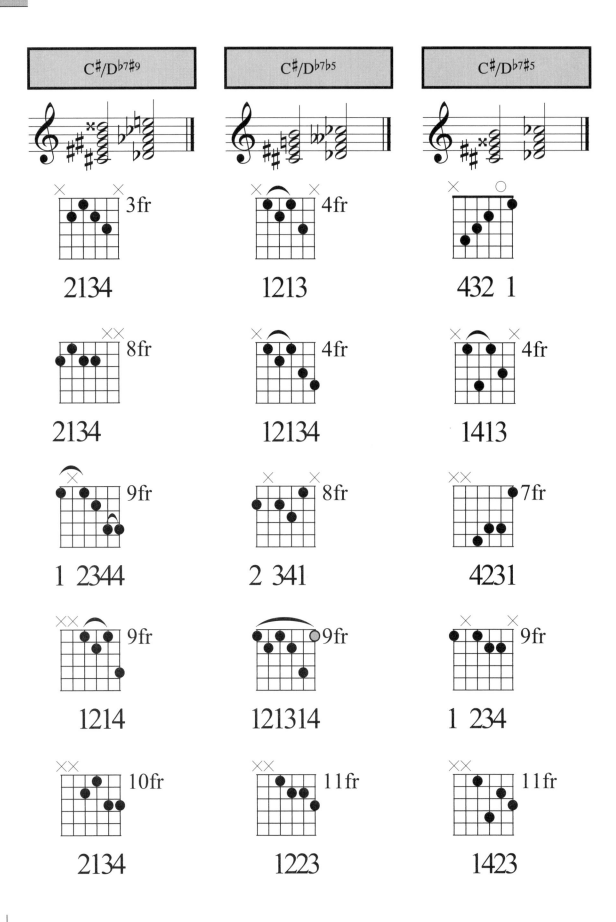

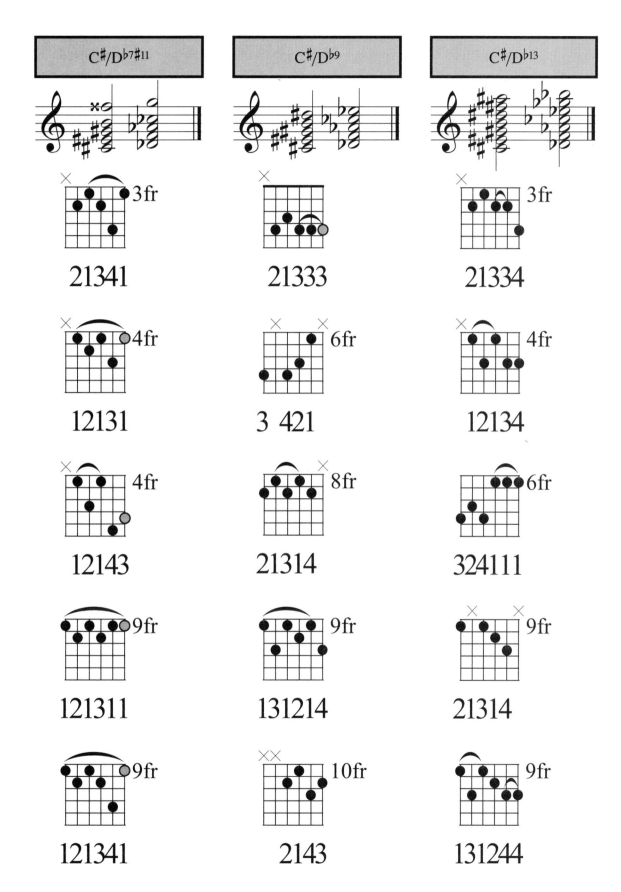

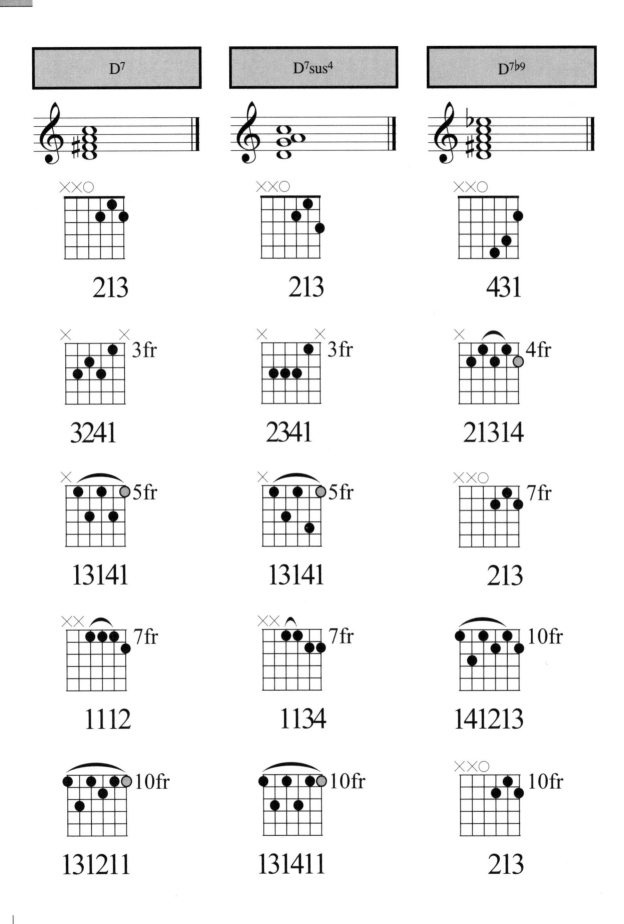

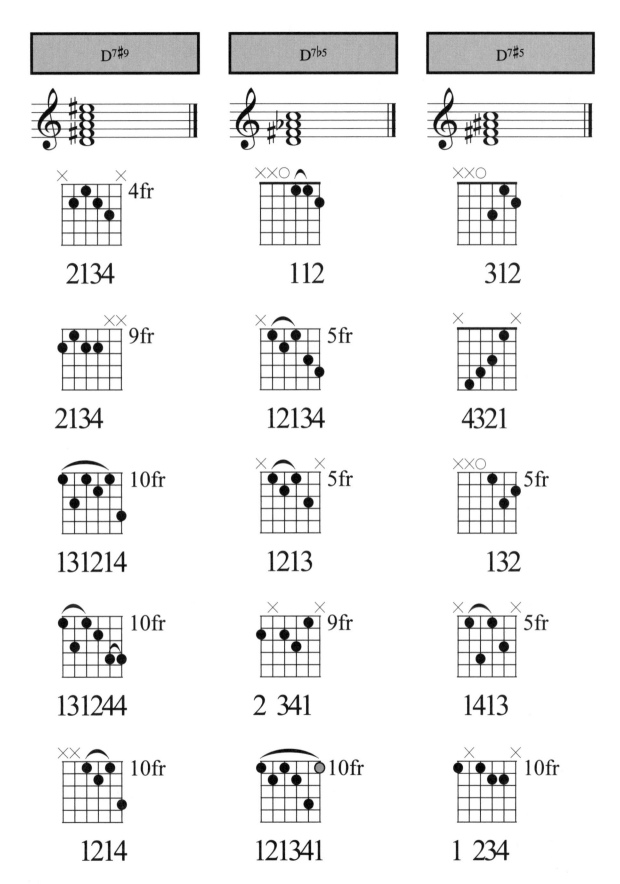

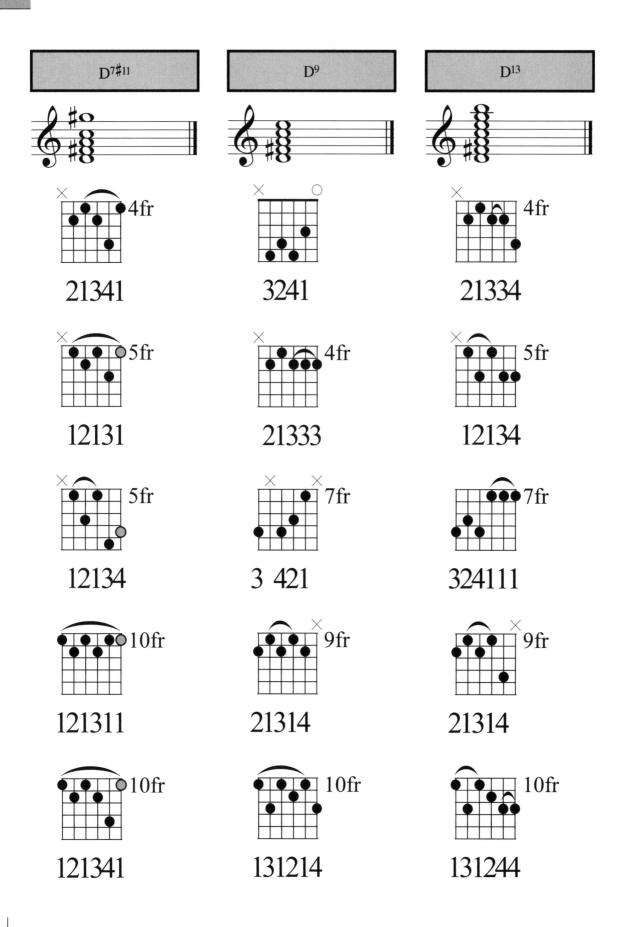

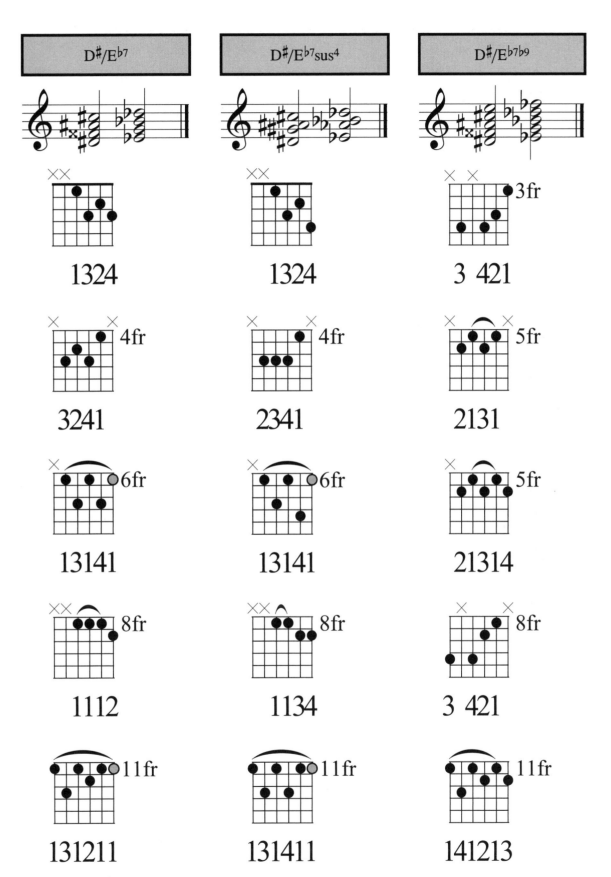

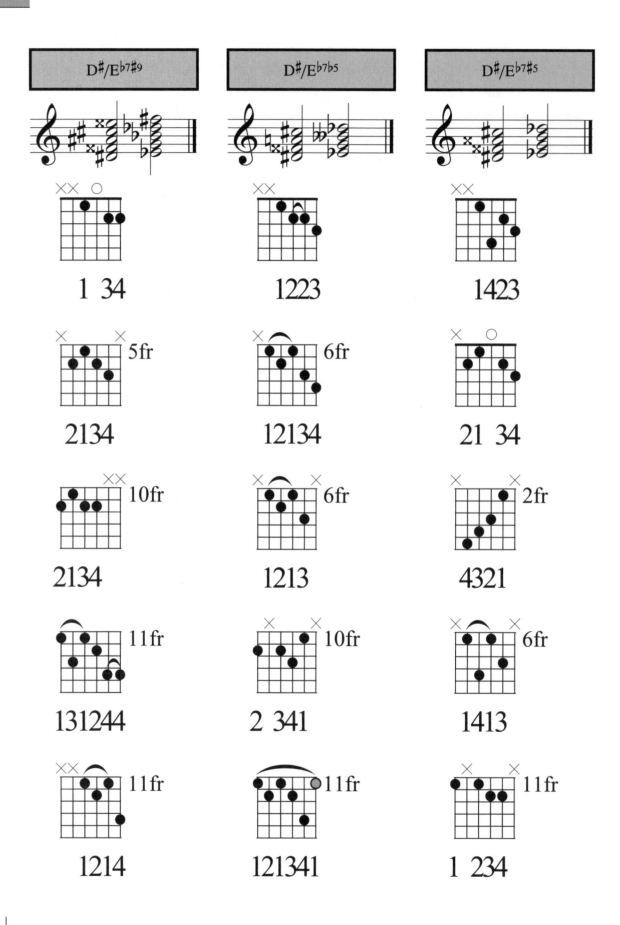

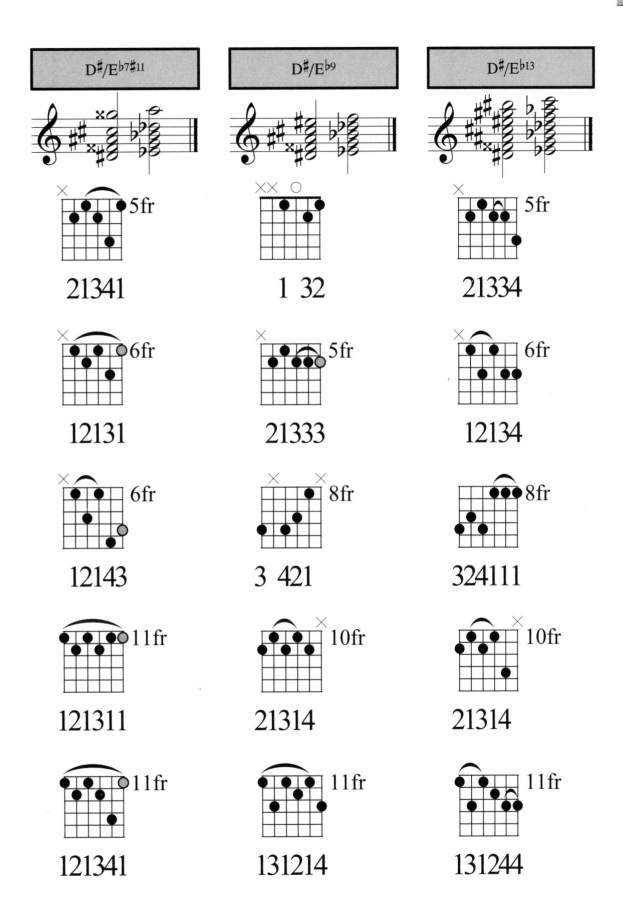

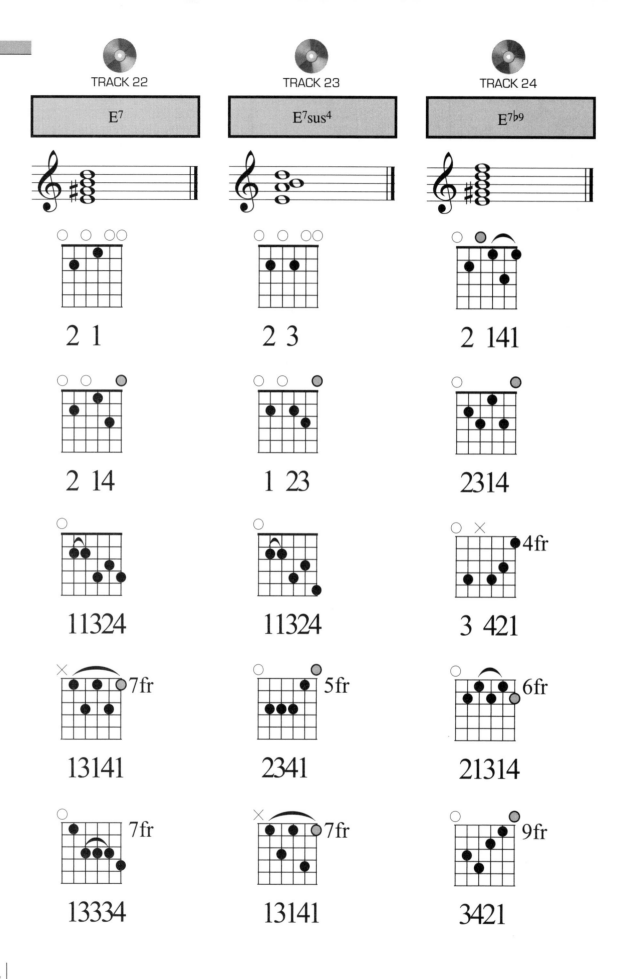

TRACK 25

TRACK 26

TRACK 27

E7#9

E7b5

E7#5

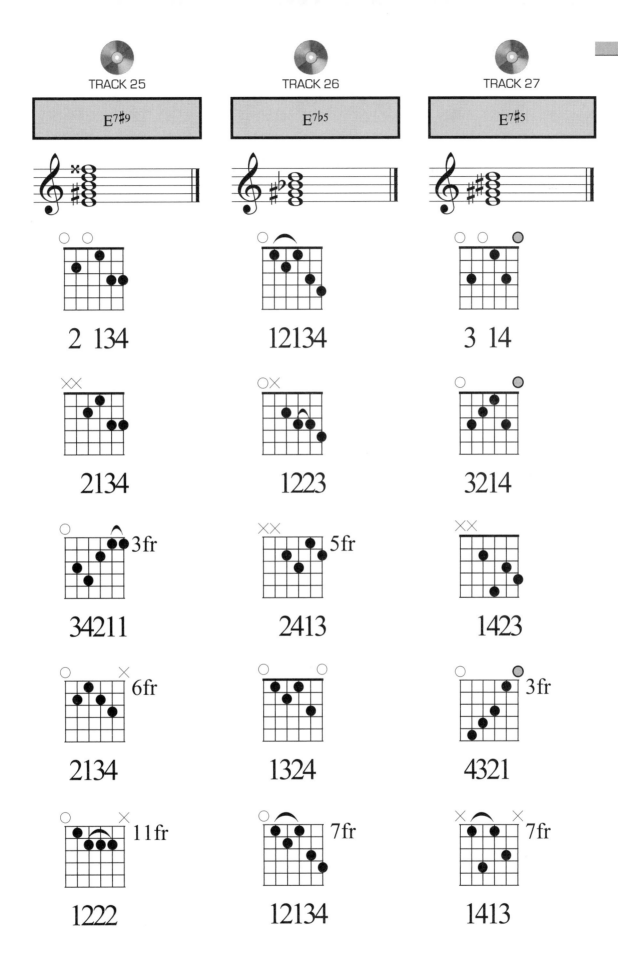

2 134

12134

3 14

2134

1223

3214

34211

2413

1423

2134   6fr

1324

4321   3fr

1222   11fr

12134   7fr

1413   7fr

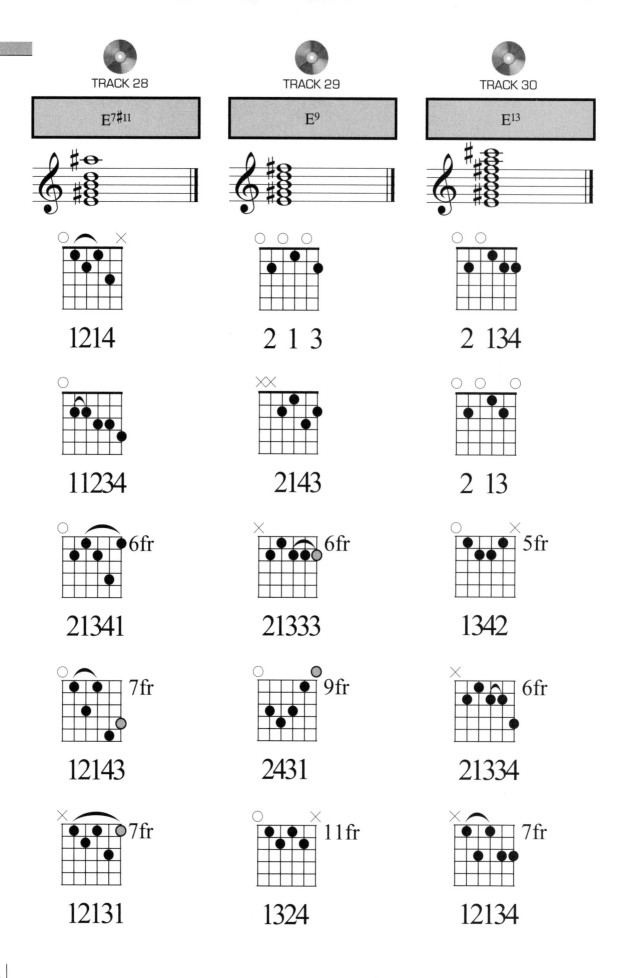

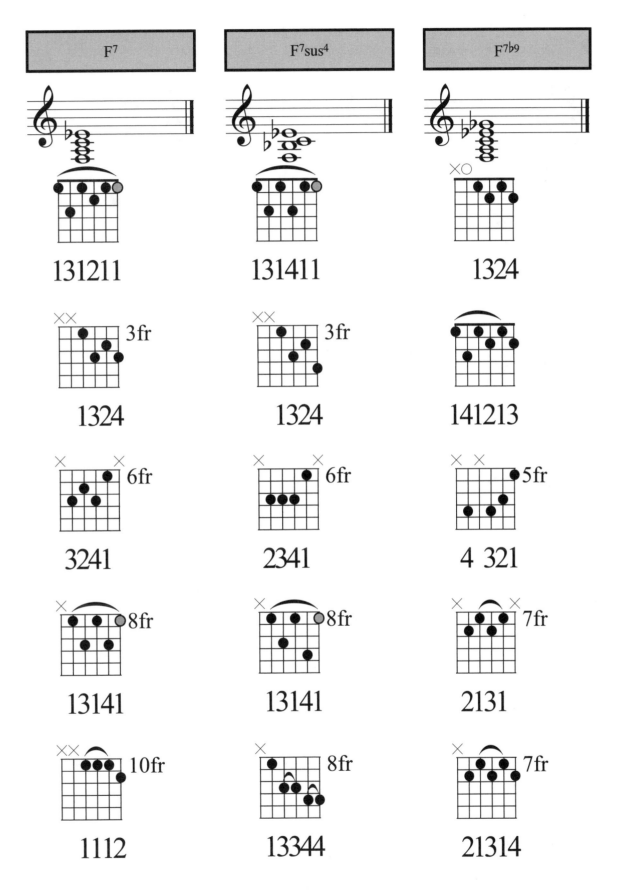

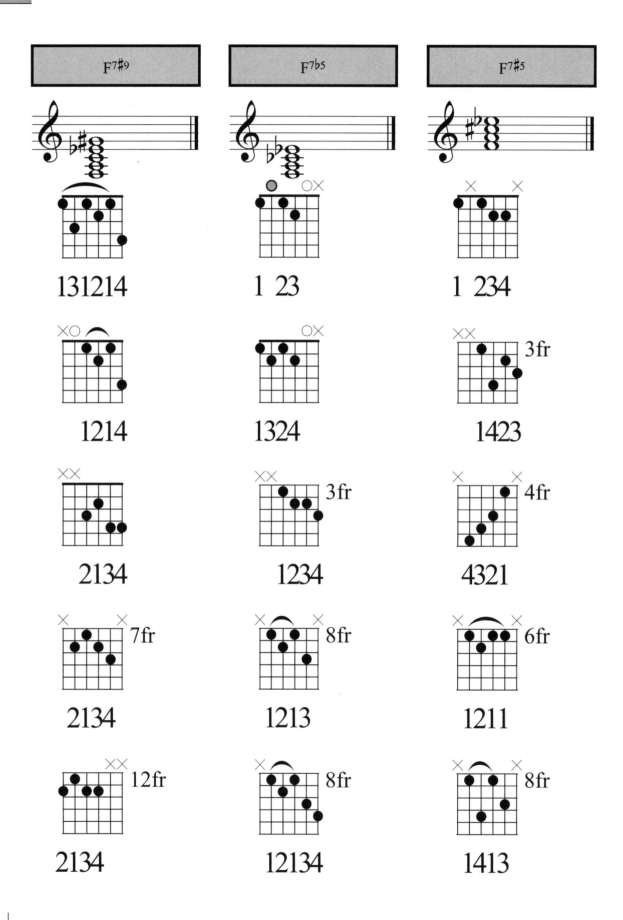

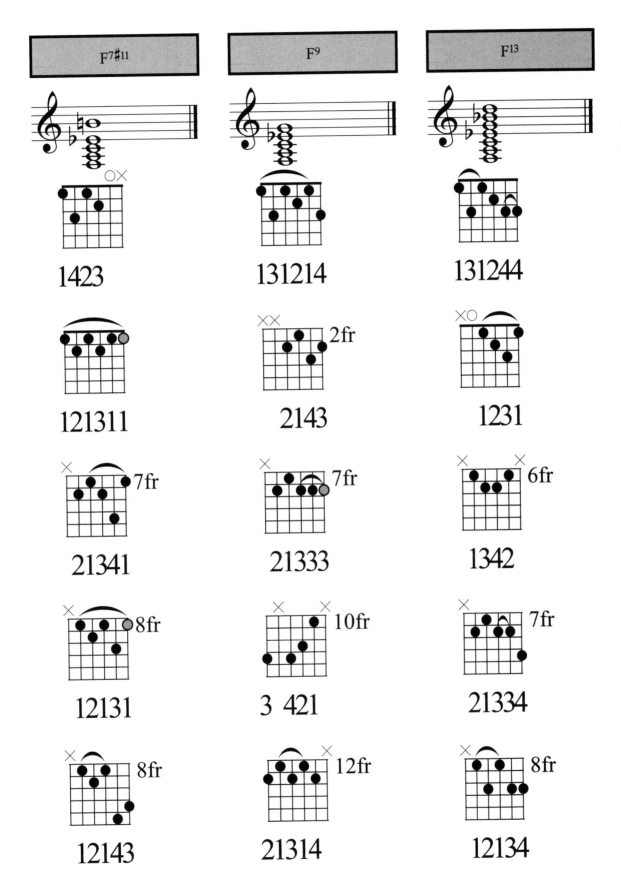

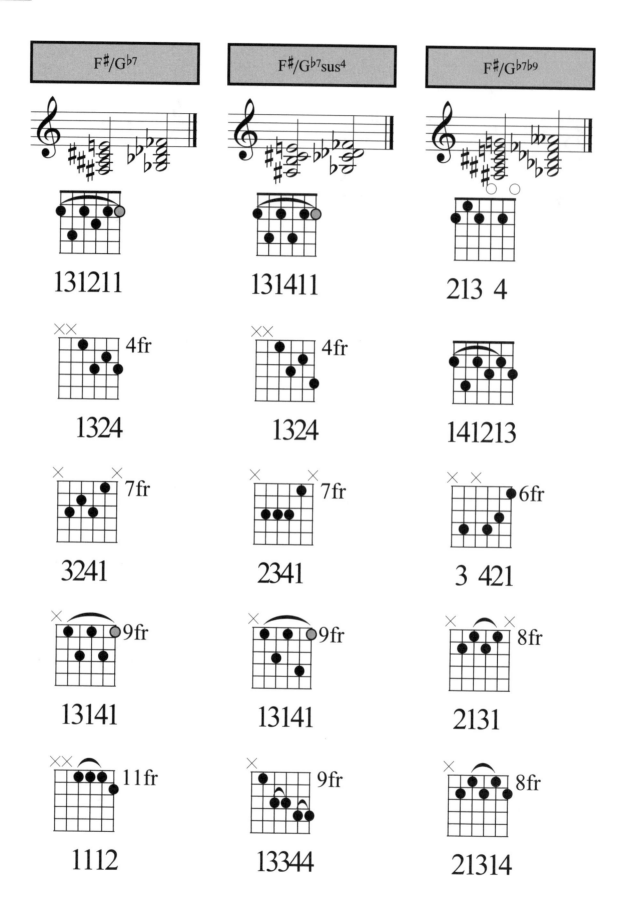

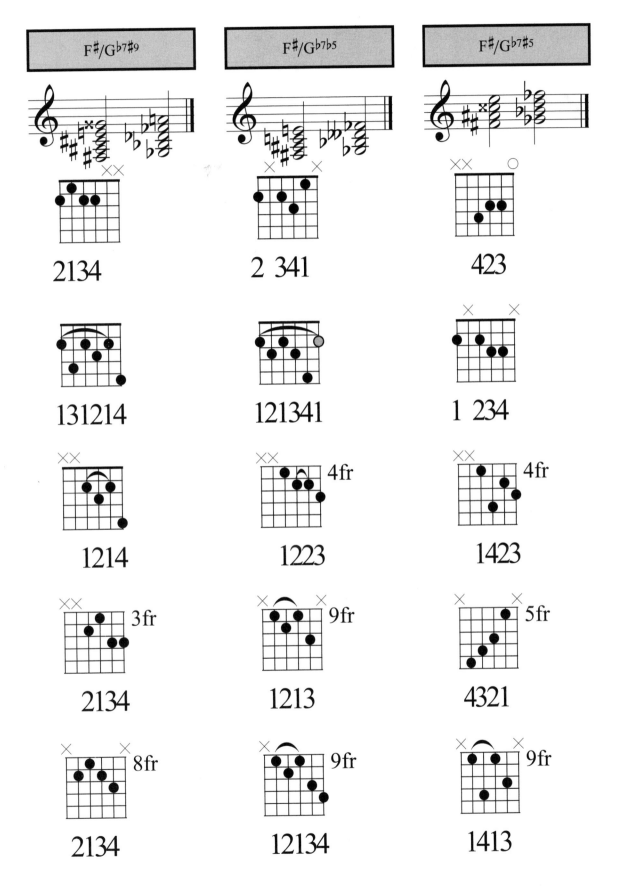

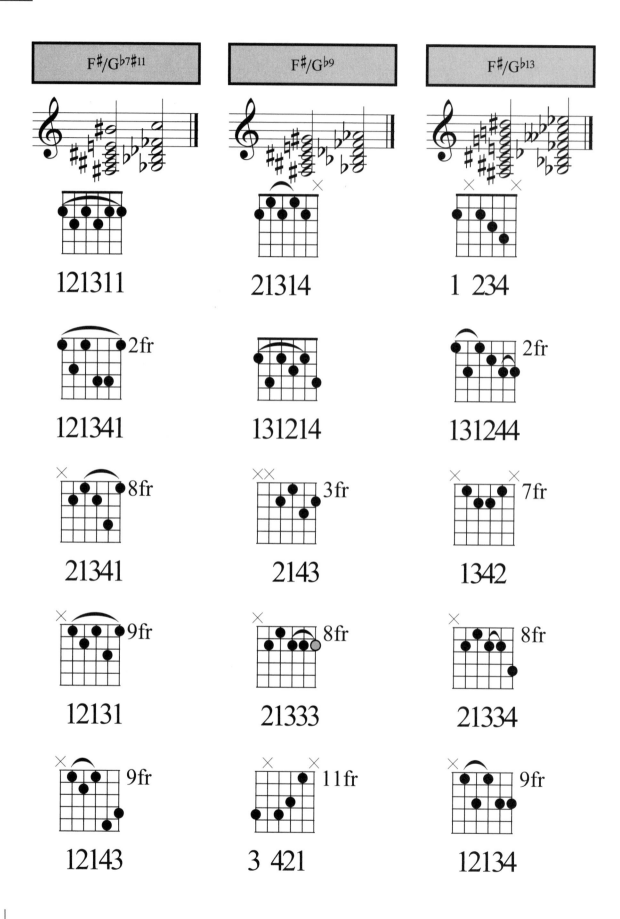

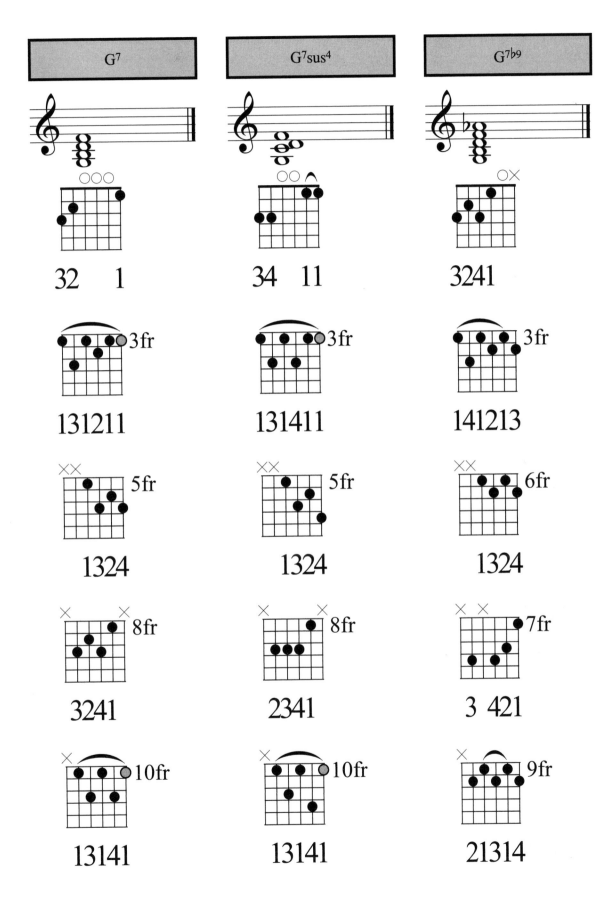

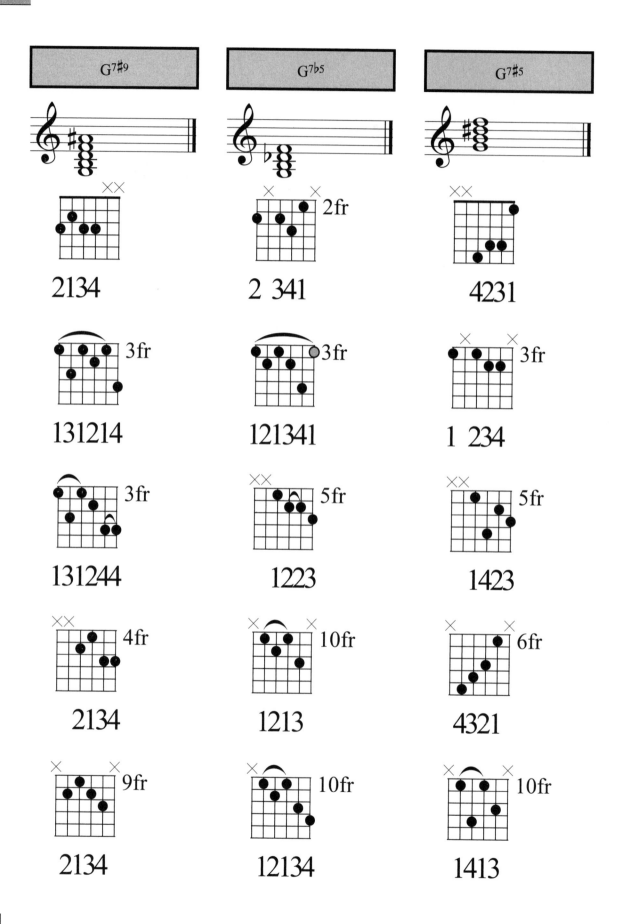

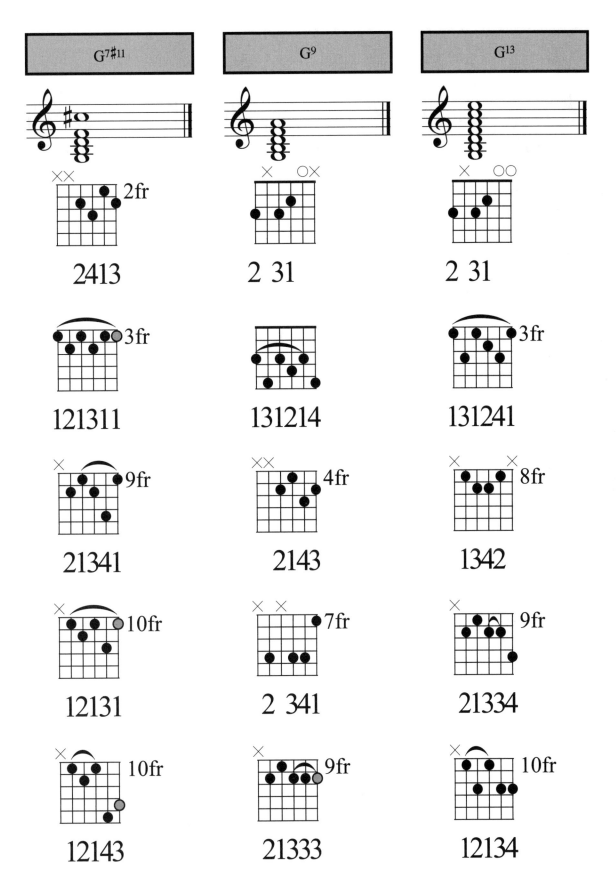

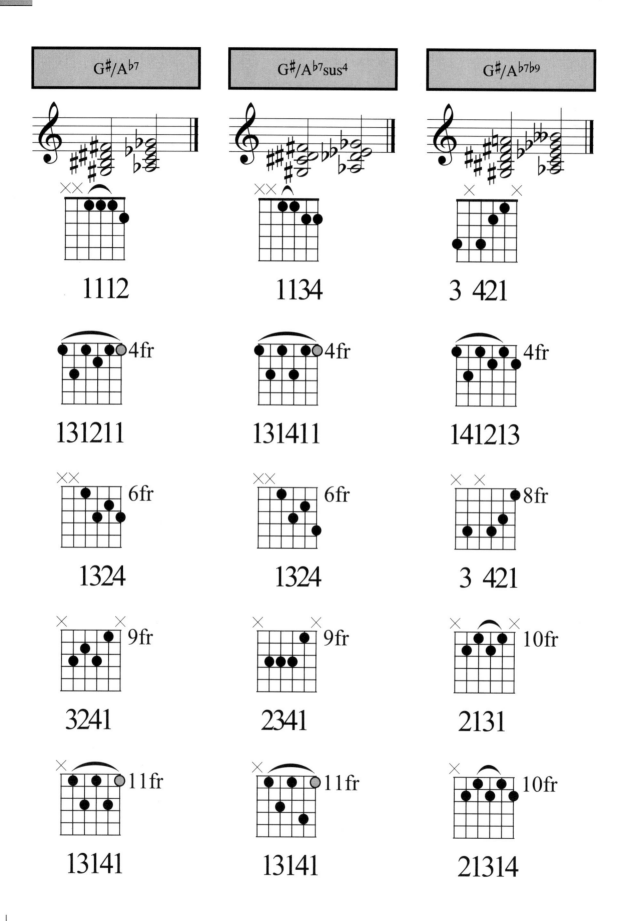

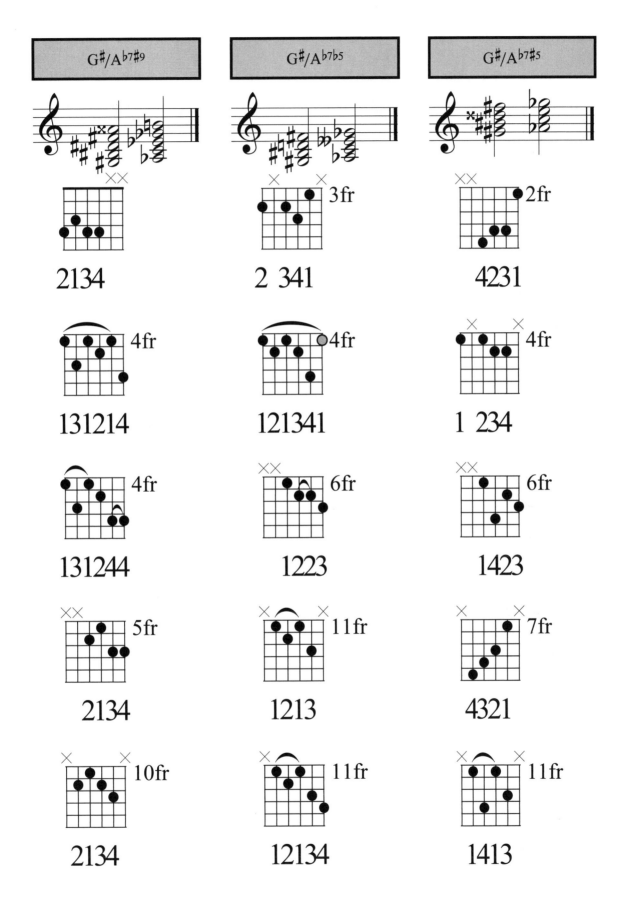

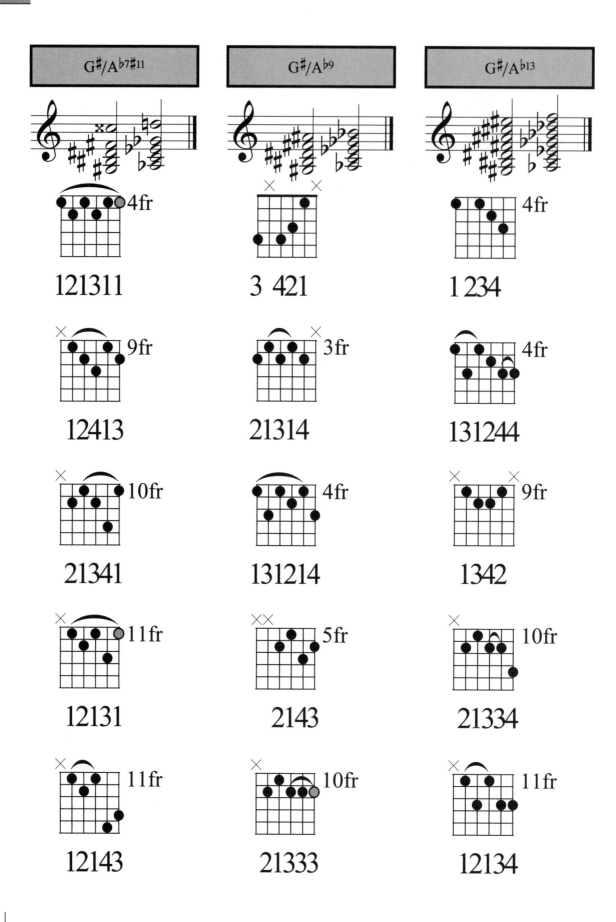

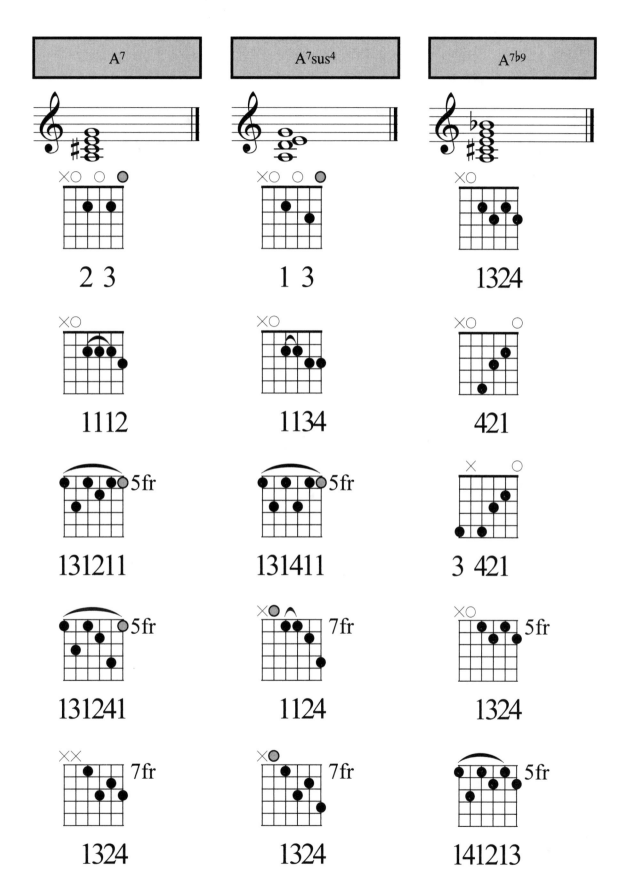

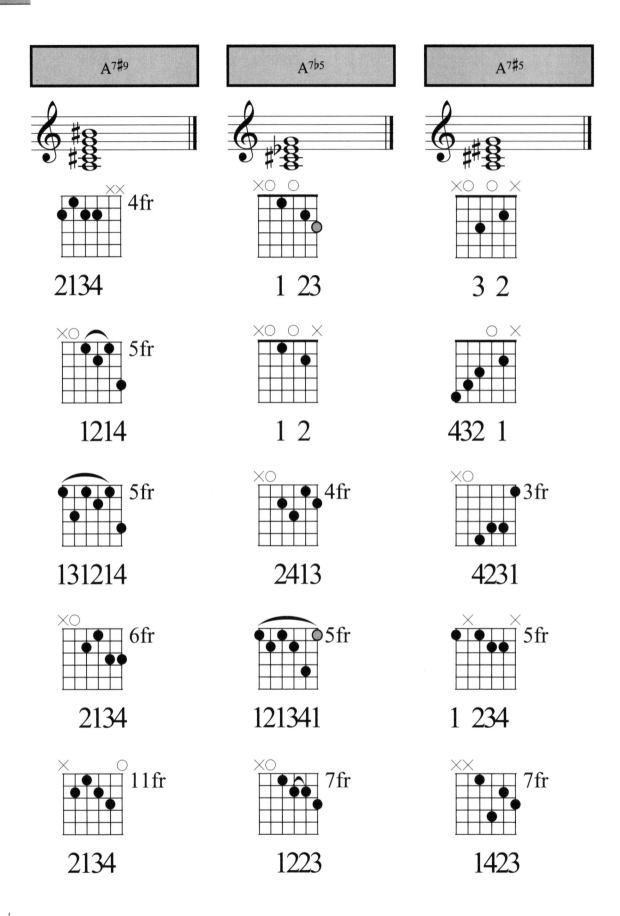

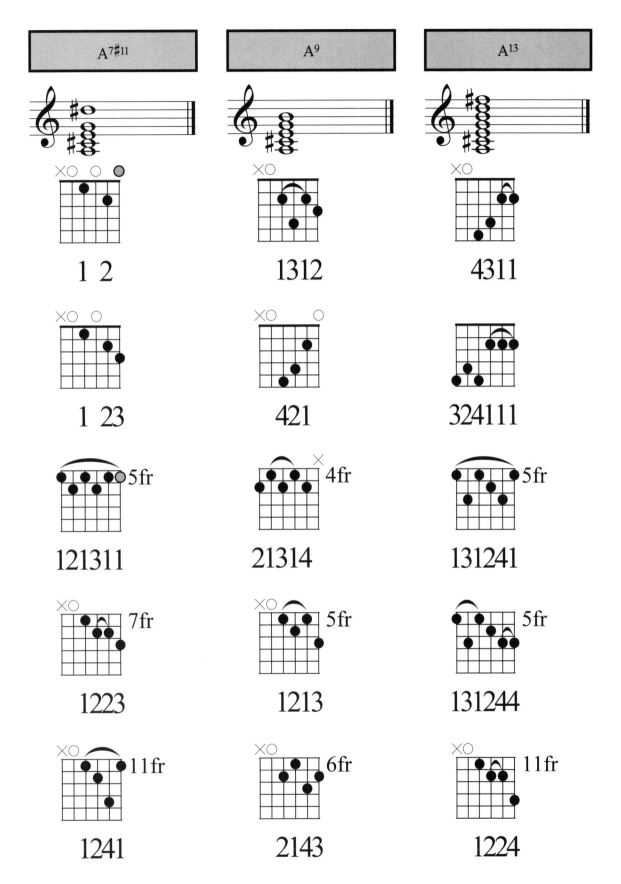

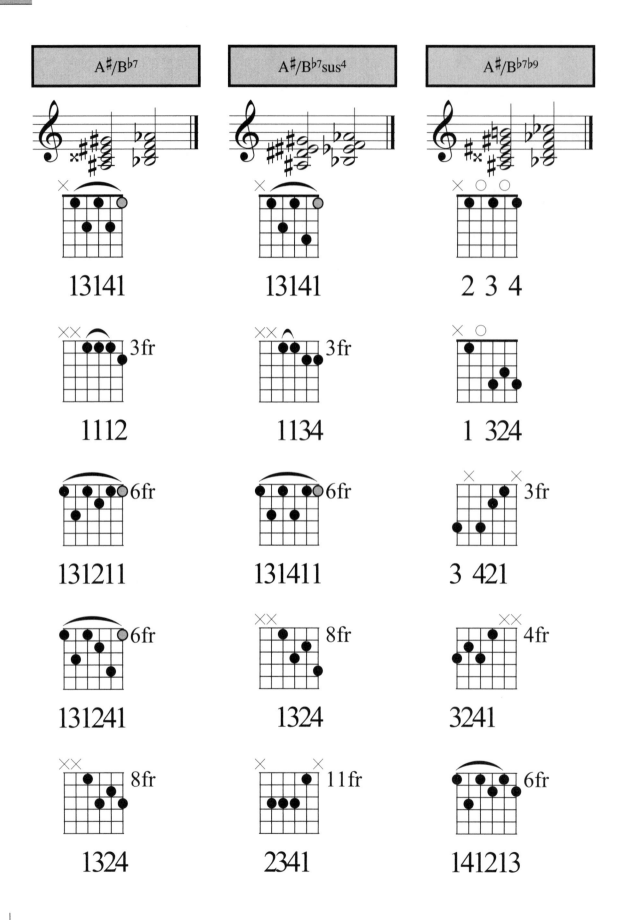

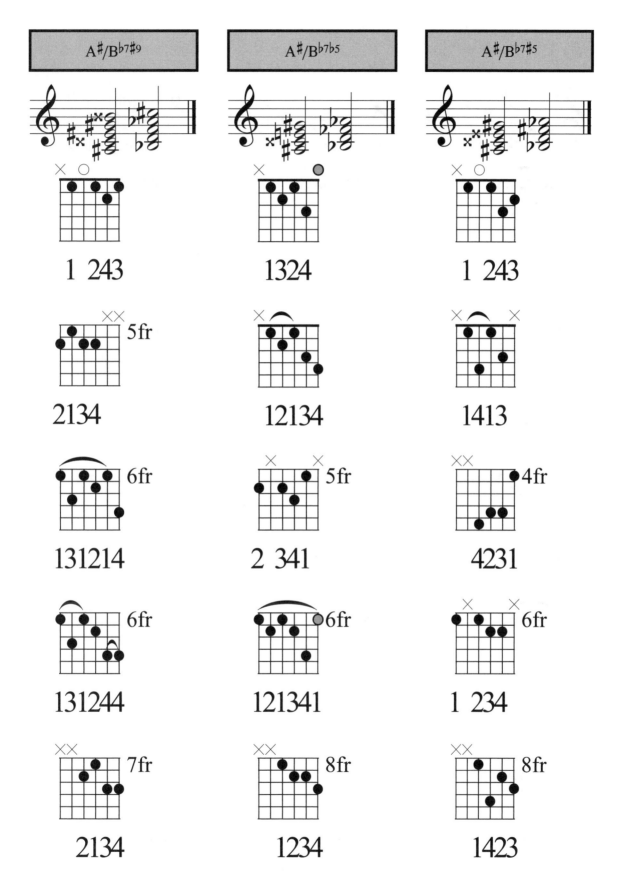

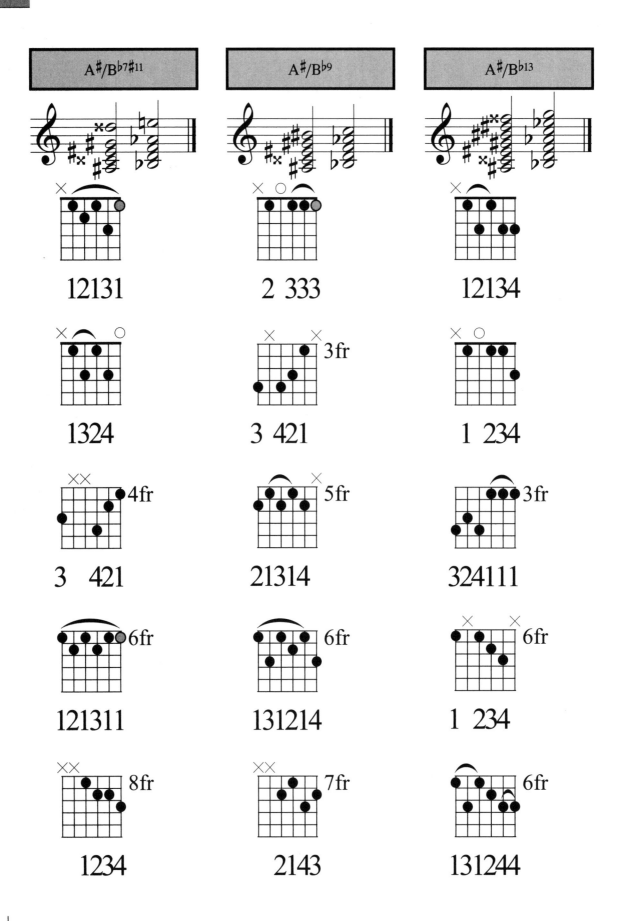

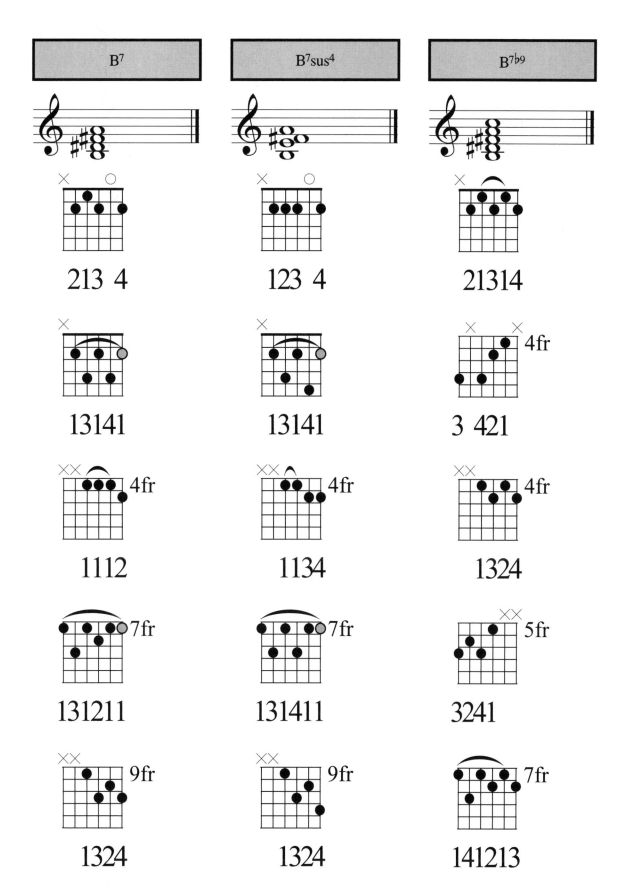

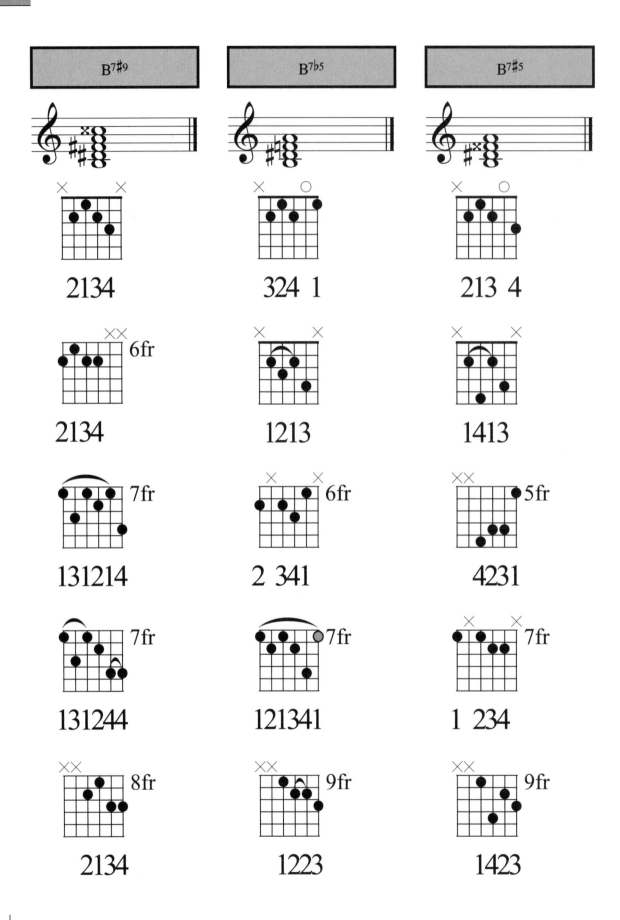

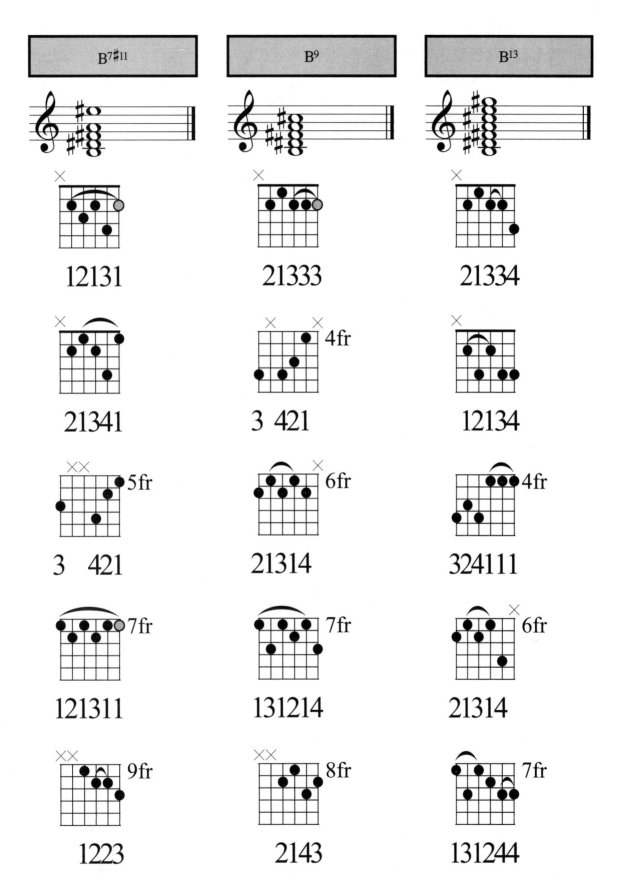

Chapter 6

Diminished Chords

Diminished chords are unique and specialized chords you don't encounter every day. Still, no book about chords would be complete without them. Diminished chords have been around since the earliest forms of classical music and have stuck around in popular music as well. They are colorful and suspenseful. The diminished seventh chord is "symmetric," because the distance between each note is exactly the same (in this case, a ♭ third). As you explore this chapter, you'll see that many of the same fingerings repeat over and over again, as diminished chords take full advantage of the unique tuning of the guitar.

C° DIMINISHED	C°7 FULL DIMINISHED	Cø HALF DIMINISHED

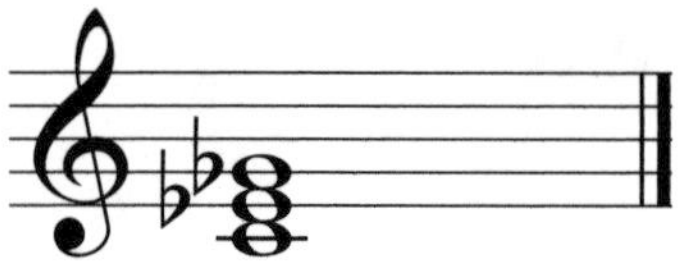

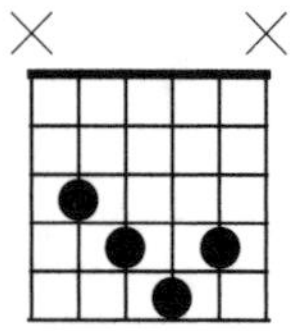

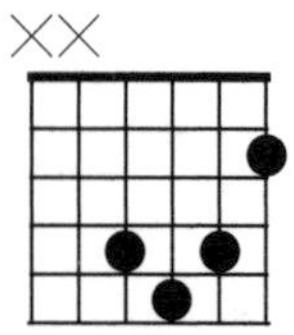

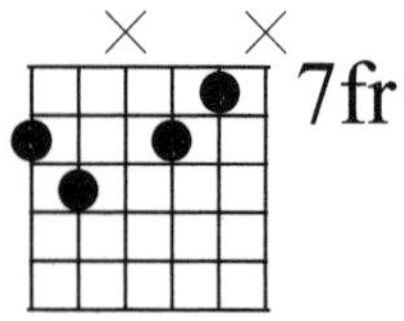

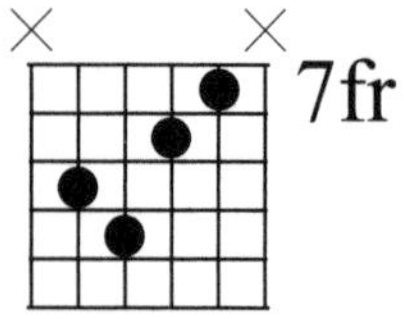

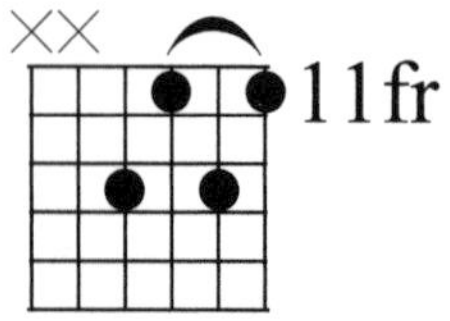

1243 | 23141 | 2 131

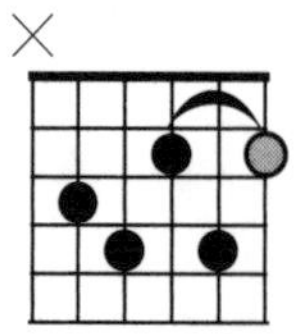

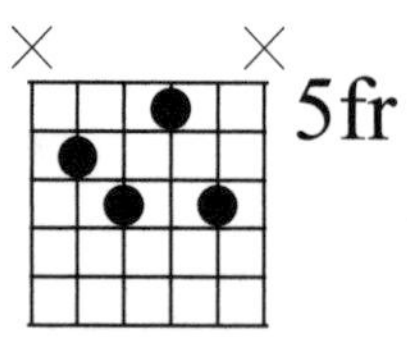

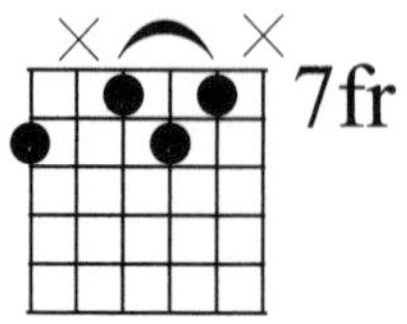

2431 | 2314 | 2 341

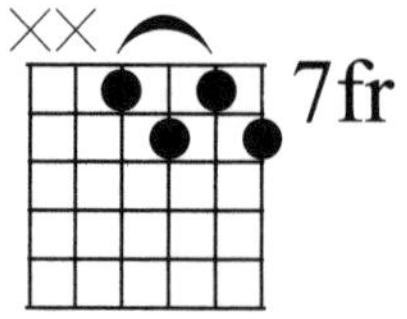

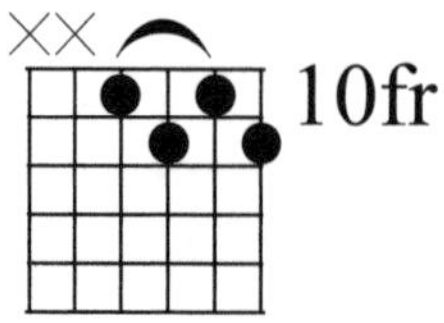

34 21 | 2 131 | 1324

3421 | 1324 | 2 341

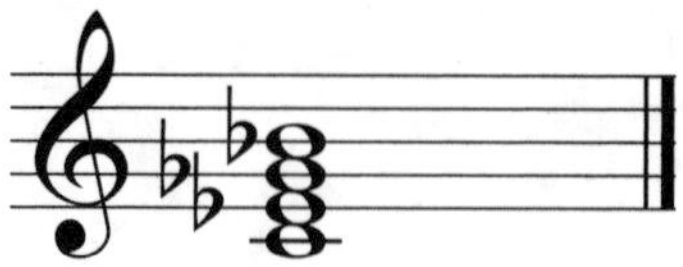

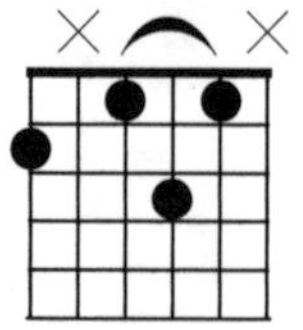

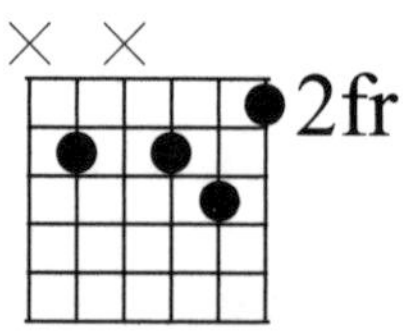

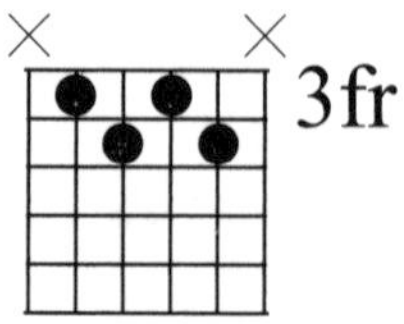

3141 | 1324 | 1222

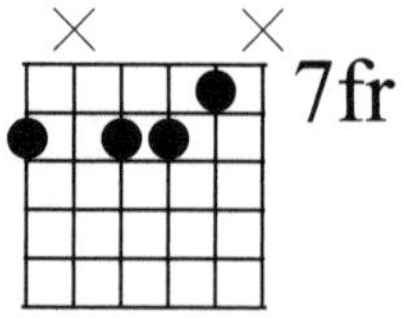

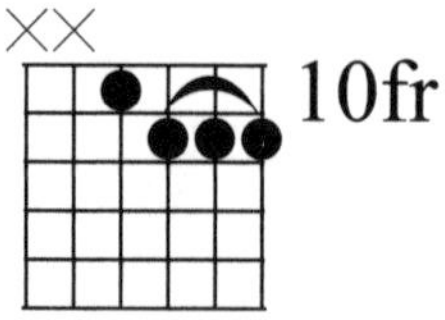

C#/D♭° DIMINISHED

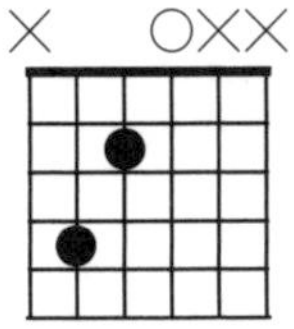

31

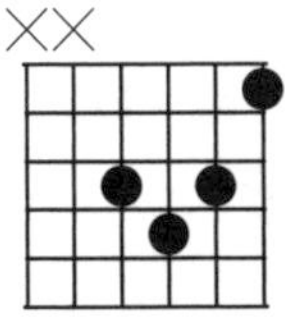

2431

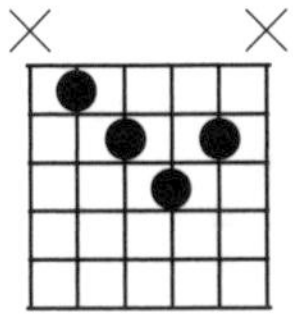

1243

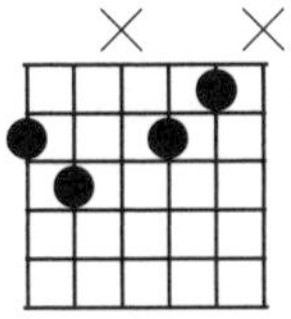

24 31

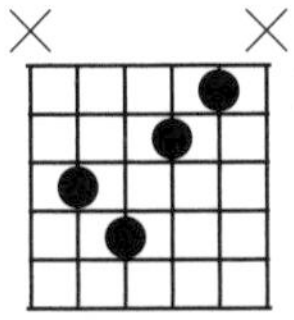

3421

C#/D♭°7 FULL DIMINISHED

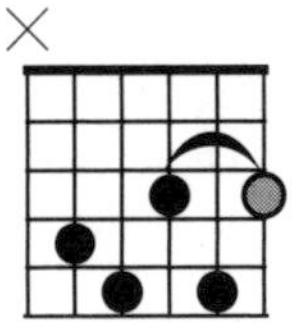

23141

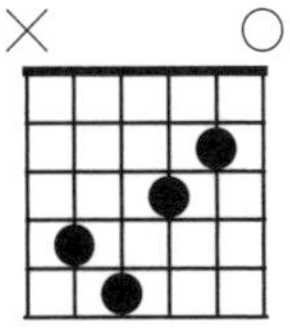

3421

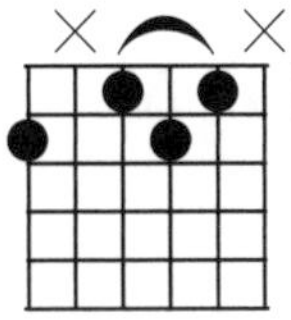

2 131

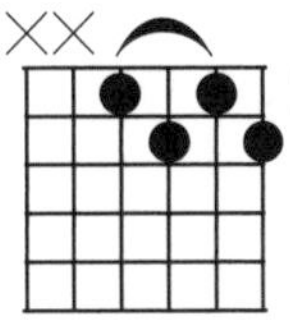

1324

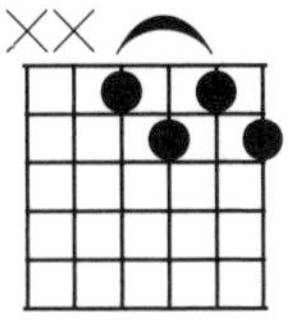

1324

C#/D♭ø HALF DIMINISHED

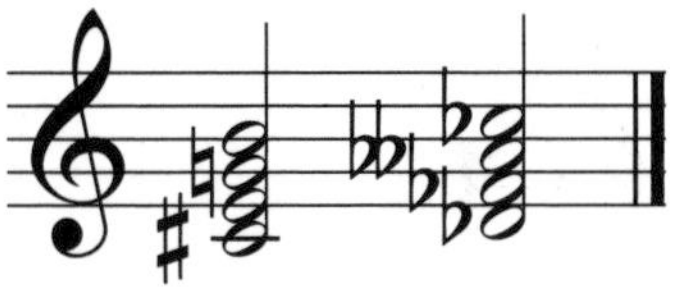

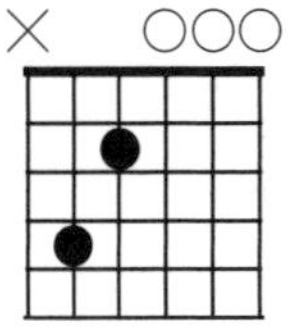

31

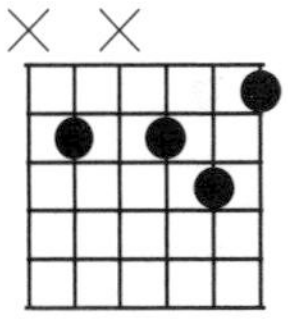

2 341

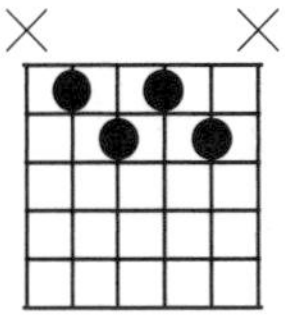

1324

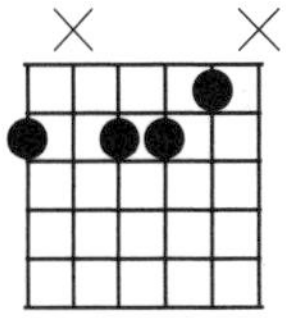

2 341

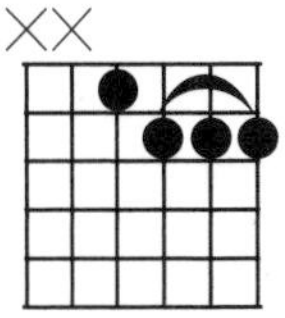

1222

D° DIMINISHED	D°7 FULL DIMINISHED	D∅ HALF DIMINISHED

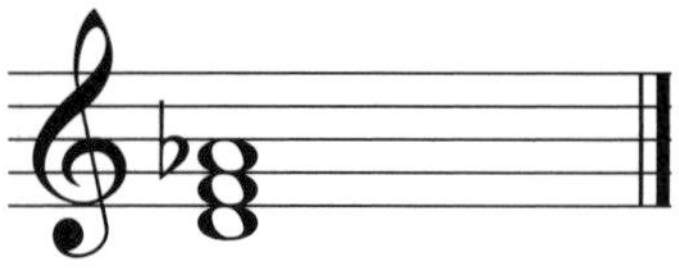

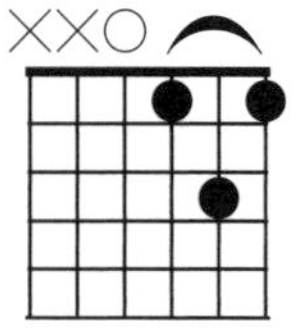

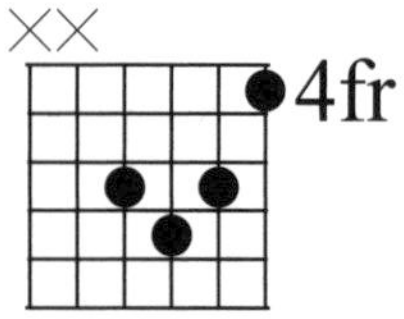

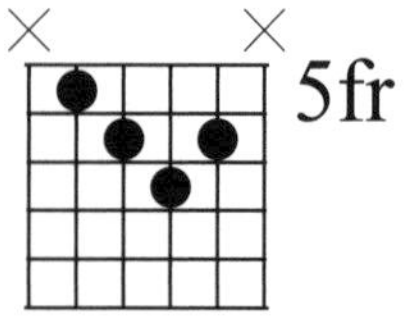

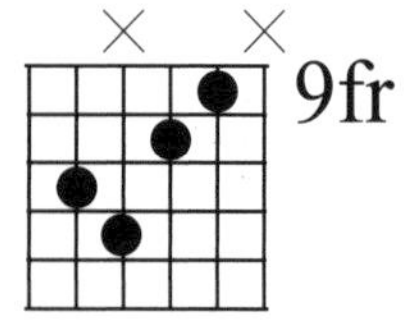

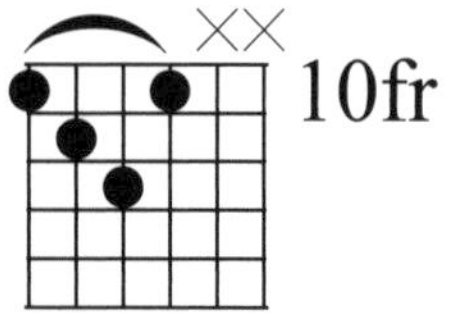

131

1 2

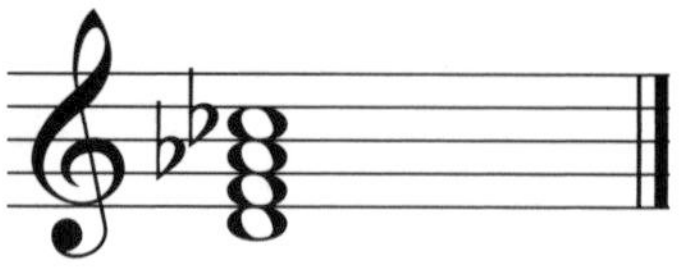

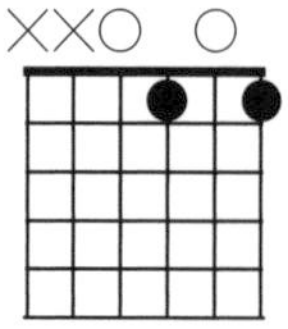

111

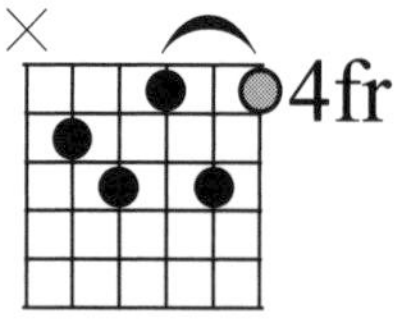

2431

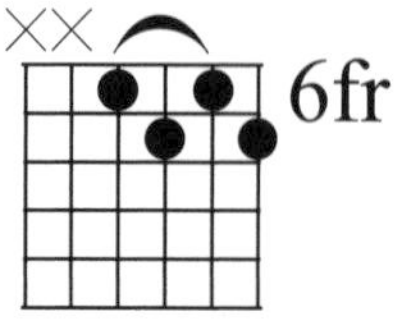

23141

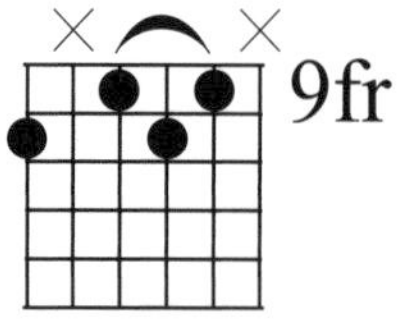

2 341

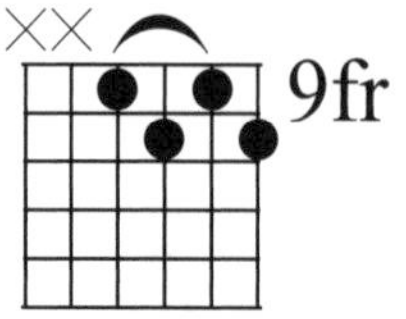

1243

1324

1324

3421

2 131

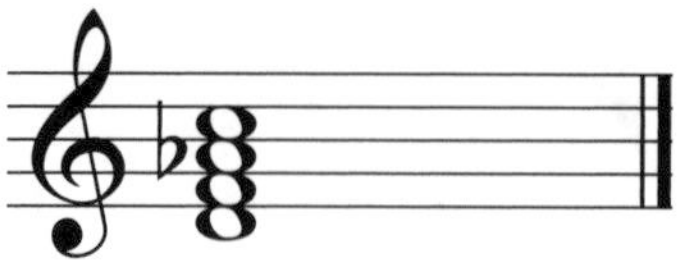

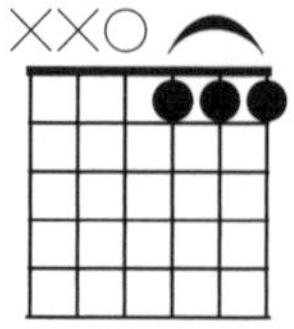

321

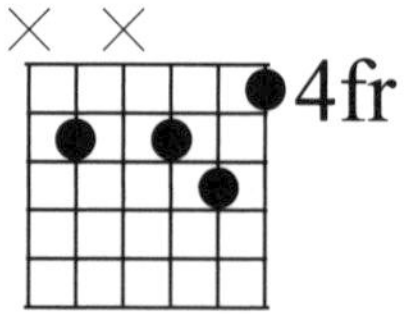

1231

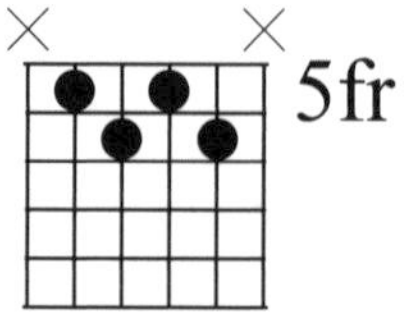

1324

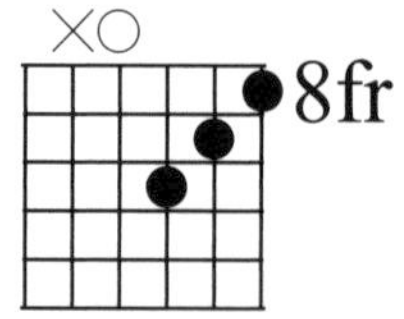

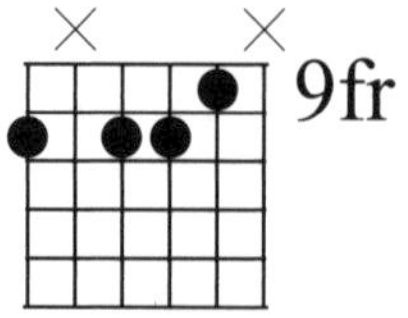

2 341

D#/E♭° DIMINISHED	D#/E♭°7 FULL DIMINISHED	D#/E♭ø HALF DIMINISHED

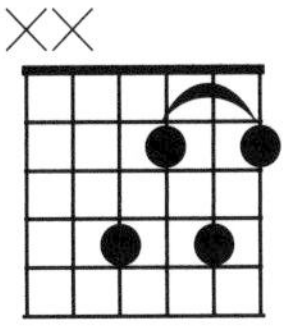

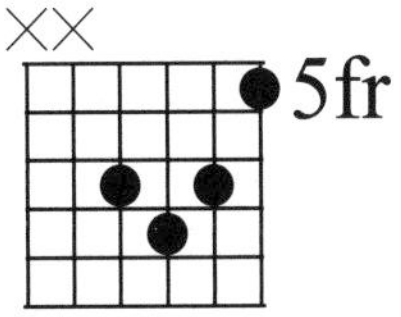

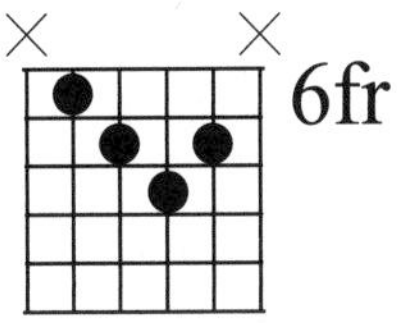

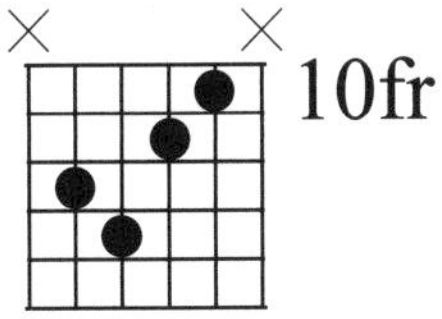

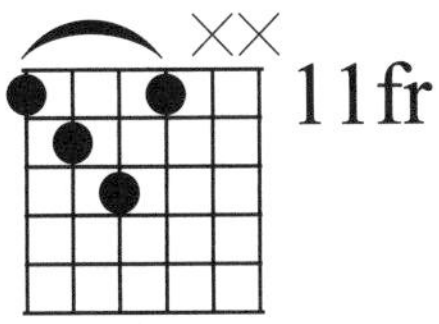

3141

1324

1222

2431 (5fr)

23141 (5fr)

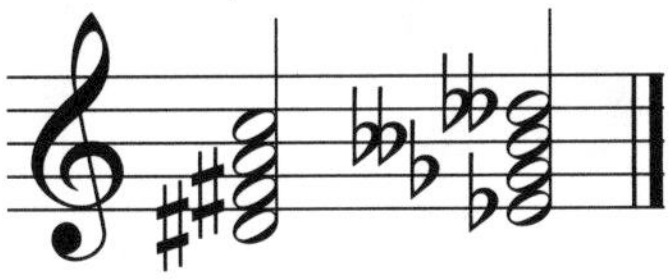

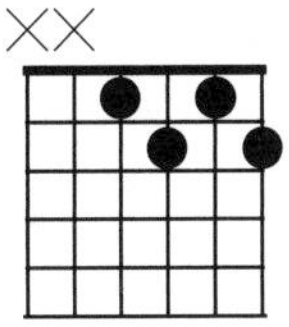

2 341 (5fr)

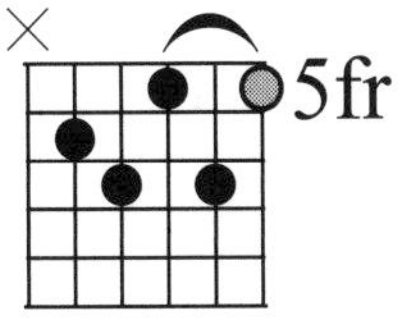

1243 (6fr)

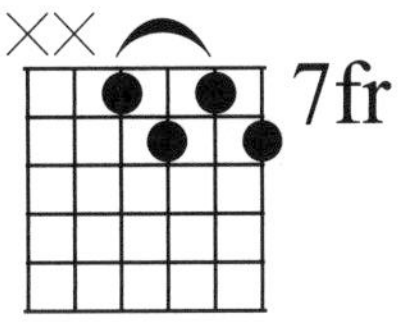

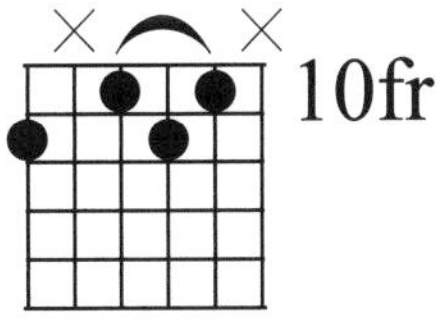

1324 (7fr)

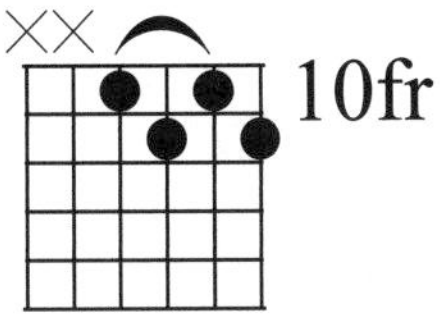

1324 (6fr)

3421 (10fr)

2 131 (10fr)

3   421 (9fr)

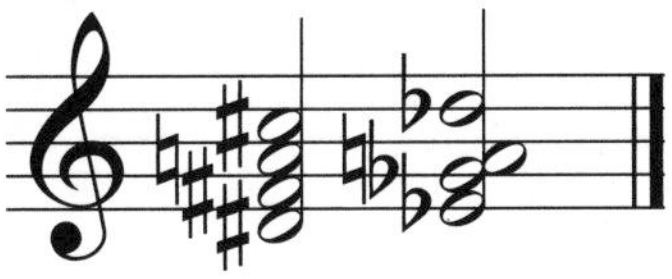

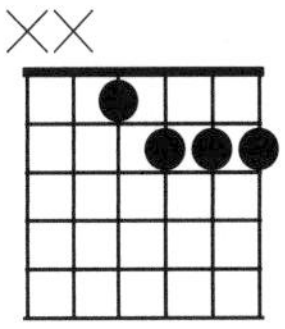

1231 (11fr)

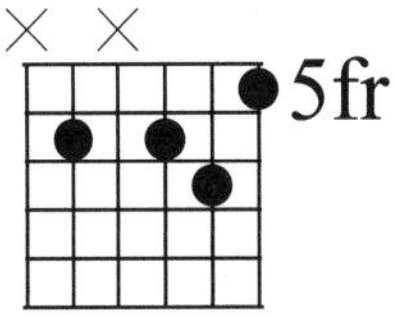

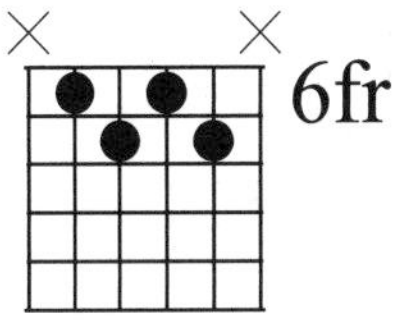

1324 (10fr)

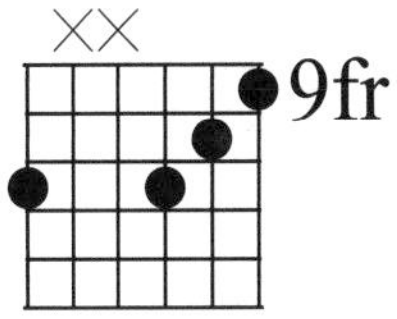

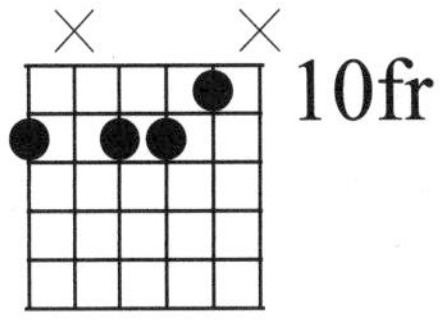

2 341 (10fr)

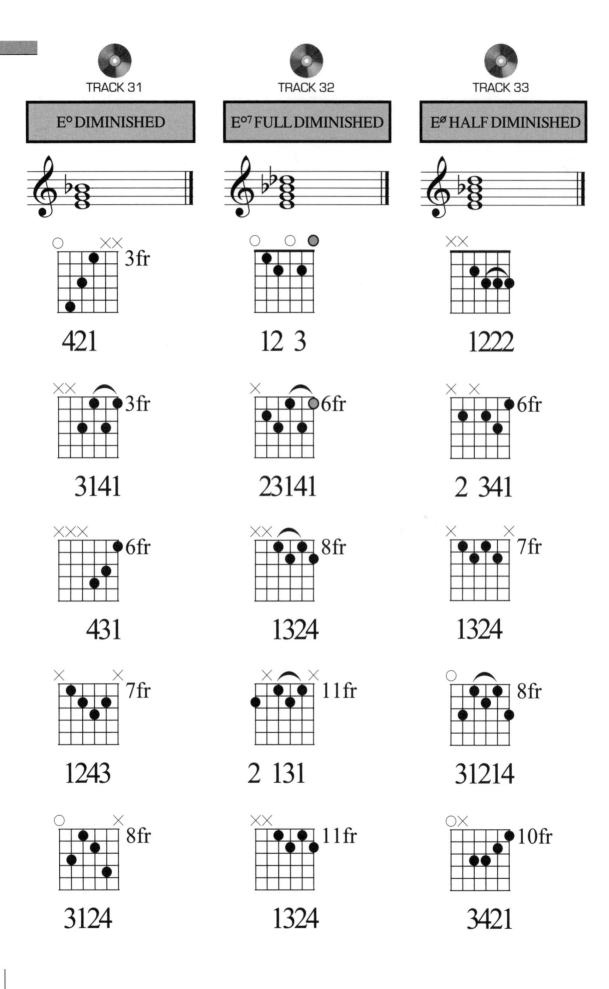

F° DIMINISHED

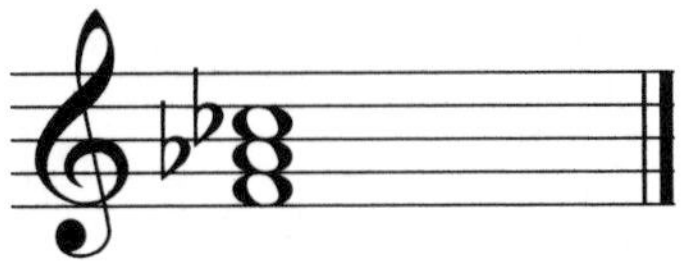

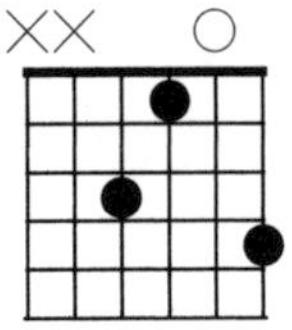

31 4

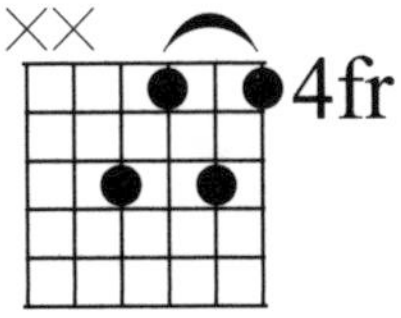

3141

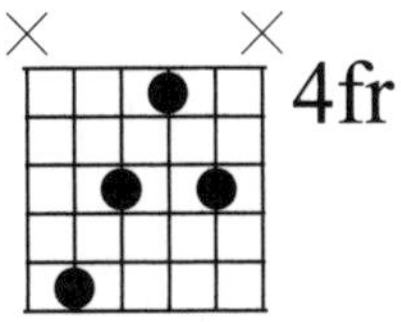

4213

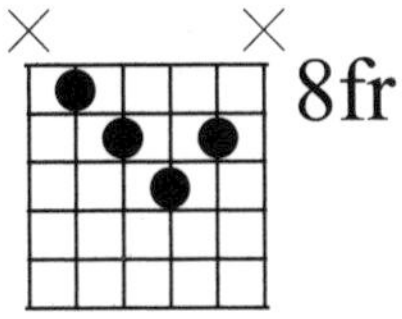

1243

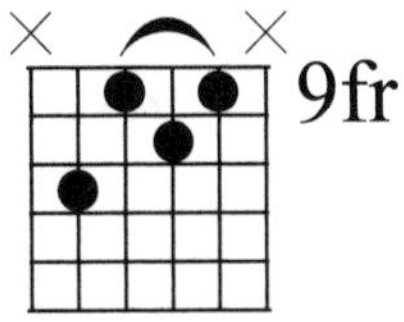

3121

F°7 FULL DIMINISHED

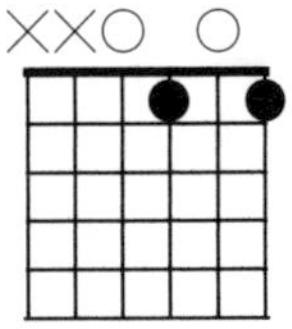

1 2

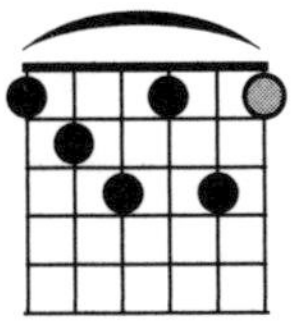

123141

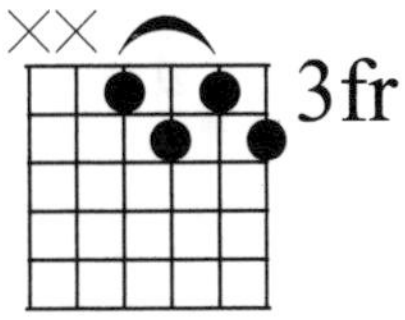

1324

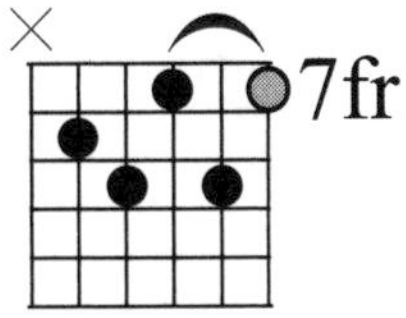

23141

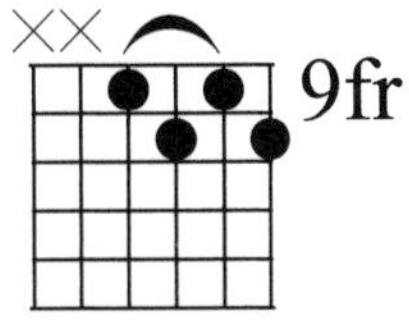

1324

Fø HALF DIMINISHED

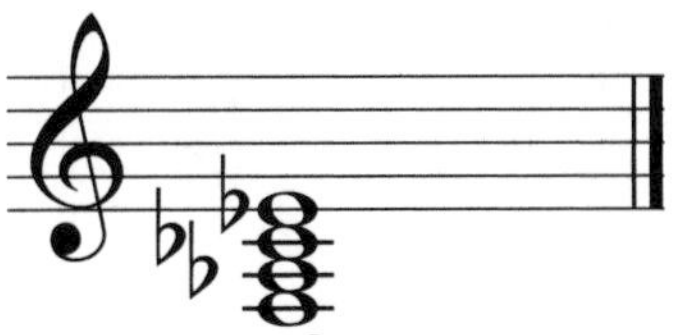

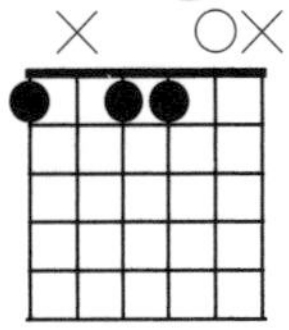

2 34

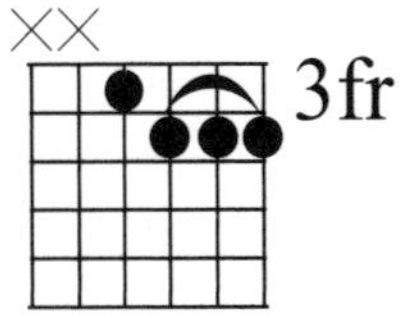

1222

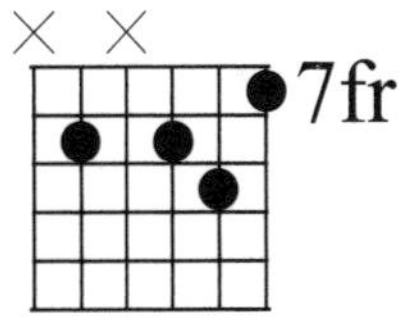

2 341

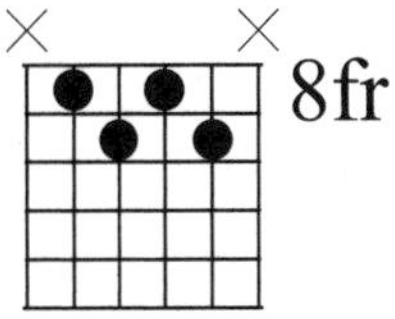

1324

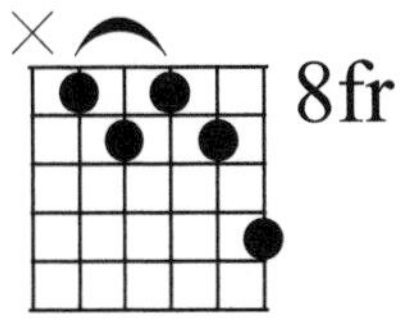

12134

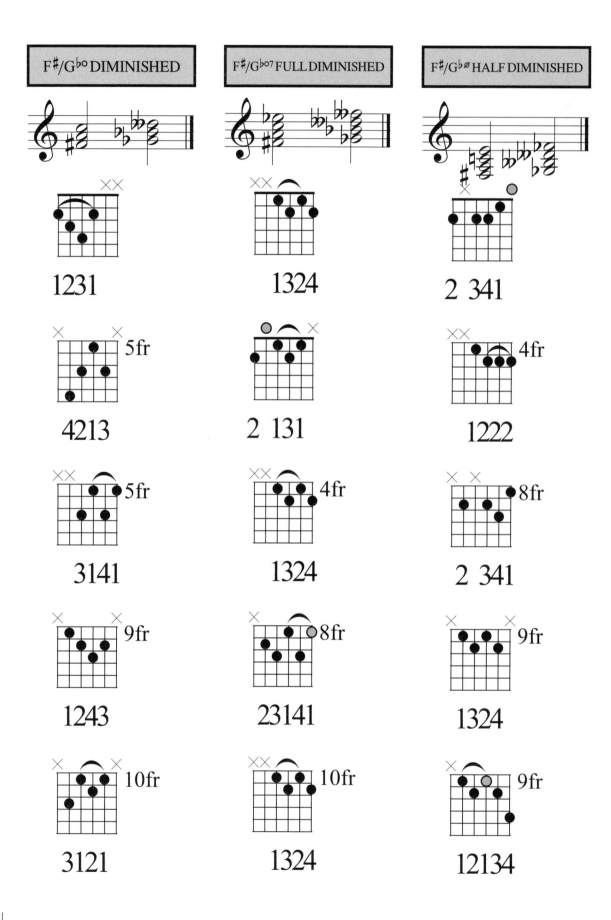

G° DIMINISHED	G°7 FULL DIMINISHED	Gø HALF DIMINISHED

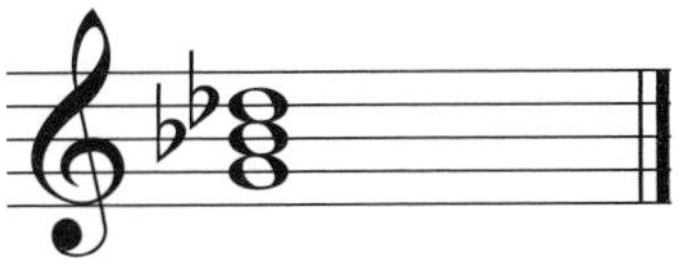

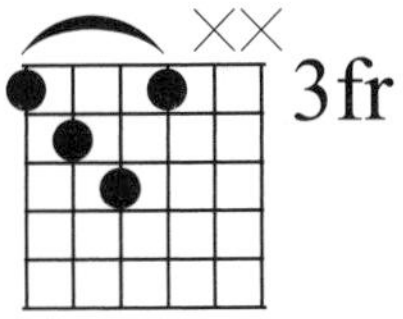

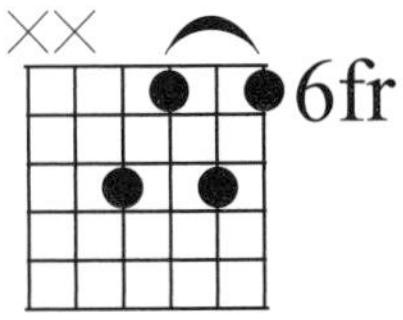

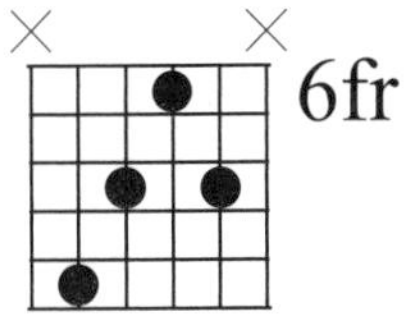

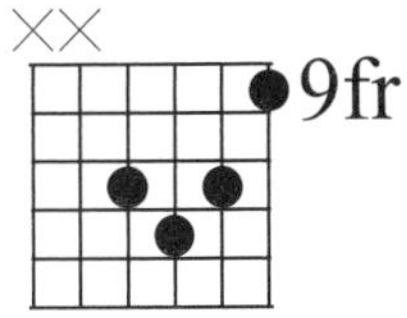

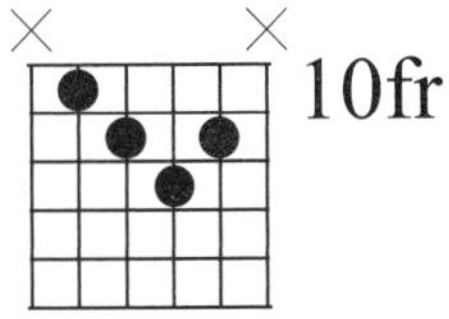

1231   2 131   2 341

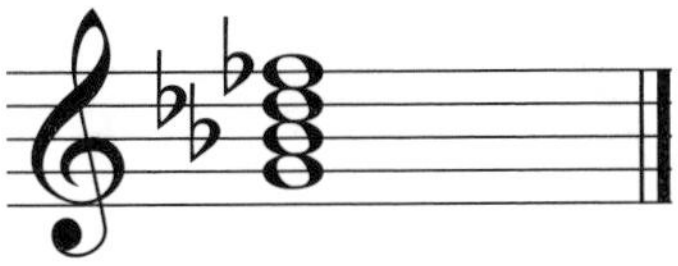

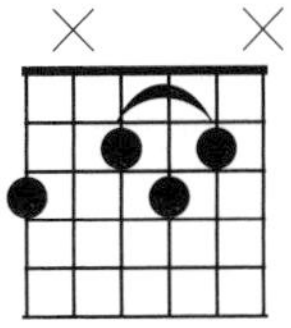

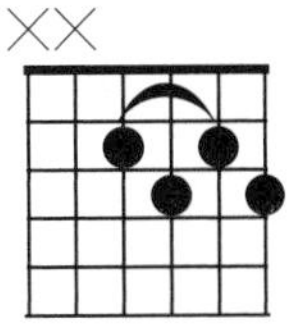

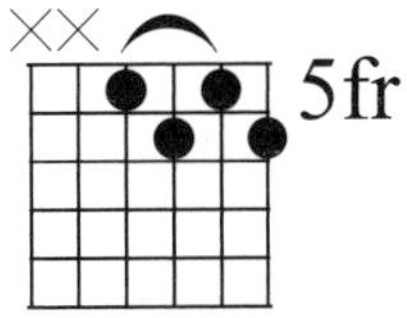

3141   1324   1222

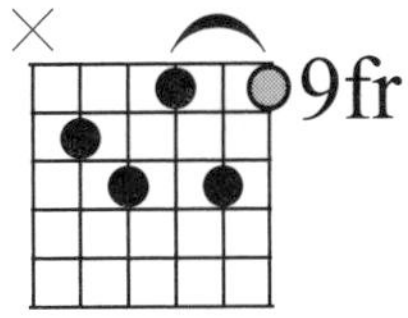

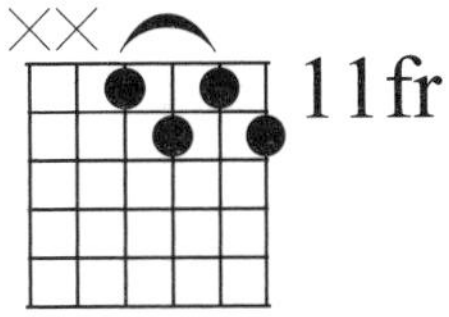

4213   1324   2 341

2431   24131   1324

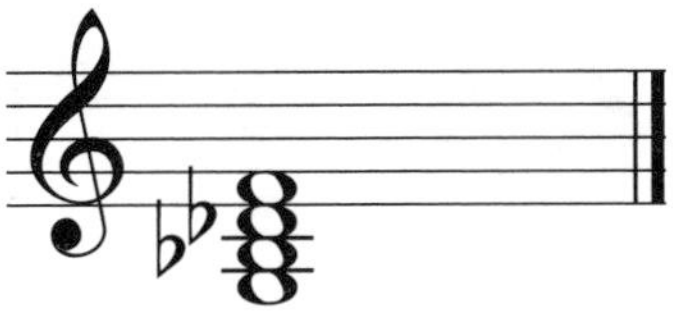

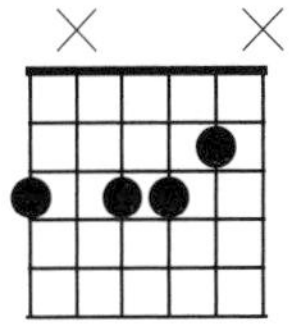

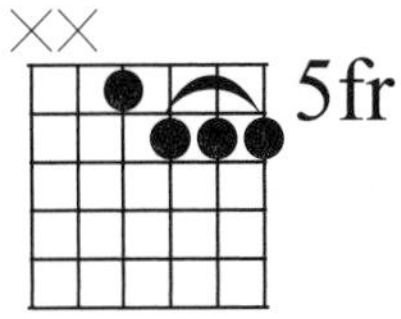

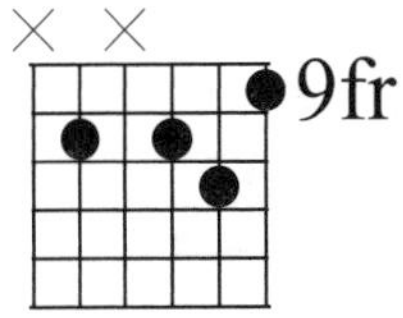

1243   1324   12134

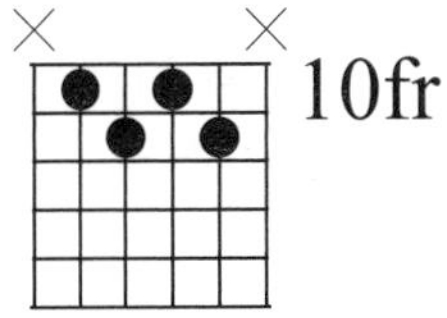

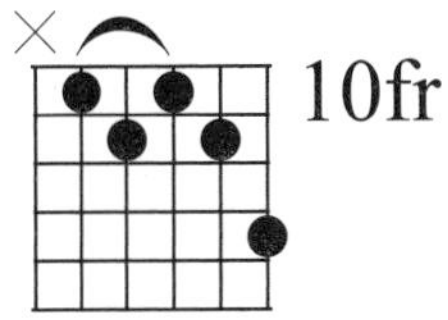

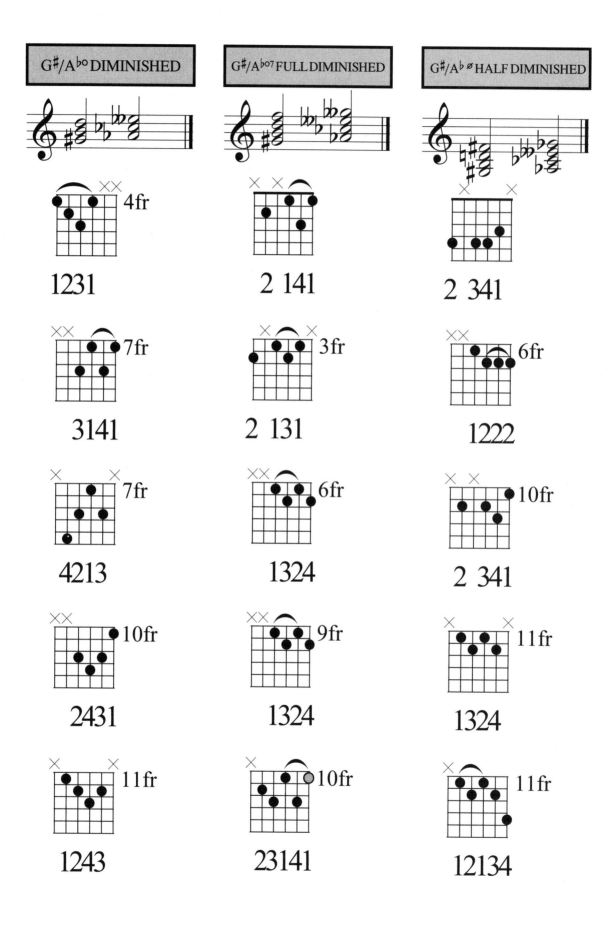

A° DIMINISHED	A°7 FULL DIMINISHED	A⌀ HALF DIMINISHED

132

1324

1 2

3214

2 131

1214

421

1324

3421

1231

421

2 341

3141

1324

1222

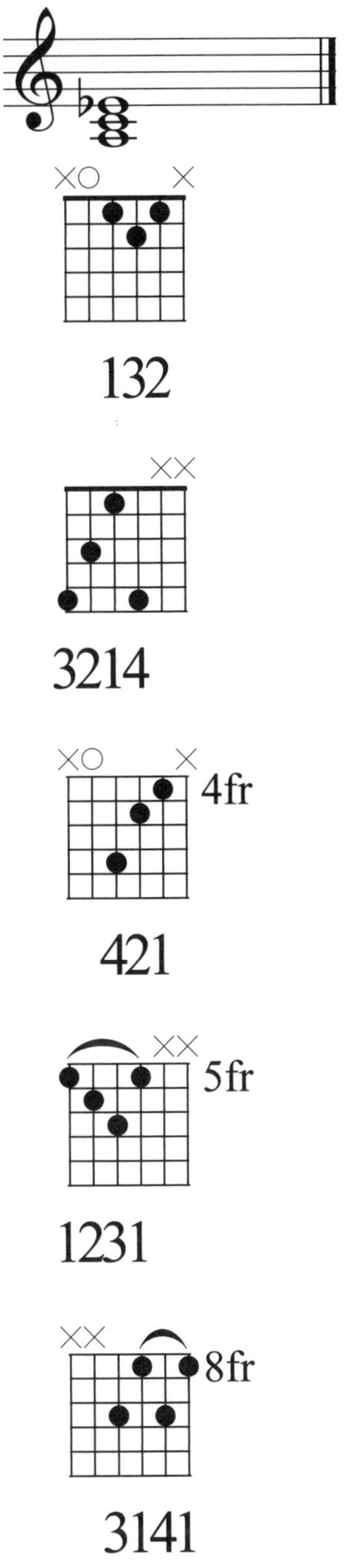

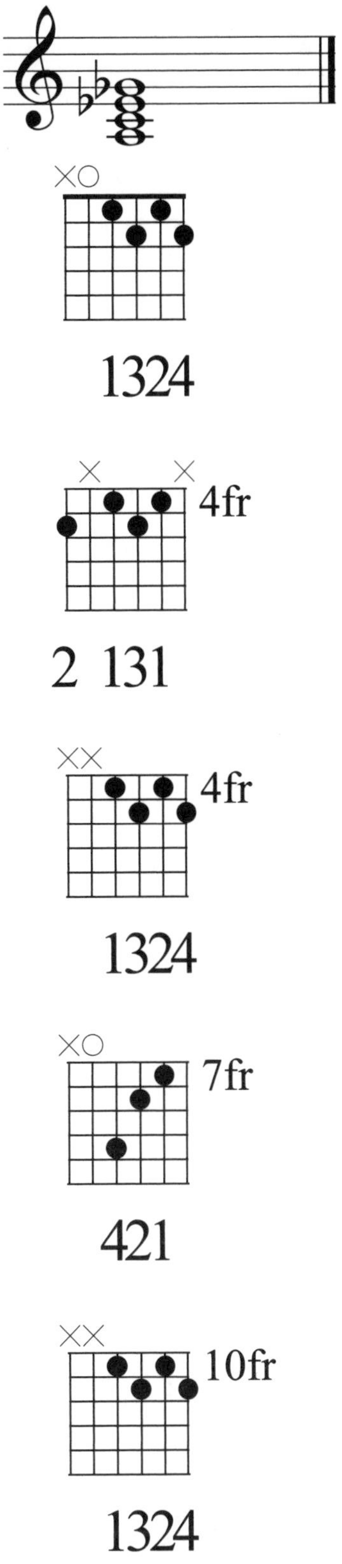

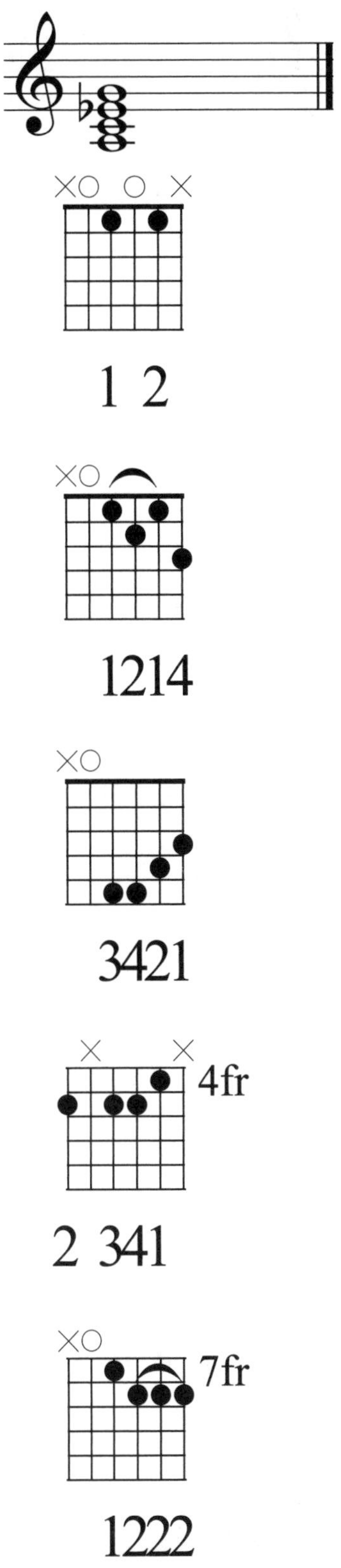

A#/B♭° DIMINISHED

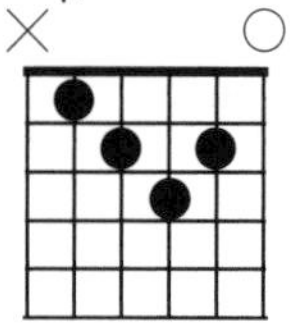

1243

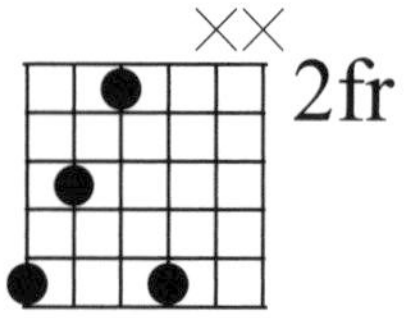

3214

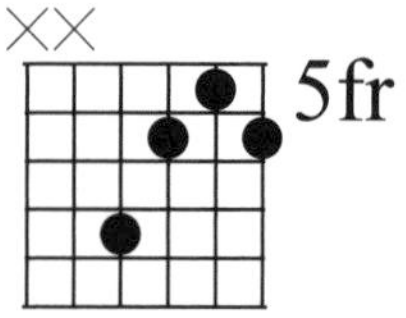

4213

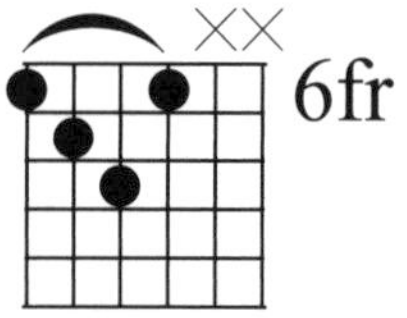

1231

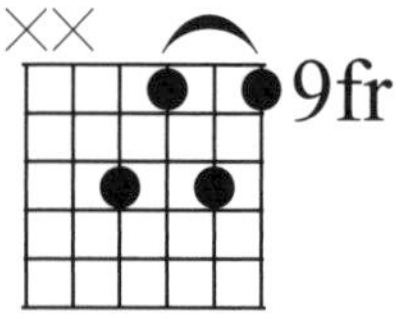

3141

A#/B♭°7 FULL DIMINISHED

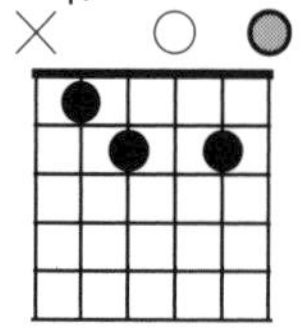

23 4

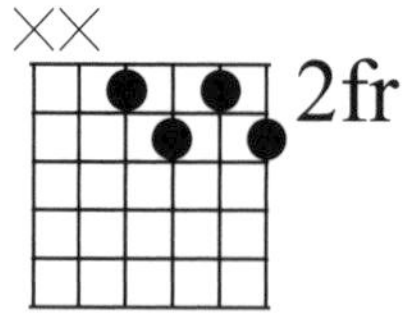

1324

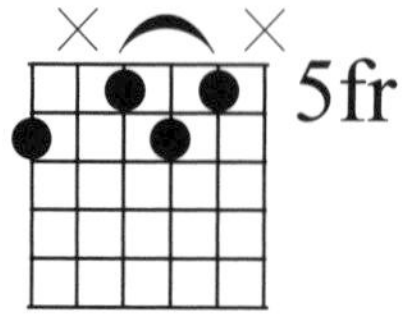

2 131

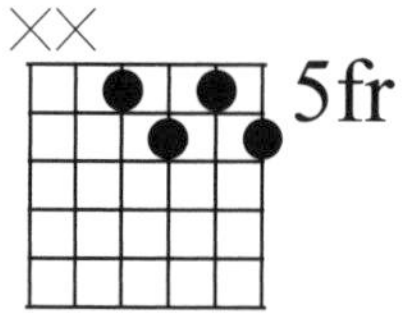

1324

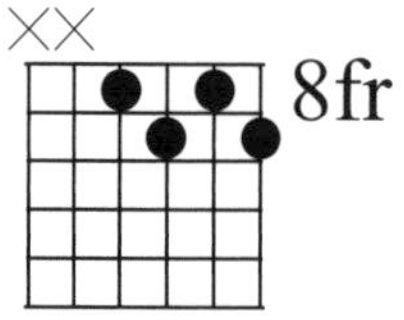

1324

A#/B♭ø HALF DIMINISHED

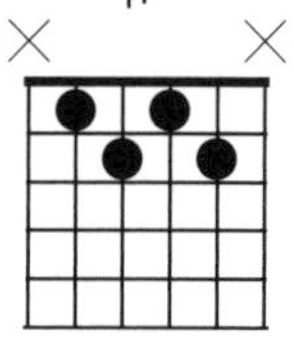

1324

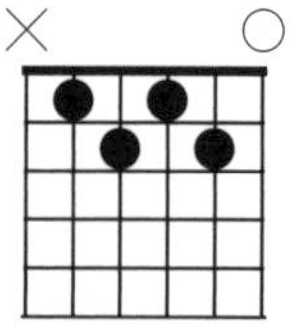

1324

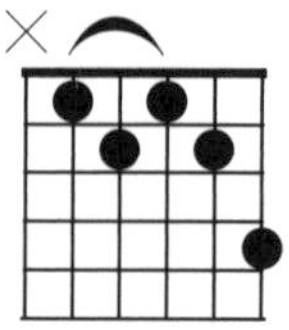

12134

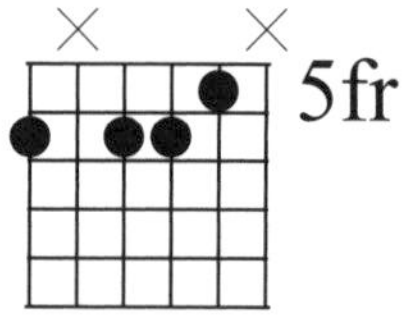

2 341

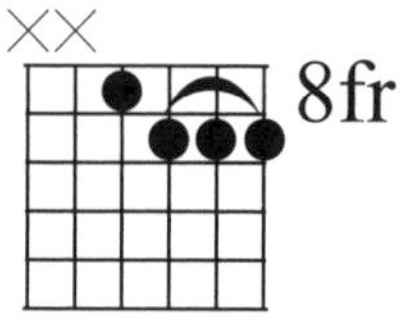

1222

B° DIMINISHED	B°7 FULL DIMINISHED	Bø HALF DIMINISHED

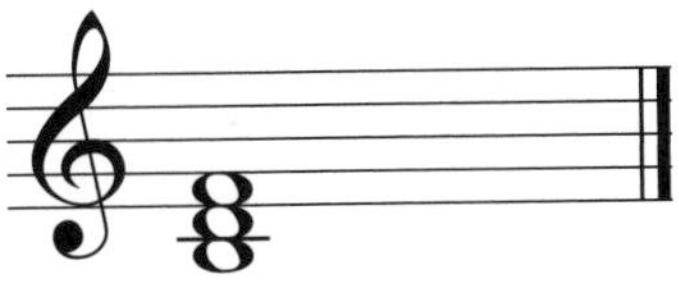

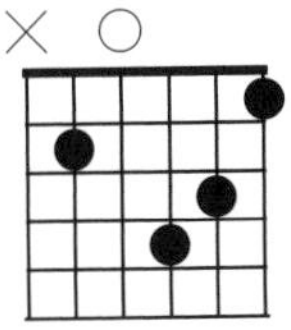

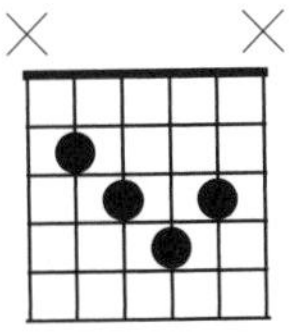

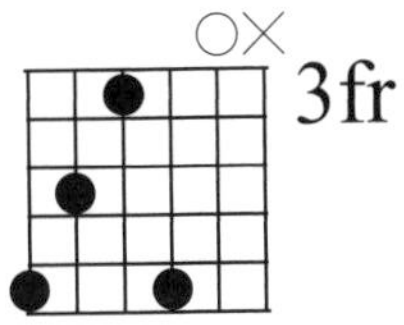

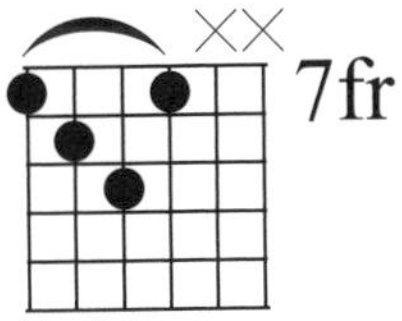

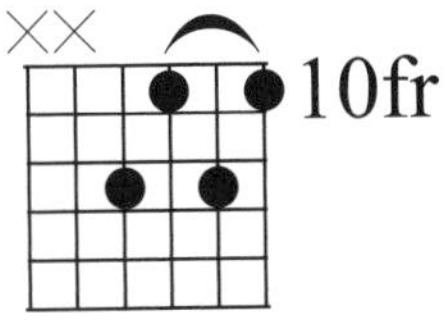

2 431

23141

2 3 1

1243

1324

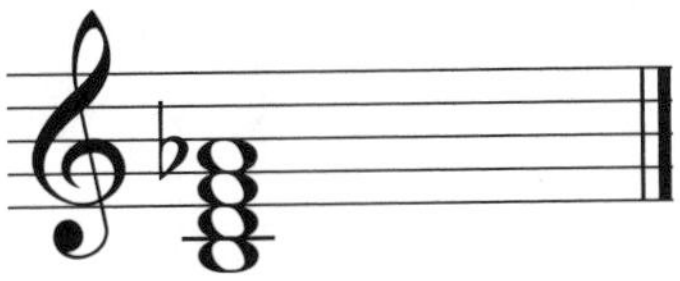

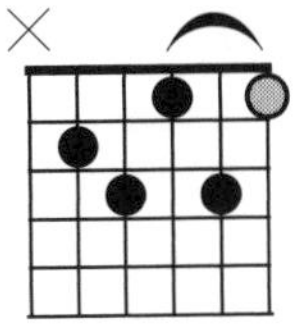

1324

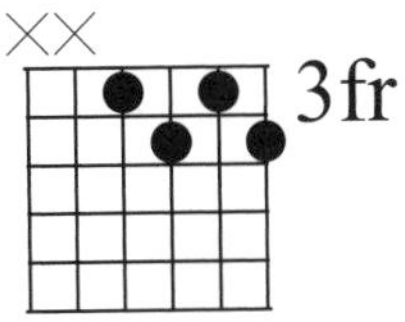

3214 (3fr)

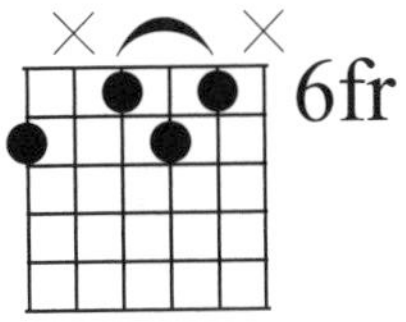

2 131 (6fr)

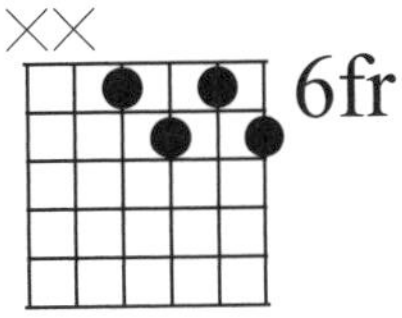

3 421 (5fr)

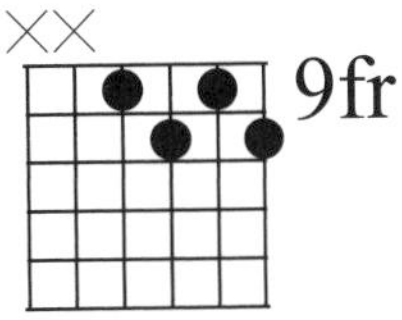

1231 (7fr)

1324 (6fr)

2 341 (6fr)

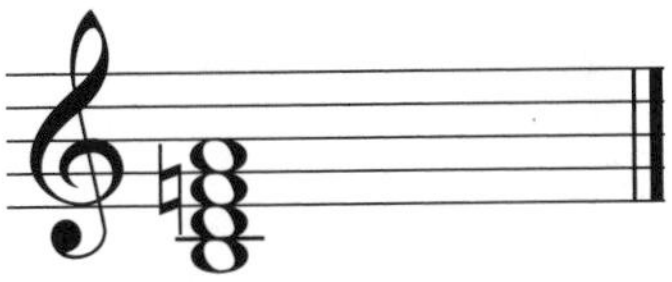

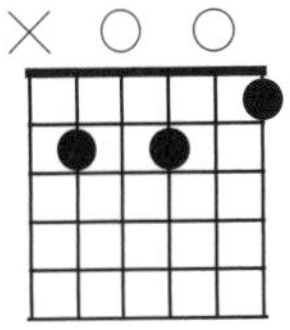

3141 (10fr)

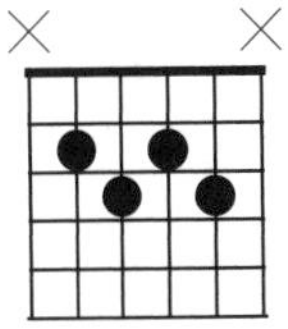

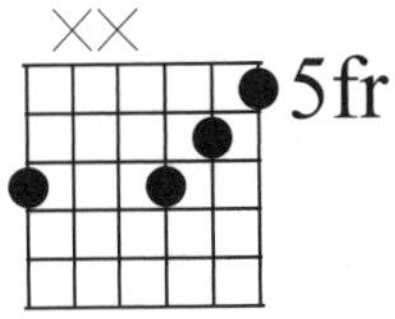

1324 (9fr)

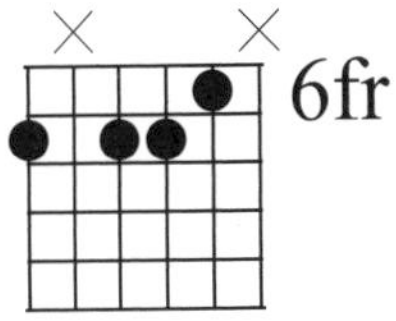

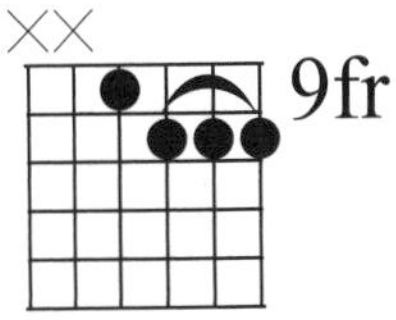

1222 (9fr)

7

Chapter 7

Augmented Chords

Augmented chords do not naturally occur in major or minor scales, but nonetheless, composers and modern artists have found uses for them. Like the diminished seventh chords, the augmented triad is symmetric, so look for repeating shapes. If you want to impart an unusual color to your music, give the augmented chords a chance.

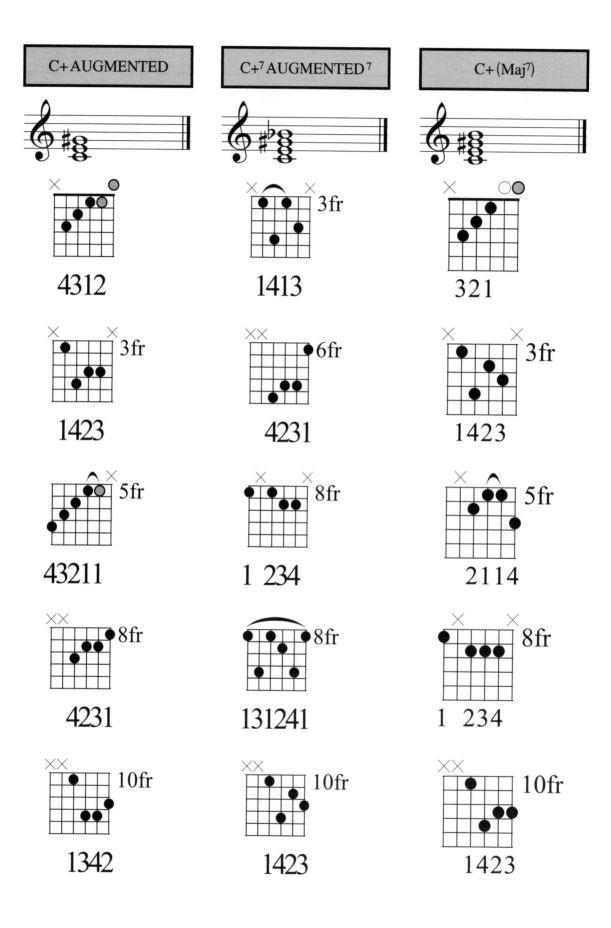

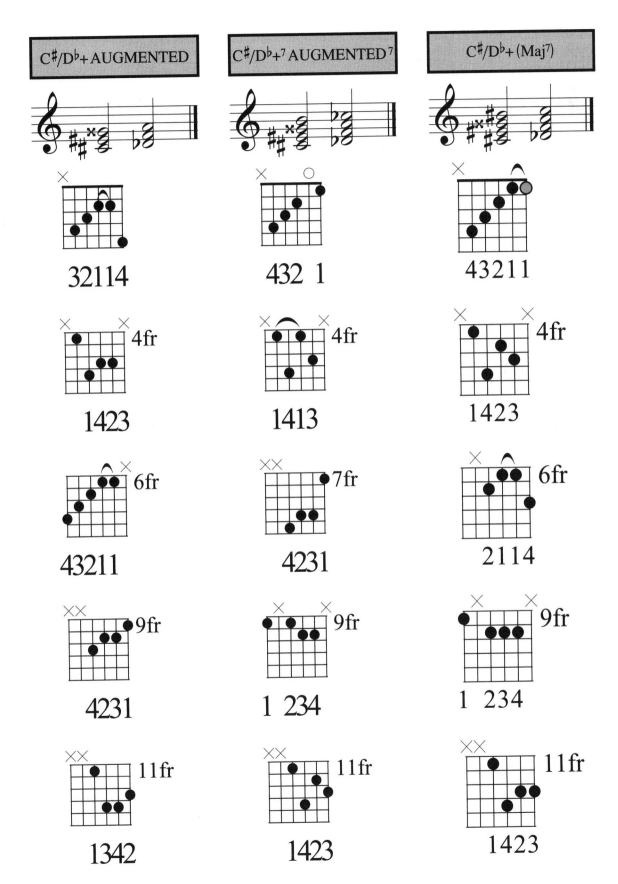

D Augmented Chords

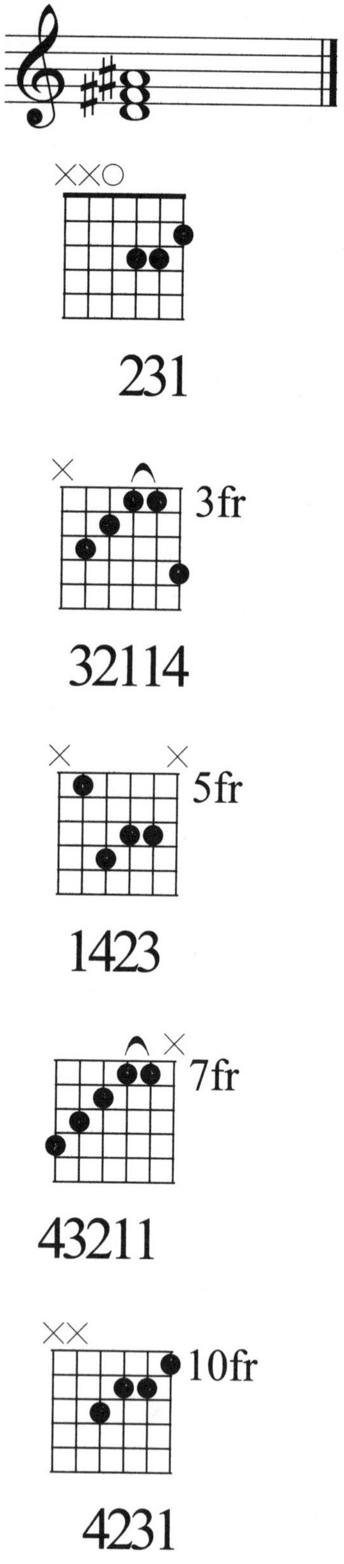

D+ AUGMENTED	D+⁷ AUGMENTED⁷	D+ (Maj⁷)

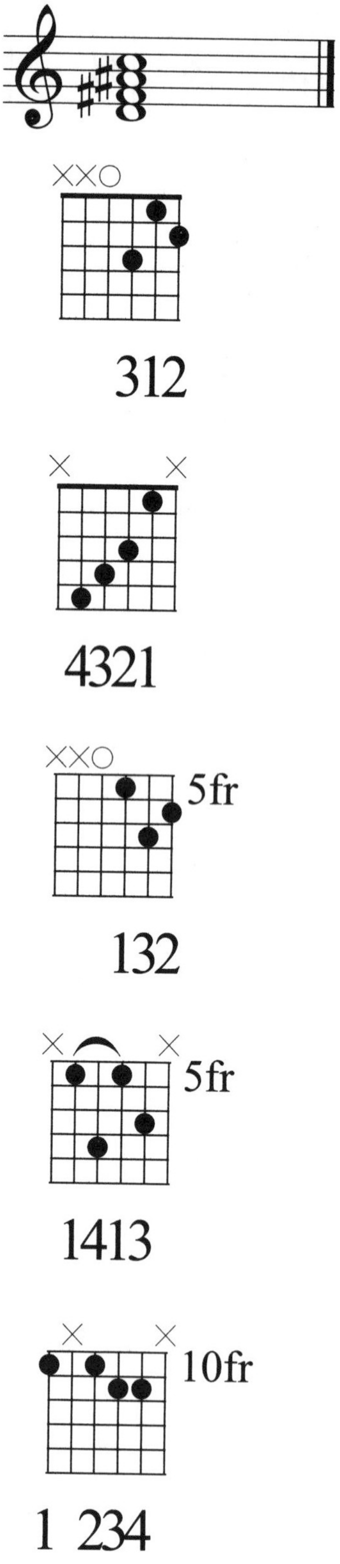

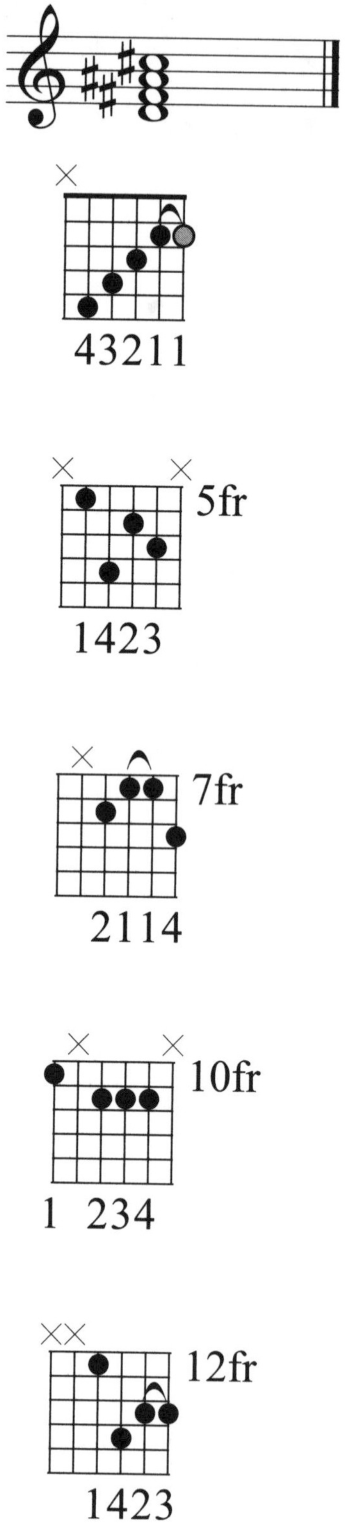

231   312   43211

32114   4321   1423 (5fr)

1423 (5fr)   132 (5fr)   2114 (7fr)

43211 (7fr)   1413 (5fr)   1 234 (10fr)

4231 (10fr)   1 234 (10fr)   1423 (12fr)

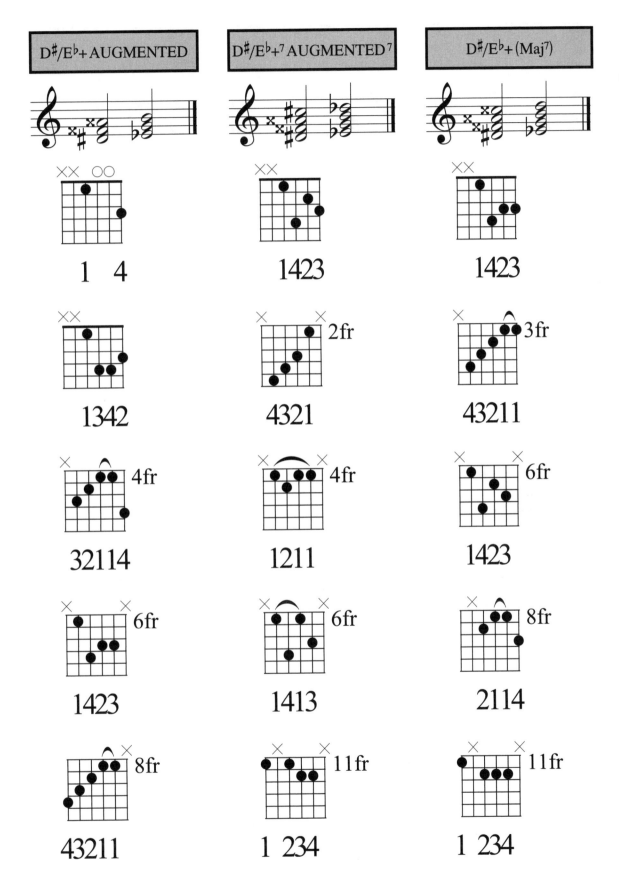

| D#/Eb+ AUGMENTED | D#/Eb+7 AUGMENTED 7 | D#/Eb+ (Maj7) |

1 4

1423

1423

1342

4321

43211

32114

1211

1423

1423

1413

2114

43211

1 234

1 234

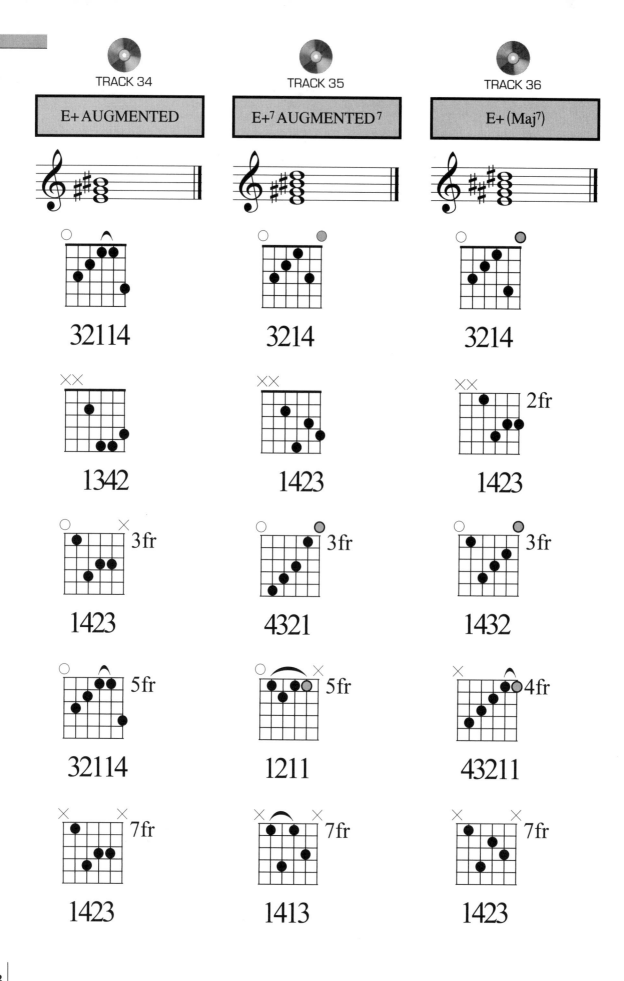

F+ AUGMENTED

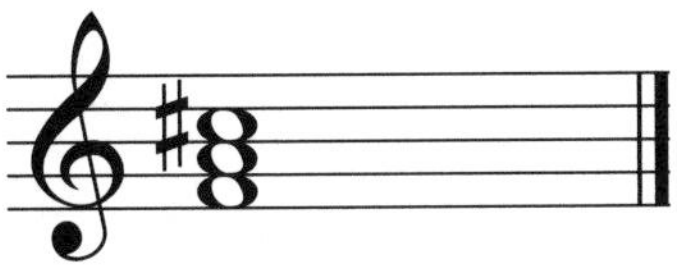

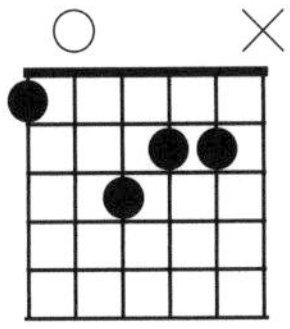

1 423

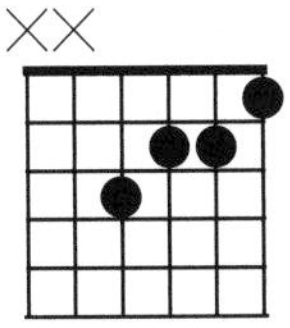

4231

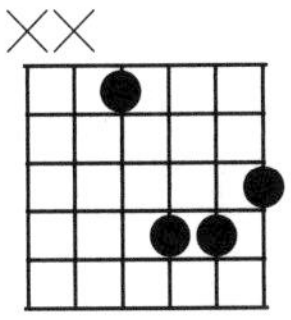

1342

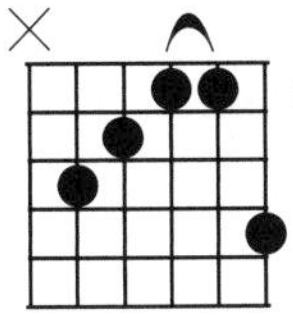

32114

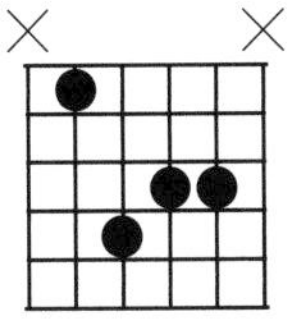

1423

F+7 AUGMENTED7

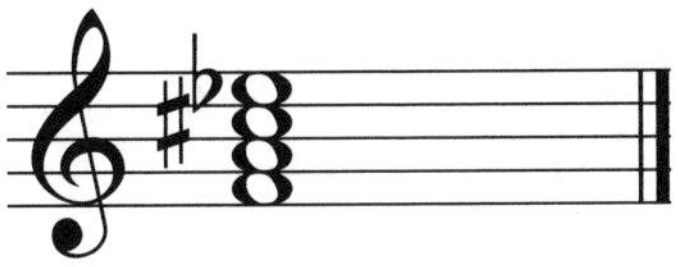

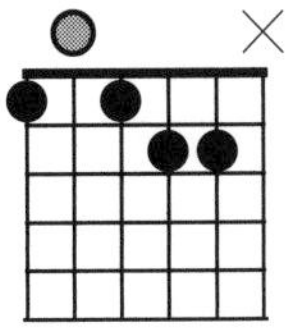

1 234

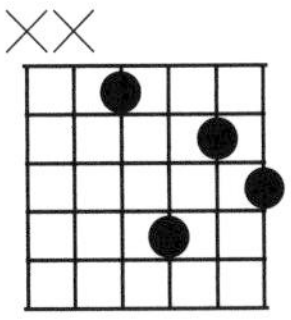

1423 3fr

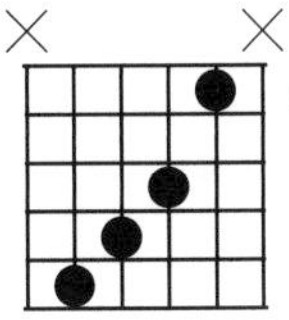

4321 4fr

1211 6fr

1413 8fr

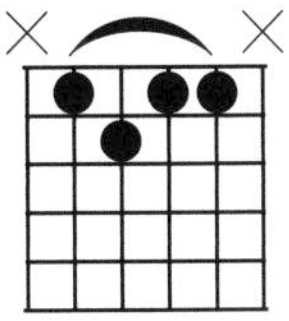

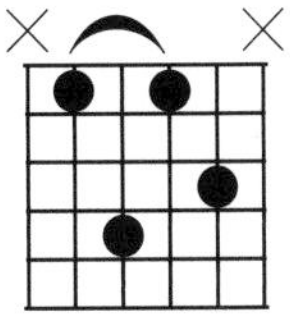

F+ (Maj7)

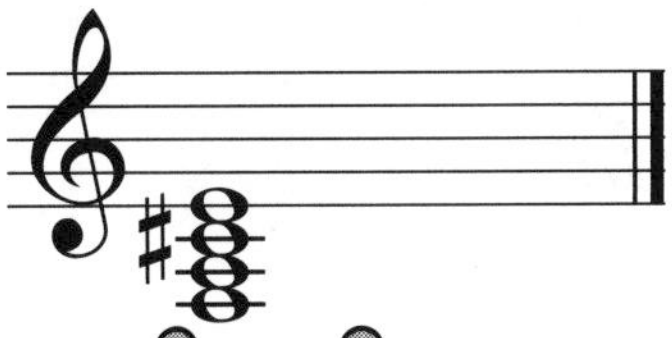

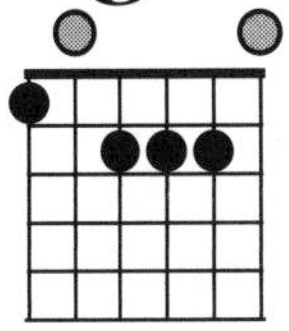

1 234

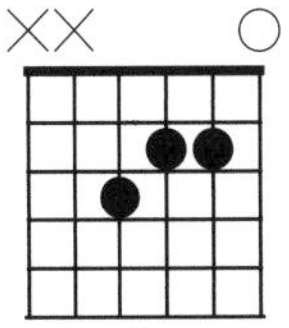

321

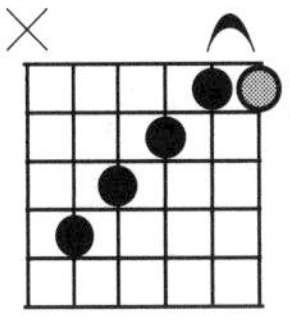

43211 5fr

1423 8fr

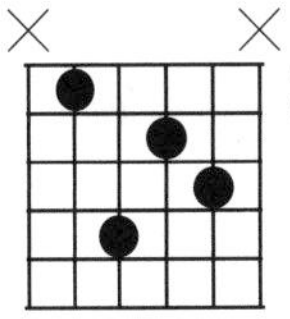

4321 9fr

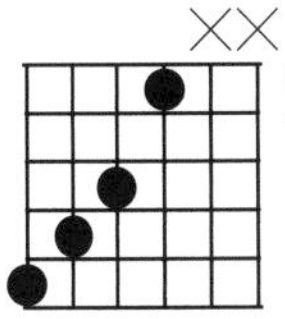

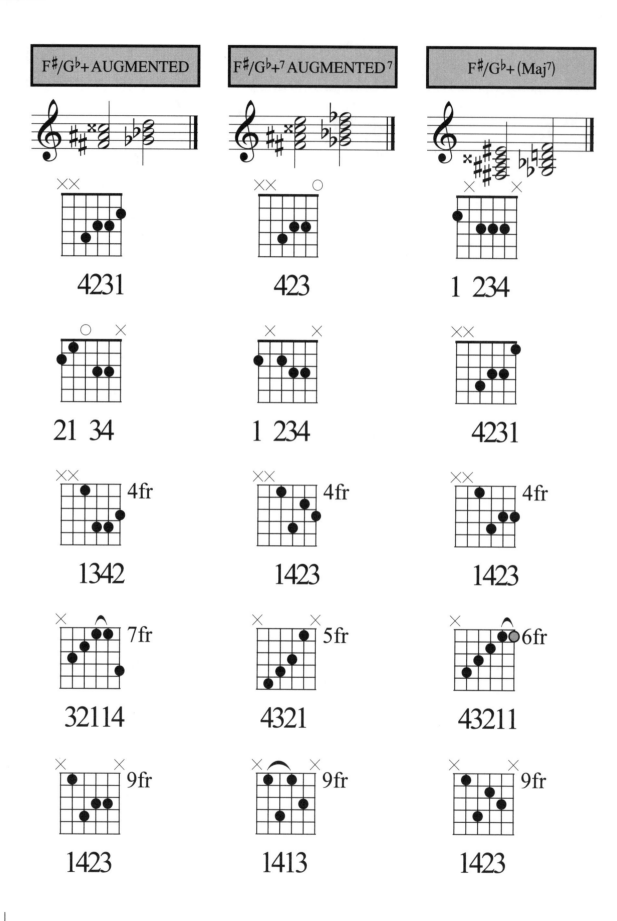

G+ AUGMENTED

321 4

G+⁷ AUGMENTED⁷

1 234

G+ (Maj⁷)

1 234

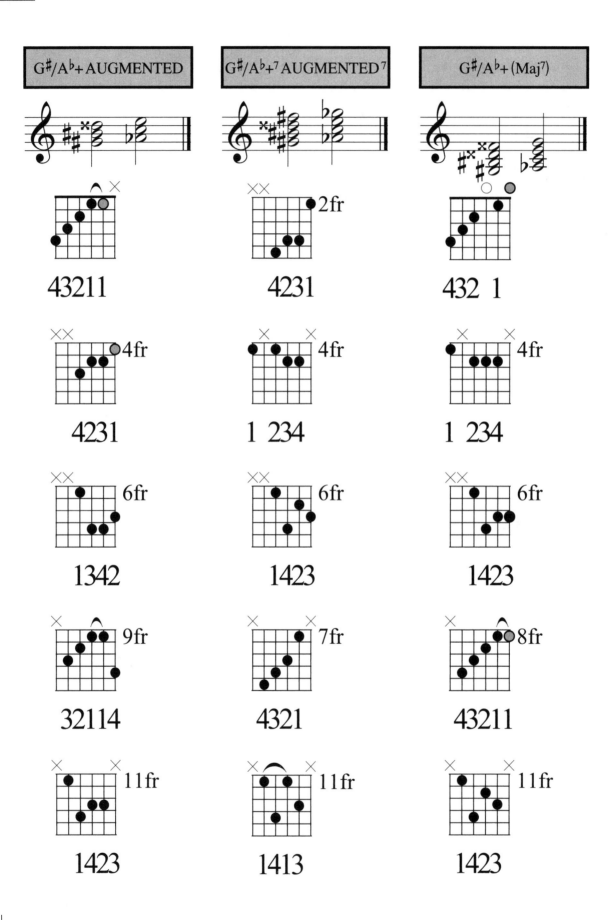

A+ AUGMENTED

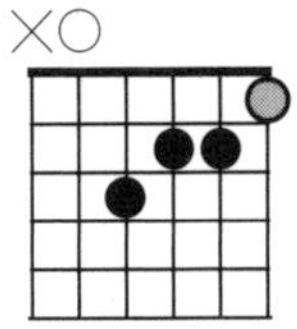

4231

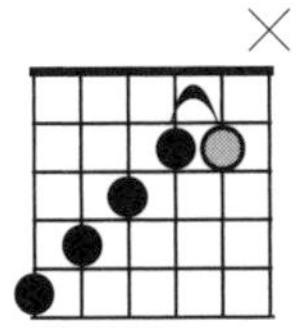

43211

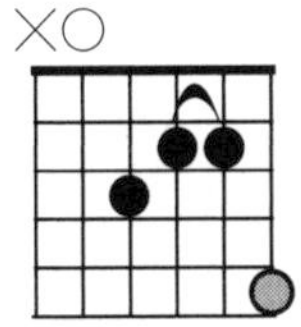

2114

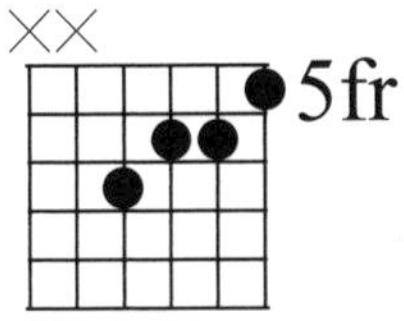

4231

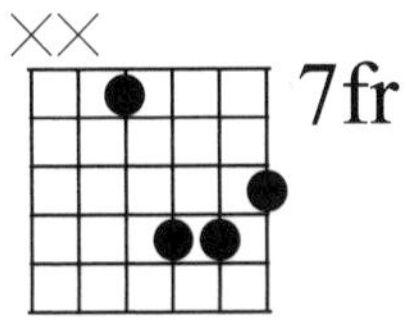

1342

A+7 AUGMENTED7

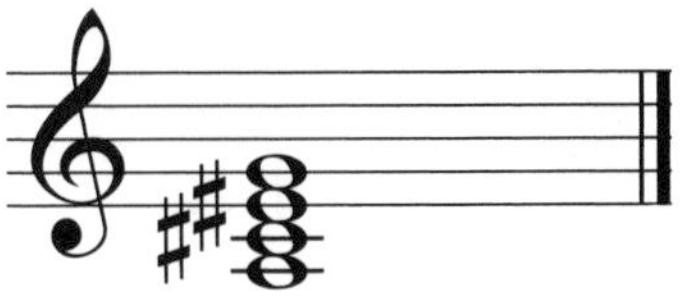

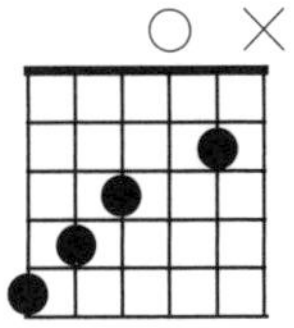

432 1

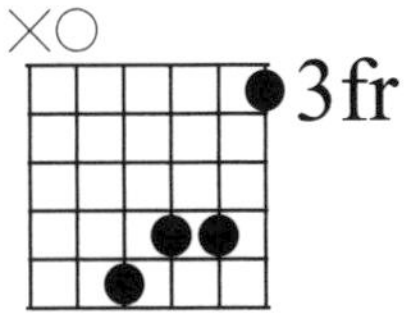

4231

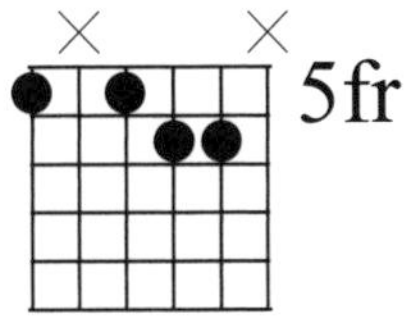

1 234

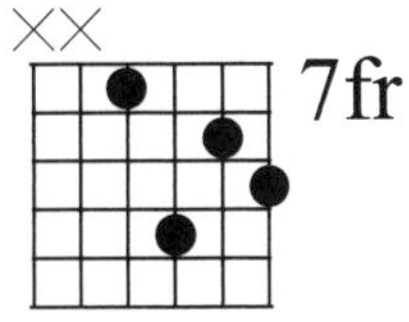

1423

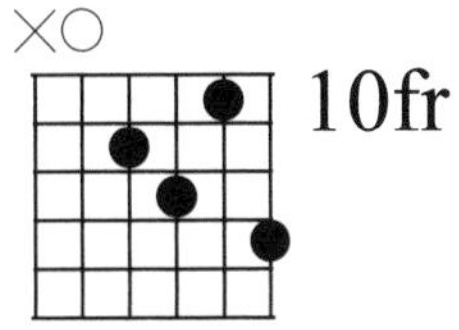

2314

A+ (Maj7)

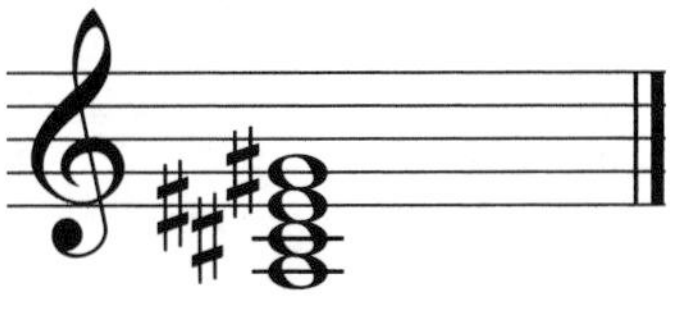

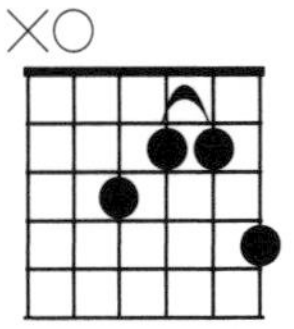

2114

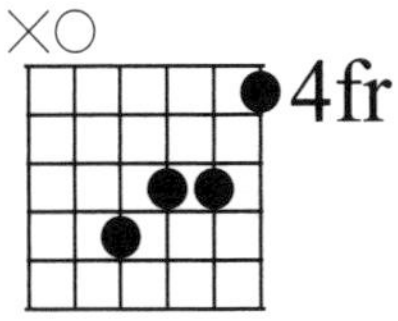

4231

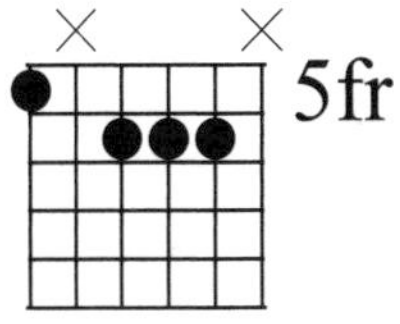

1 234

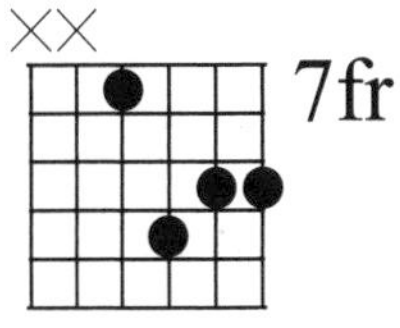

1423

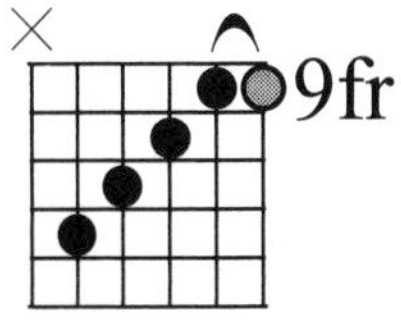

43211

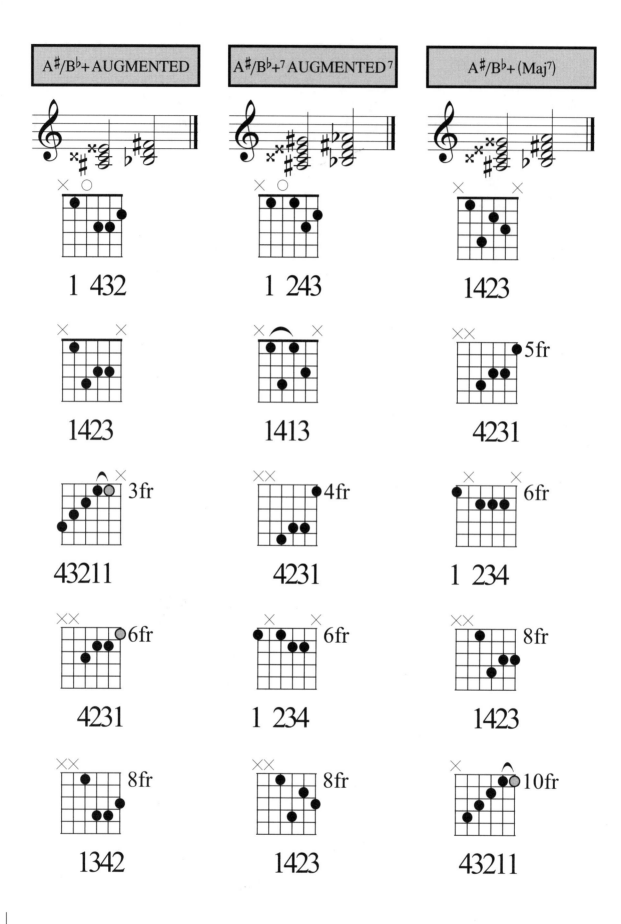

B+ AUGMENTED

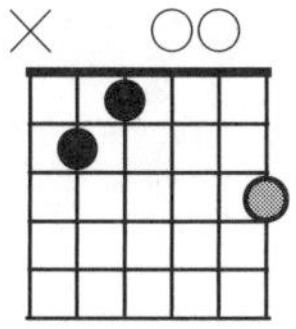

21 4

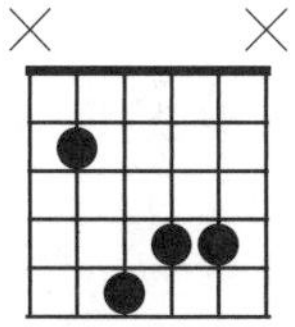

1423

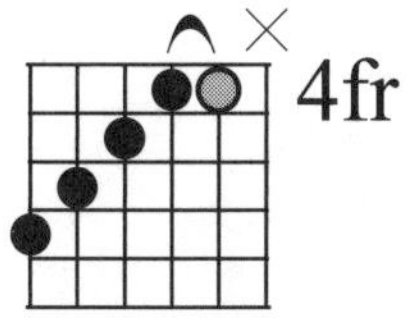

43211

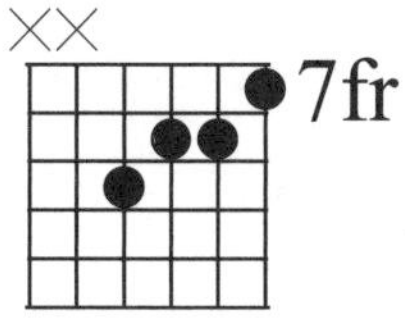

4231

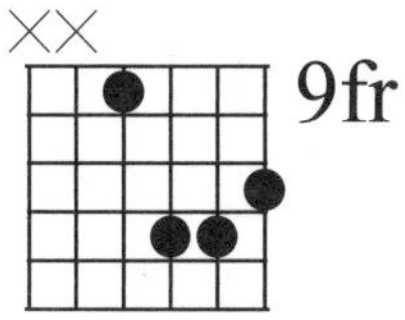

1342

B+⁷ AUGMENTED⁷

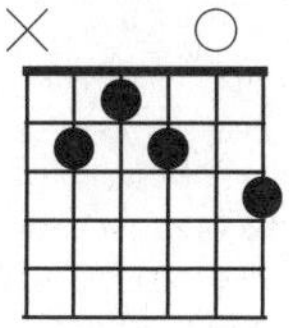

213 4

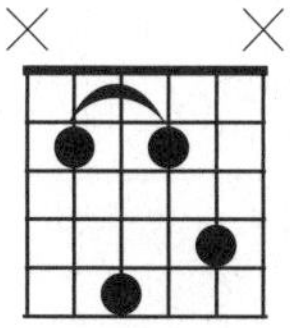

1413

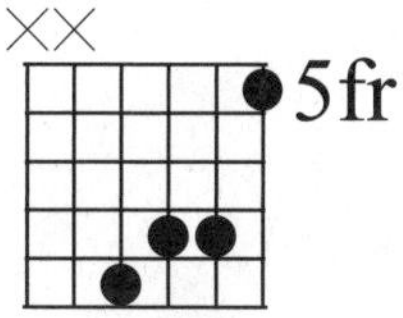

4231

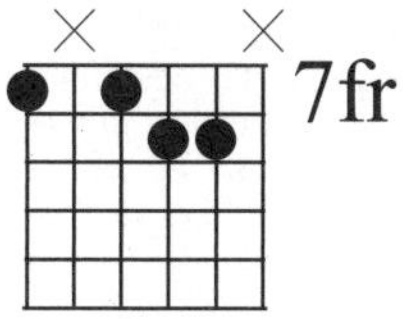

1 234

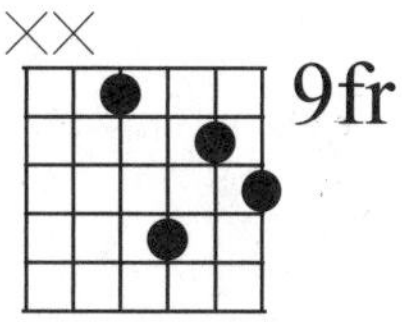

1423

B+ (Maj⁷)

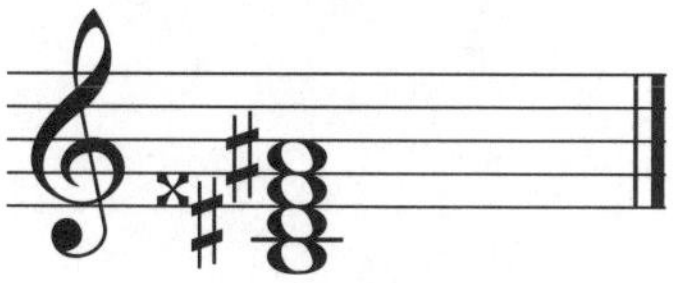

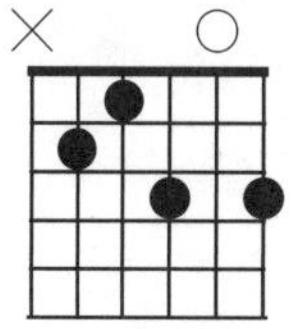

213 4

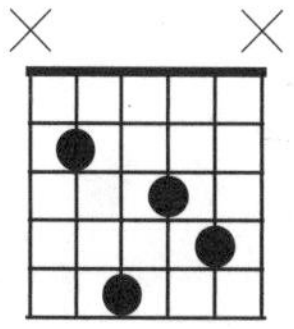

1423

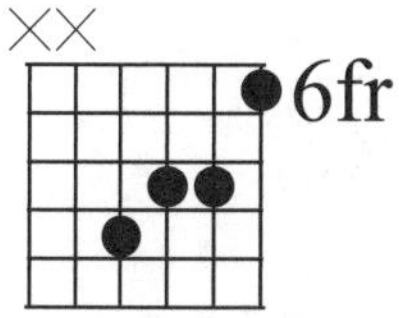

4231

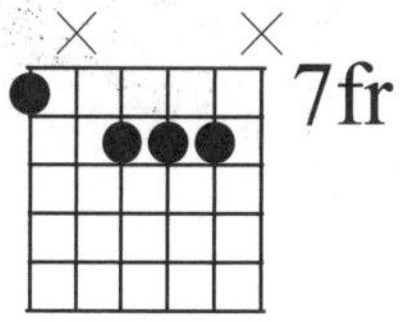

1 234

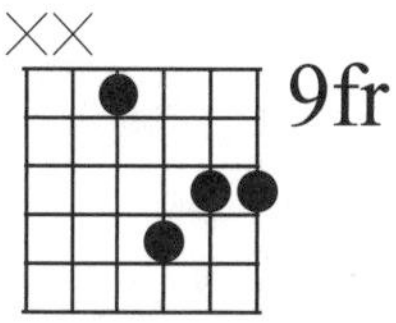

1423

Chapter 8

Special Chords

Here are the chords that don't fit anywhere else. Power chords are the staple of rock, punk, and just about every form of music composed after 1940. Suspended chords are as common as apple pie and exist in two varieties: sus 2 and sus 4. Suspended chords often resolve to major chords with the same root, but they don't have to.

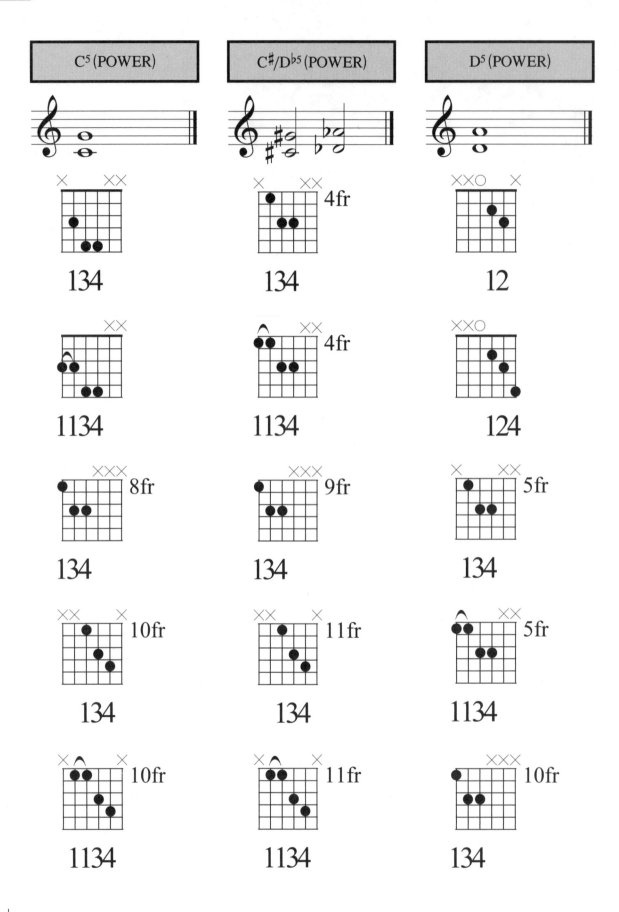

TRACK 37

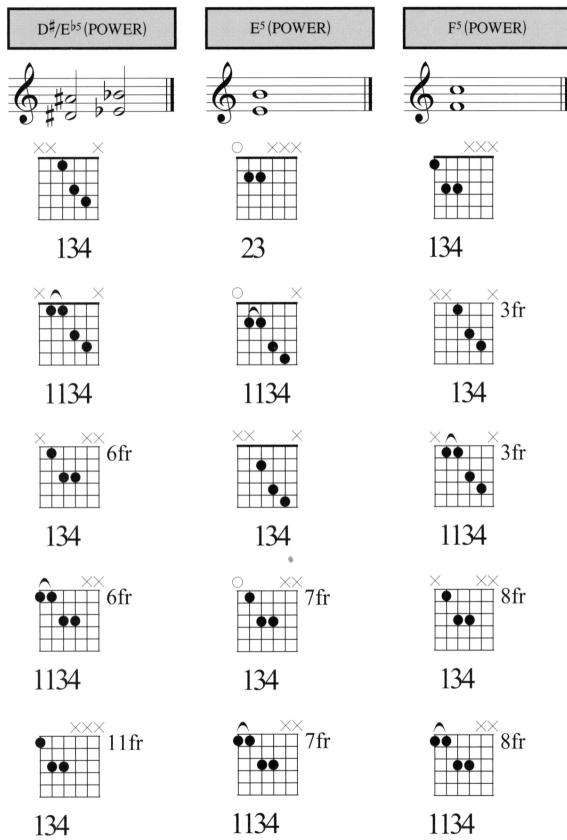

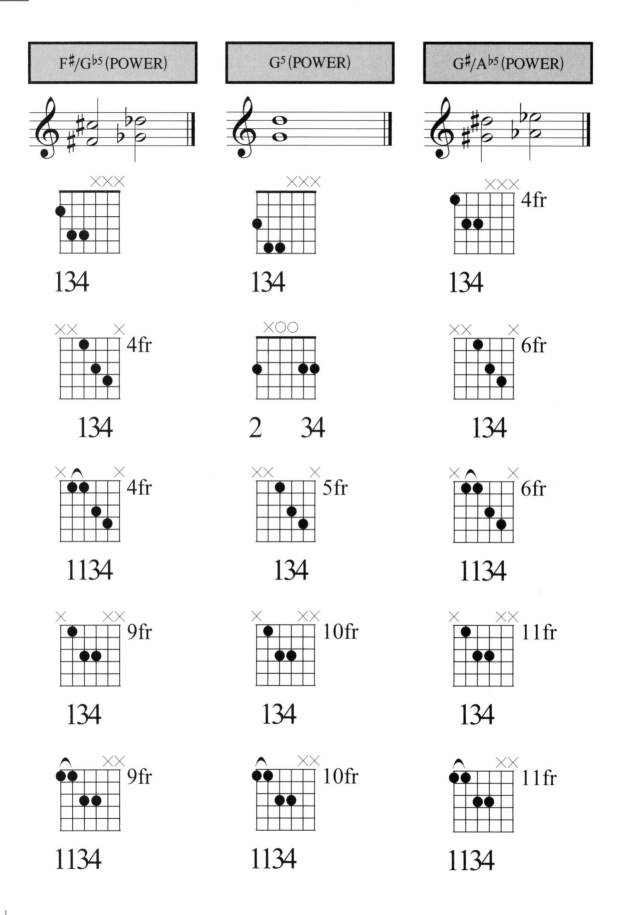

A⁵ (POWER)	A♯/B♭⁵ (POWER)	B⁵ (POWER)
23	134	134
1134	1134	1134
134 (5fr)	134 (6fr)	134 (7fr)
134 (7fr)	134 (8fr)	134 (9fr)
1134 (7fr)	1134 (8fr)	1134 (9fr)

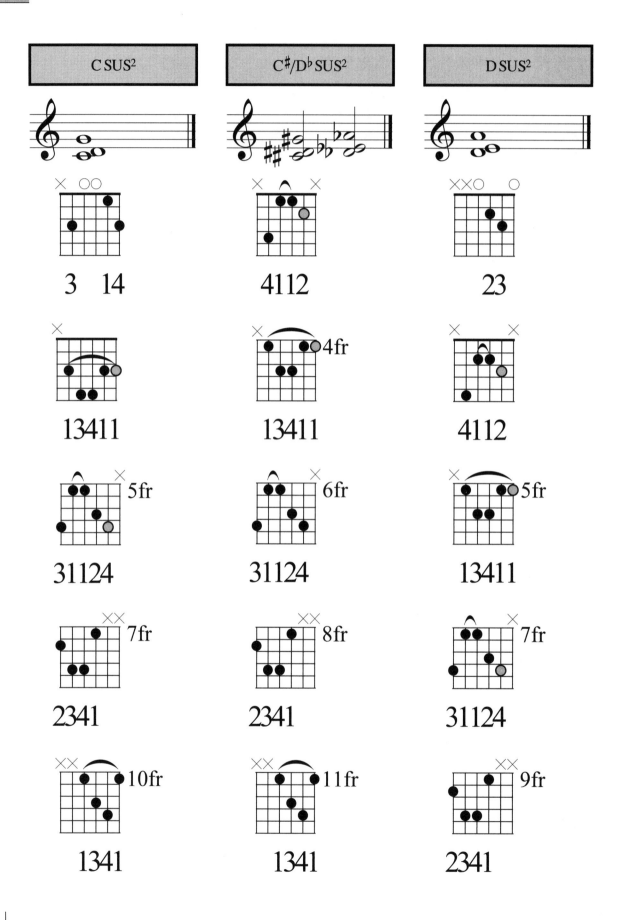

TRACK 38

Sus 2 Chords

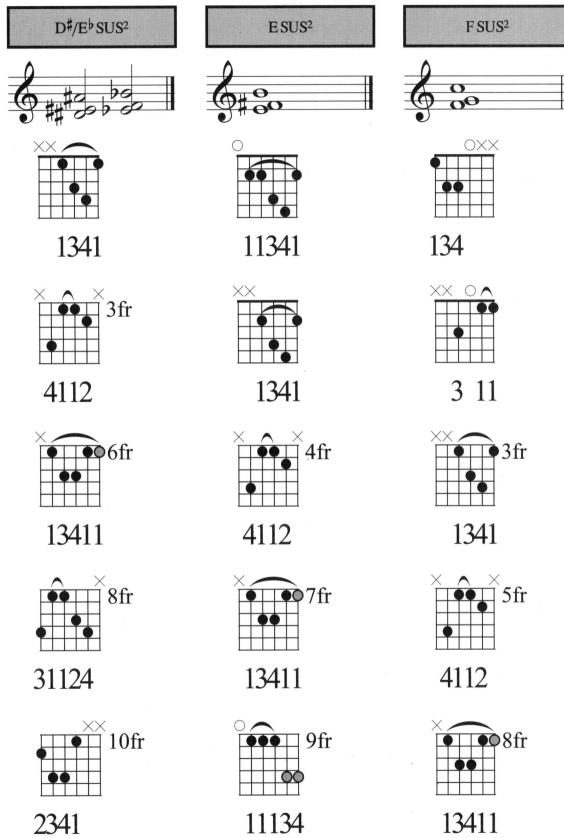

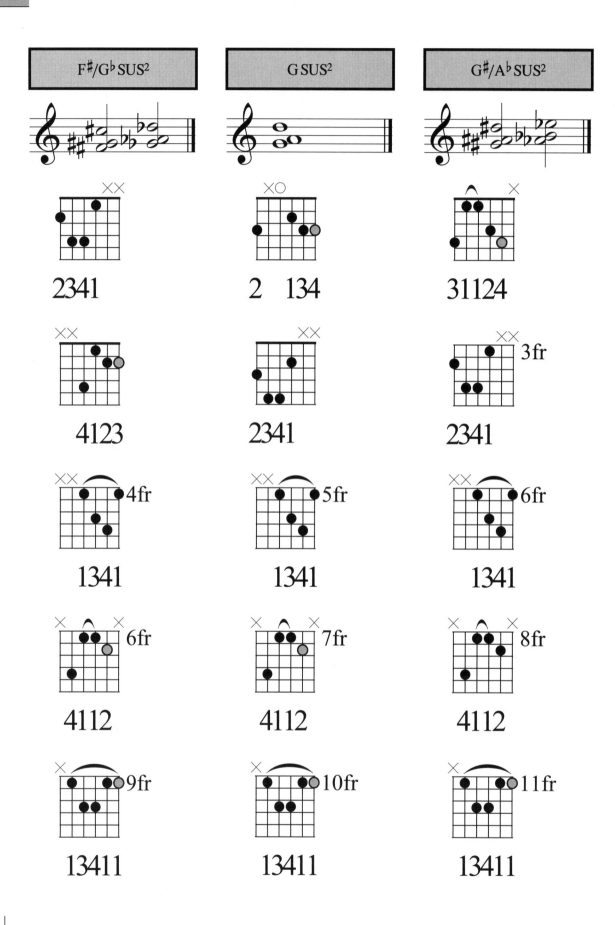

A SUS²	A#/B♭ SUS²	B SUS²

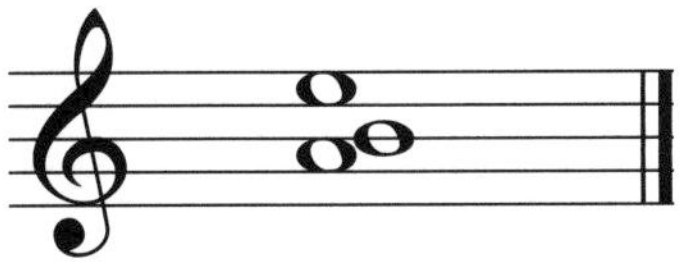

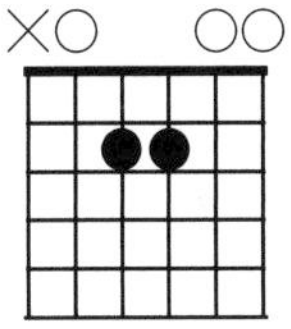

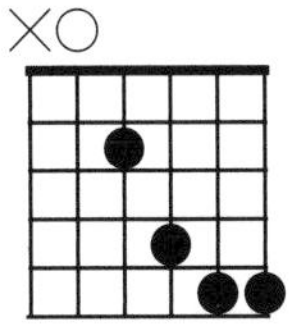

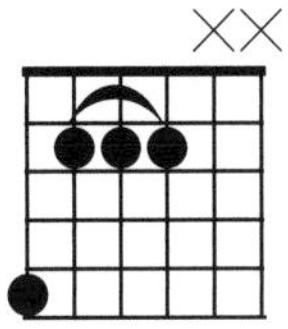

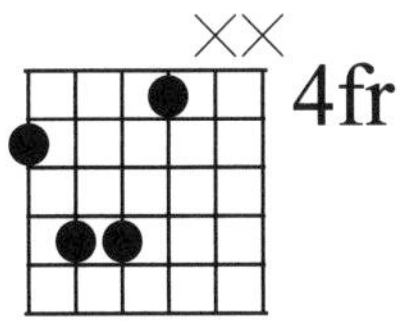

23 13411 13411

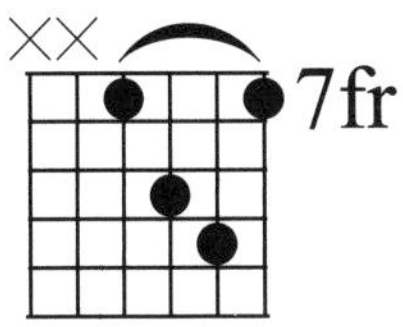

1234 31124 31124

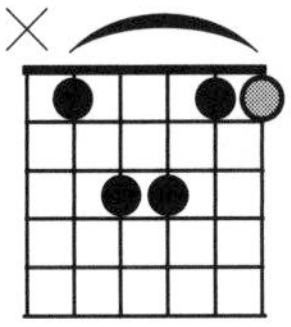

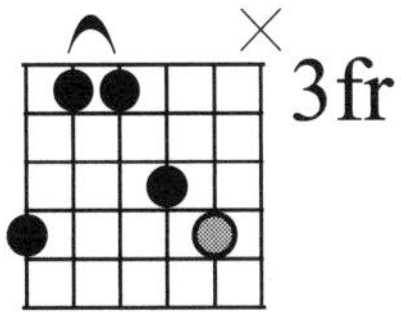

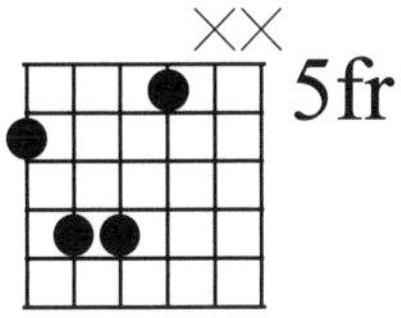

4111 2341 2341

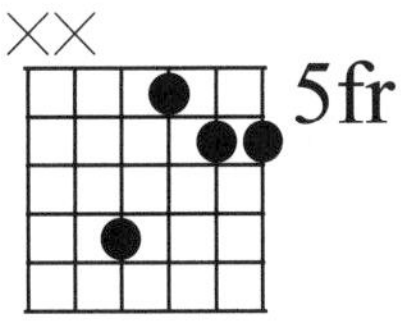

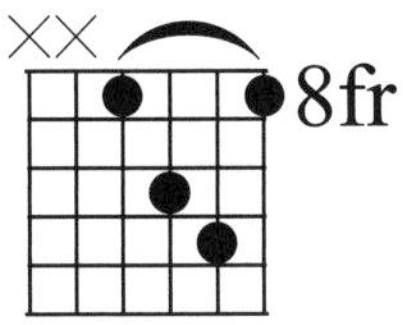

2341 4123 4123

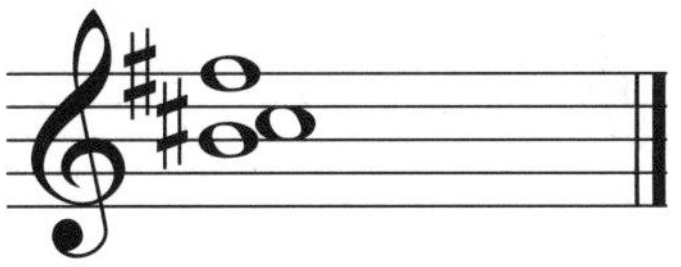

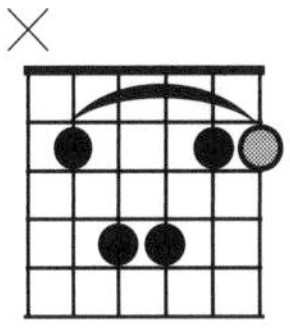

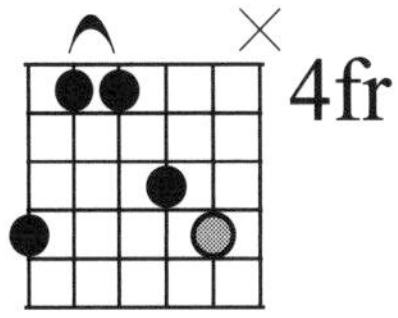

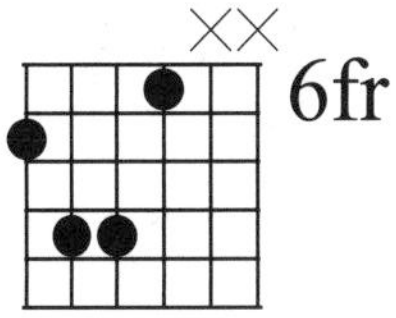

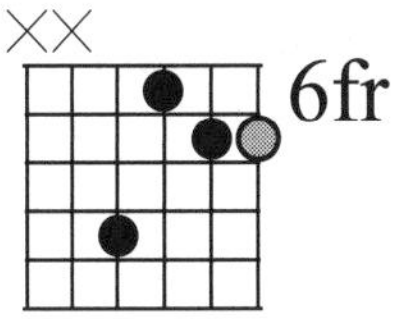

1341 1341 1341

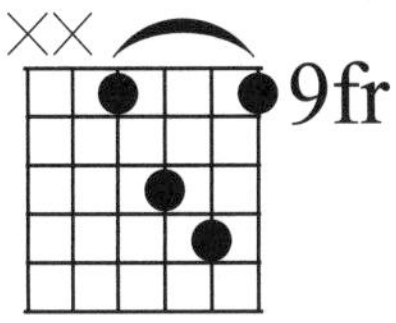

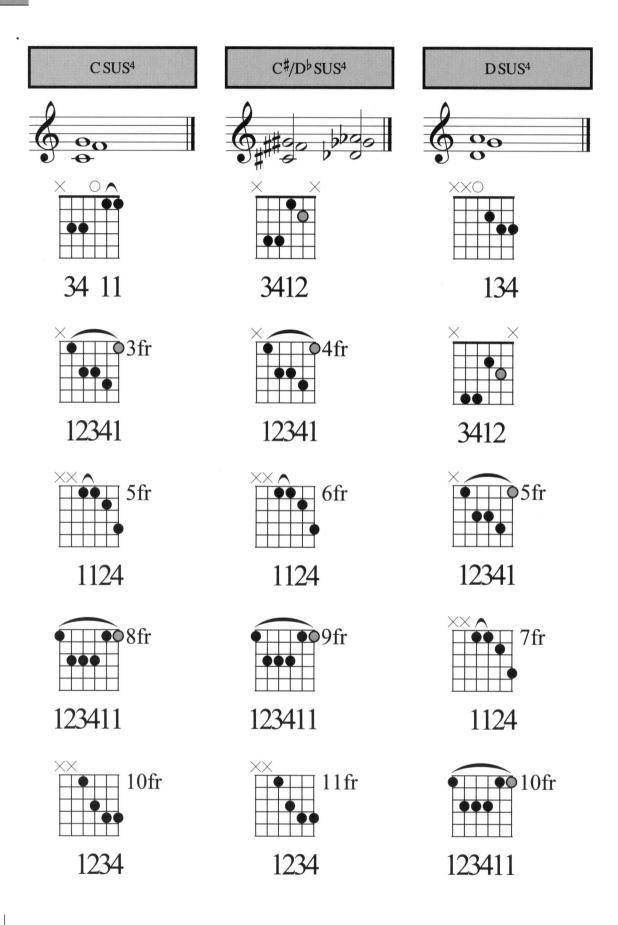

TRACK 39

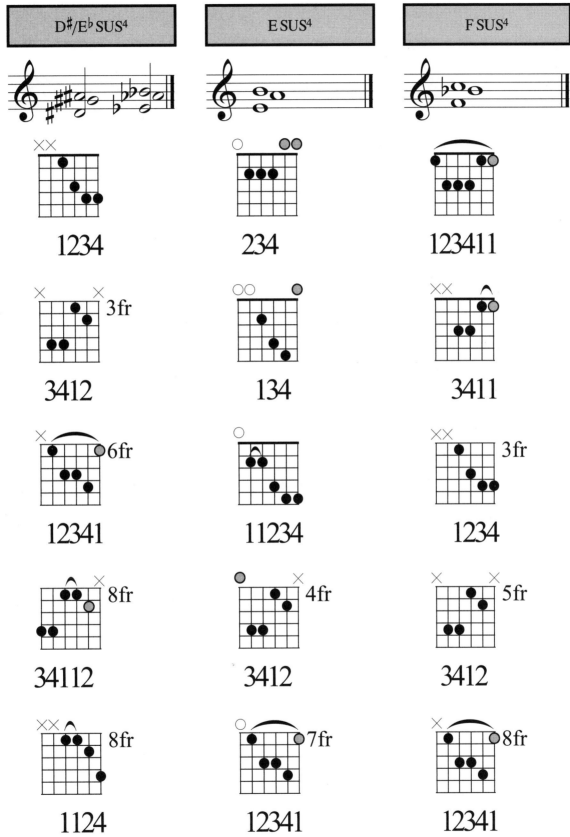

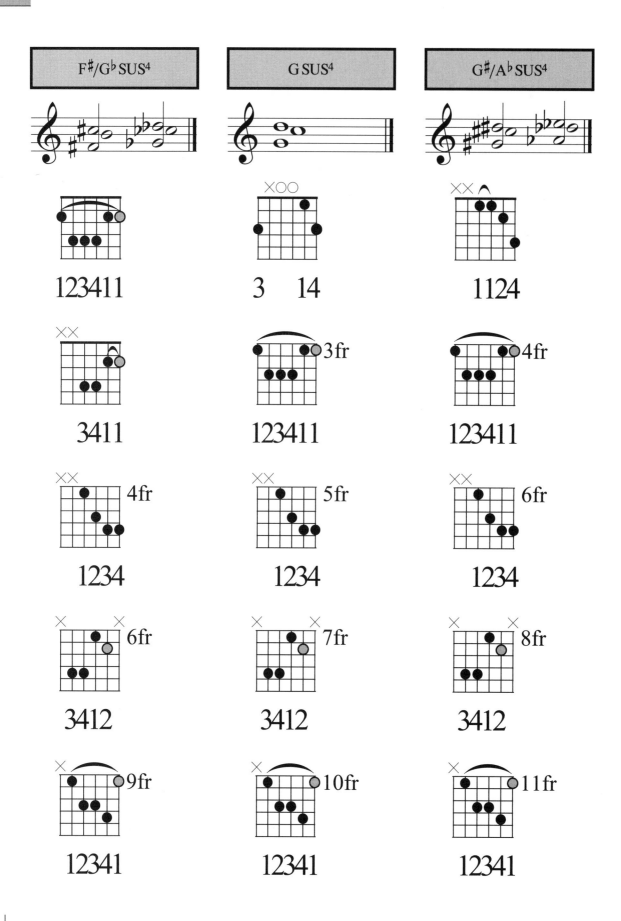

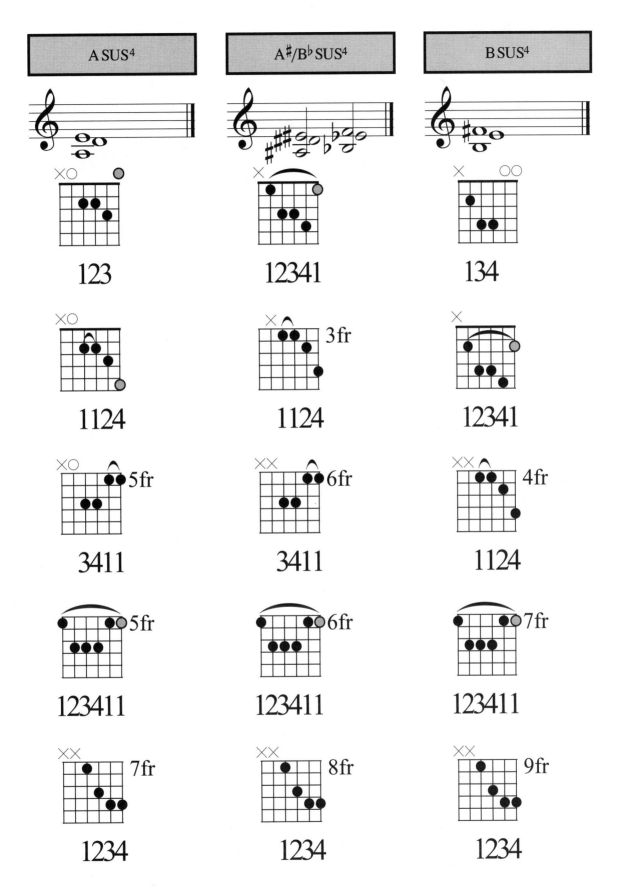

Chapter 9

Common Chord Progressions

Let's put your chords to work. Here you will find five styles of music: blues, rock, jazz, folk/country, and classical. For each style, I will demonstrate typical ways to use the chords in sequence—typical ways for the chords to group together. Some will be simple, and some will highlight the lesser-known voicings scattered throughout this book, which are worth integrating into your music. No matter what style you play, this chapter will give you a clearer picture of how to use the information provided in this book.

TRACK 40

Blues Progressions

Figure 9.1 is a very standard blues progression using open chords.

Figure 9.1

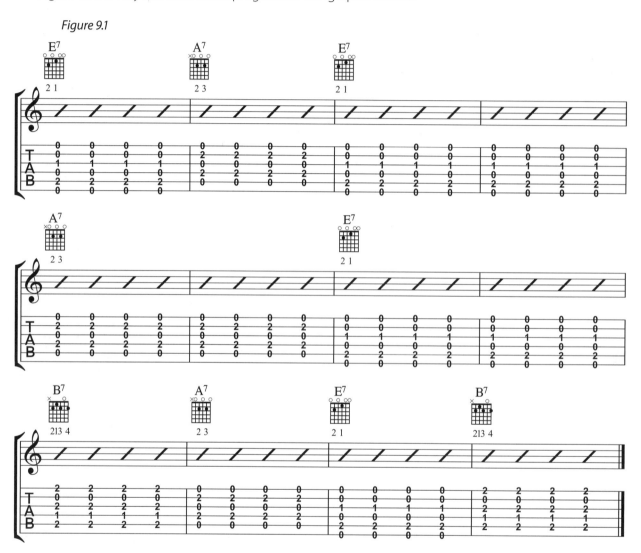

TRACK 41

The next thing you'll want to do when playing blues is to stop using open chords. The example in Figure 9.2 uses barre chord shapes across the neck. Notice how different they sound.

Figure 9.2

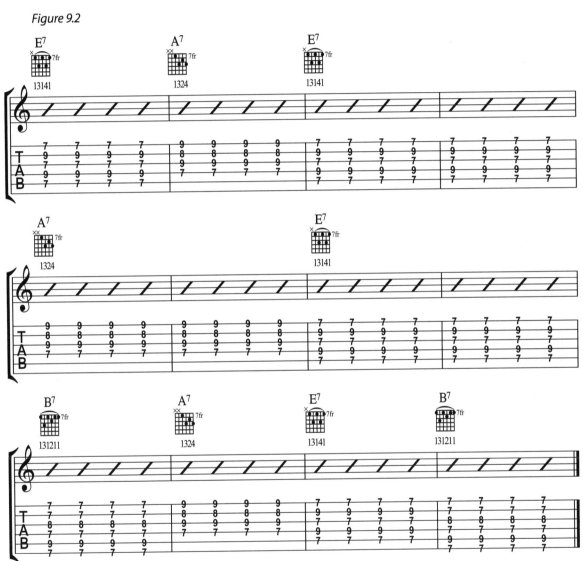

TRACK 42

The next step in your evolution is to try some substitute chords. Here I threw in some ninth and thirteenth chords. This is still the same basic progression, but see how much "fancier" it sounds (Figure 9.3).

Figure 9.3

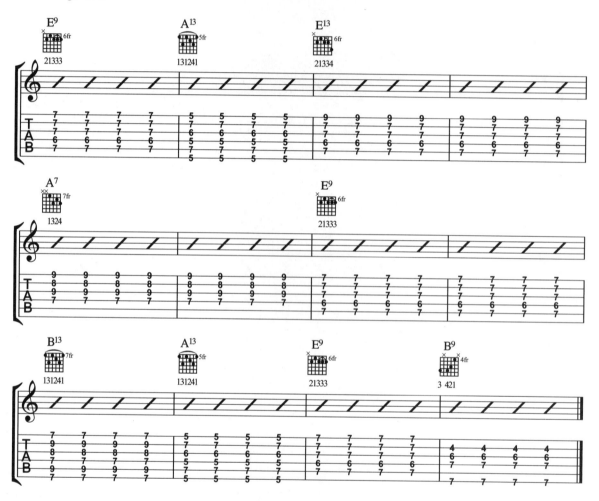

TRACK 43

Now it's time to really go to town and use some of the more obscure chords found in the book. Again, notice that I kept everything the same but altered the types of chords used. It's amazing how much variation you can achieve from this basic foundation (see Figure 9.4).

Figure 9.4

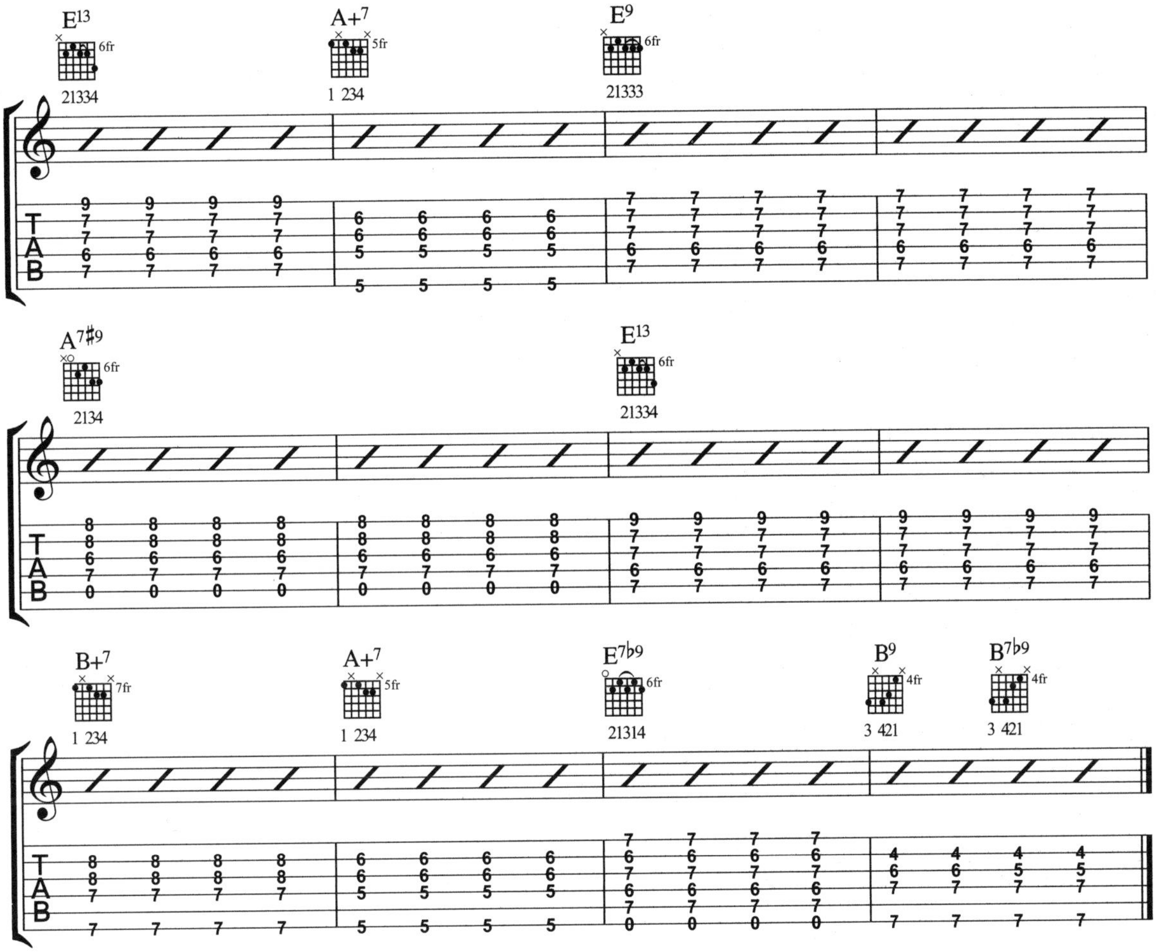

TRACK 44

Basic Rock Progressions

Figure 9.5 shows the basic rock progression, which you've probably played a few million times by now.

Figure 9.5

TRACK 45

Again, the first thing to do is look for other shapes of the same chords. In Figure 9.6 I chose a bunch of barre chords to vary the sound.

Figure 9.6

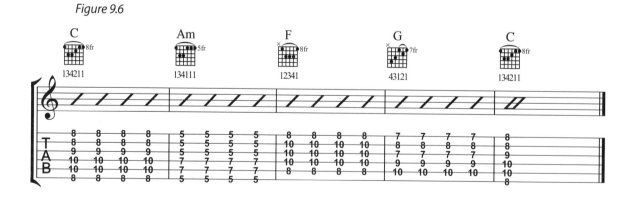

TRACK 46

In Figure 9.7, I chose chords that contained open strings. I kept the basic chords the same, but looked for more creative options. Since every chord has the same open strings, the sound is very smooth and flowing.

Figure 9.7

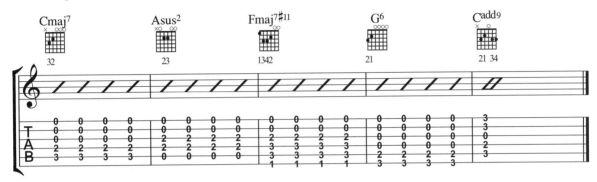

TRACK 47

For this last one (Figure 9.8), I explored different types of the basic chords. Simple chords can transform into more colorful choices simply by looking in the same section and choosing other chords. Listen to how this progression has elevated from mundane to ethereal.

Figure 9.8

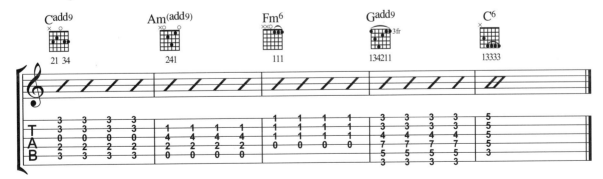

TRACK 48

Basic Jazz Progressions

Here is a very basic jazz progression (Figure 9.9). I chose simple jazz voicings that are all pretty low on the neck. Though this is more than "passable" as a jazz chord example, it is easy to do even more.

Figure 9.9

TRACK 49

Simply choosing other voicings for the chords that are present and making sure that you keep the chords relatively close to one another yields another interesting sound. It's amazing how different your music can sound simply by choosing alternate locations for the chords you already know (see Figure 9.10).

Figure 9.10

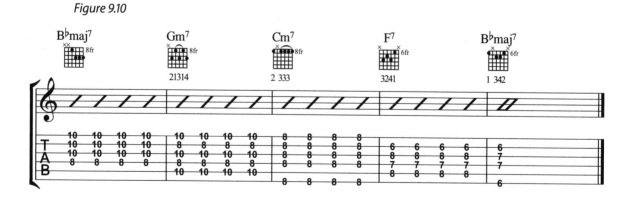

TRACK 50

In the example in Figure 9.11, I changed the G minor chord to G7 and used a new set of voicings. Changing the "quality" of a chord is a common occurrence in jazz music. Listen to how different this example sounds from the others!

Figure 9.11

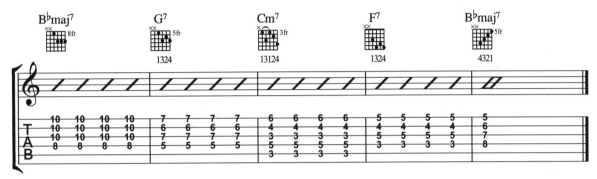

TRACK 51

Of course, I saved the most advanced for last. I chose extended and altered chords based on the original progressions. By doing this, you get a sound that is more closely associated with modern jazz (see Figure 9.12).

Figure 9.12

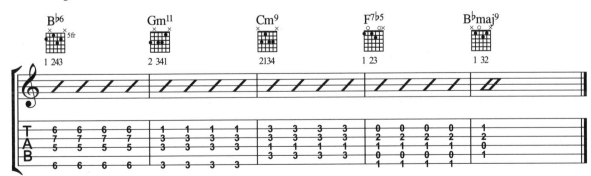

Basic Folk/Country Progressions

This set of chords shows you the kinds of chords you find in folk and country: open chords. The examples follow the same harmonic configuration in each example (I, IV, V, I) but do so in four different keys. The roman numerals are a way that musicians name chords. I is the first note of the scale, and so on. A sample I, IV, V progression in C major would be a C chord, an F chord, and a G chord. It is common to use numbers when talking about chord progressions. While this may seem limiting, you'd be amazed at how much mileage musicians get out of three simple chords in a few different keys. Feel free to start with the progressions and look for alternate voicings throughout the book to make them your own.

TRACK 52

Figure 9.13

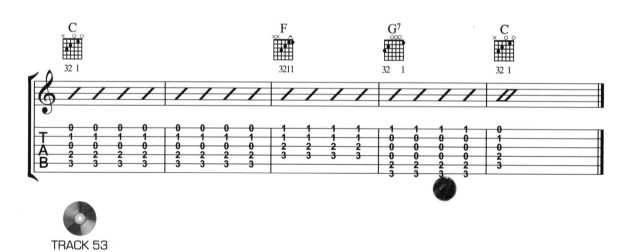

TRACK 53

Figure 9.14

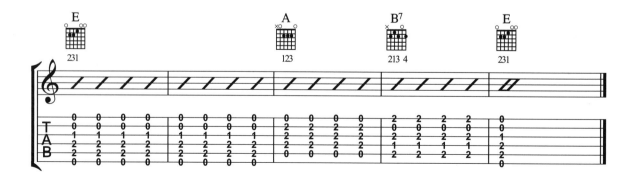

204

TRACK 54

Figure 9.15

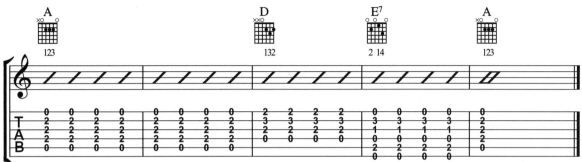

TRACK 55

Figure 9.16

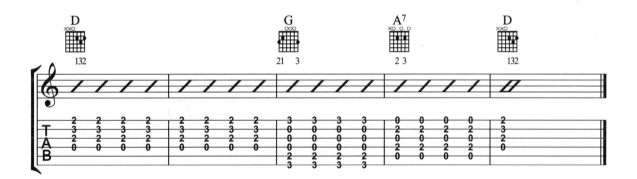

Classical Style Progressions

The next sets of progressions are in classical style. Not only is "classical" a style of music; it's also a way of playing the guitar with your right-hand fingers. What you'll notice is that the chords in the next examples have no chord boxes, but only music and tablature. Pay attention to the chord symbols and compare them with how you normally play those chords. It's amazing to see the difference in how these chords look from what you are used to. Because classical guitar is played entirely with your fingers, without a pick, the types of chords you can play will sound quite different from the standard "freshman fifteen" chords that you learn at first.

Of course, classical guitar is too big of a topic to cover in four examples! Just notice how the chords are used and how they sound in comparison to the folk/country progressions. Both use simple triads. The four progressions are standard classical style progressions found all over classical guitar literature. You can enjoy them even if you've never played classical guitar.

TRACK 56

Figure 9.17

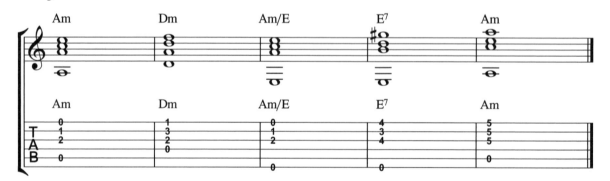

TRACK 57

Figure 9.18

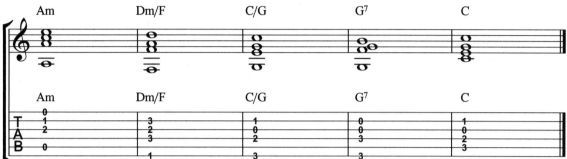

TRACK 58

Figure 9.19

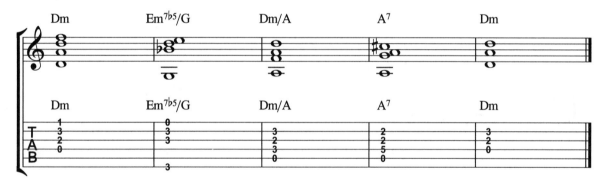

TRACK 59

Figure 9.20

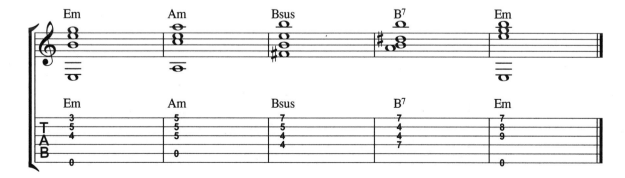

Appendix

CD Tracks

Here is a list of the tracks on the CD and their corresponding chords.

TRACK # CHORD TYPE

1.	E Major
2.	E Major 7
3.	E Major 7 ♯ 11
4.	E Major 7 ♯ 5
5.	E Major 9
6.	E Major 13
7.	E 6
8.	E 6/9
9.	E Major Add 9
10.	E Minor
11.	E Minor 7
12.	E Minor 7 ♭ 5
13.	E Minor/Major 7
14.	E Minor 9
15.	E Minor 9/Major 7
16.	E Minor 11
17.	E Minor 13
18.	E Minor 6
19.	E Minor ♭ 6
20.	E Minor 6/9
21.	E Minor Add 9
22.	E 7
23.	E 7 sus 4
24.	E 7 ♭ 9
25.	E 7 ♯ 9
26.	E 7 ♭ 5
27.	E 7 ♯ 5
28.	E 7 ♯ 11
29.	E 9
30.	E 13

TRACK # CHORD TYPE

31.	E Diminished
32.	E Diminished 7
33.	E Half Diminished 7
34.	E Augmented
35.	E Augmented 7
36.	E Augmented Major 7
37.	E 5 (Power)
38.	E sus 2
39.	E sus 4
40.	Blues Progression 1
41.	Blues Progression 2
42.	Blues Progression 3
43.	Blues Progression 4
44.	Rock Progression 1
45.	Rock Progression 2
46.	Rock Progression 3
47.	Rock Progression 4
48.	Jazz Progression 1
49.	Jazz Progression 2
50.	Jazz Progression 3
51.	Jazz Progression 4
52.	Folk/Country Progression 1
53.	Folk/Country Progression 2
54.	Folk/Country Progression 3
55.	Folk/Country Progression 4
56.	Classical Progression 1
57.	Classical Progression 2
58.	Classical Progression 3
59.	Classical Progression 4

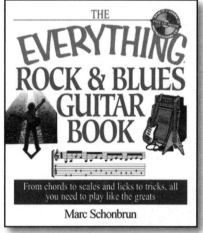